PRAISE FOR *CALLED AND CHOSEN*

"Grounded in the transformative vision of the Second Vatican Council, this volume offers a wholistic perspective on the core issues confronting lay ecclesial leaders in the US Catholic church today. As experienced leaders and seasoned scholars, the contributors use life stories and practical cases to bring theory to life. Hopeful and helpful, this book honors the pioneering work of the church's current lay leaders and encourages the next generation in this expansion of ecclesial ministry. It will be a valuable resource for use in programs of initial and ongoing leadership development. Questions at the end of each chapter provoke reflection and will provide focus for fruitful group discussion." —**Evelyn Eaton Whitehead** and **James D. Whitehead**, Institute of Pastoral Studies at Loyola University Chicago, authors of *Method in Ministry*

"*Called and Chosen* invites thoughtful reflection on the vital yet complex task of leading Catholic institutions. The various essays inspire wisdom and hope, even as they challenge readers to new depths of commitment." —**Mary C. Boys**, Skinner & McAlpin Professor of Practical Theology, Union Theological Seminary

"In spite of evidence to the contrary—scandals and crises—there is a new Pentecost breaking out in the church as lay people claim the rights and responsibilities of their baptism. But if lay leaders are to stay the course, they must ground themselves in a life-giving spirituality, one that draws from the deep waters of the Catholic treasury. *Called and Chosen* will be an invaluable resource to this good end." —**Thomas H. Groome**, Director, Institute of Religious Education and Pastoral Ministry at Boston College and author of *What Makes Us Catholic*

Called and Chosen

Toward a Spirituality for Lay Leaders

Edited by
Zeni Fox and Regina Bechtle, S.C.

A SHEED & WARD BOOK

ROWMAN & LITTLEFIELD PUBLISHERS, INC.
Lanham • *Boulder* • *New York* • *Toronto* • *Oxford*

A SHEED & WARD BOOK

ROWMAN & LITTLEFIELD PUBLISHERS, INC.

Published in the United States of America
by Rowman & Littlefield Publishers, Inc.
A wholly owned subsidary of The Rowman & Littlefield Publishing Group, Inc.
4501 Forbes Boulevard, Suite 200, Lanham, Maryland 20706
www.rowmanlittlefield.com

PO Box 317
Oxford
OX2 9RU, UK

British Library Cataloguing in Publication Information Available

Library of Congress Cataloging-in-Publication Data

Called and chosen : toward a spirituality for lay leaders / edited by Zeni Fox
and Regina Bechtle.
    p. cm.
    Includes index.
    ISBN 0-7425-3199-6 (cloth : alk. paper) — ISBN 0-7425-3200-3 (pbk. : alk. paper)
    1. Christian leadership—Catholic Church. 2. Laity—Catholic Church. I. Fox,
Zeni. II. Bechtle, Regina M.
BX1920.C259 2005
248.8'9—dc22

                                                                2004027622

Printed in the United States of America

∞™ The paper used in this publication meets the minimum requirements of
American National Standard for Information Sciences—Permanence of Paper
for Printed Library Materials, ANSI/NISO Z39.48-1992.

"We are convinced that the laity are making an indispensable contribution to the experience of the People of God and that the full import of their contribution is still in a beginning form in the post-Vatican II Church."

Called and Gifted: The American Catholic Laity, Reflections of the American Bishops Commemorating the Fifteenth Anniversary of the Issuance of the *Decree on the Apostolate of the Laity*, 1980

"The laity's call to holiness is a gift from the Holy Spirit. Their response is a gift to the Church and to the world."

Called and Gifted for the Third Millennium, Reflections of the U.S. Catholic Bishops on the Thirtieth Anniversary of the *Decree on the Apostolate of the Laity* and the Fifteenth Anniversary of *Called and Gifted*, 1995

Contents

Foreword

H. Richard McCord

"Today the Roman Catholic Church in the United States is on the verge of either an irreversible decline or a thoroughgoing transformation." So begins Peter Steinfels in the opening pages of his book, *A People Adrift: The Crisis of the Roman Catholic Church in America*. I agree with him, as do many others. We stand at a crossroads. Will we choose the right path forward? This is a question for and about leadership.

Called and Chosen: Toward a Spirituality for Lay Leaders responds to the question in such a way as to set the reader on a path leading away from decline toward transformation. It helps in constructing a bridge between problem diagnosis and solution. Its focus on church institutional leadership by laypersons is not the entire solution. It is, however, a necessary component of any solution. Without a vision the people will perish. Without leaders the institution will perish. But with a leader who has a vision, the institution and the people it serves will all have a very good chance of surviving and thriving.

Again, Peter Steinfels writes:

> Every great church renewal has had an institutional expression and every great church failure has institutional sources. Mystical, intellectual, and charitable energies operate within institutional frameworks, indeed sometimes spring from the frustrations of institutional shortcomings. The Catholic Church can succeed as an institution while failing as a church. But it cannot succeed as a church while failing as an institution.[1]

Obviously, we need both a successful church and a successful institution, that is, an institutional church true to its calling. This will not happen without leadership. What kind of leadership specifically? The premise of this

book is that spiritual formation is an essential, even distinguishing, characteristic of the church leader. This is true for both clergy and lay. But inasmuch
as laity are entering church leadership positions in greater numbers today—
and often without the benefit of a period of formation normally offered in
seminary or novitiate—what perspectives, questions, and resources are ger-
mane to the spiritual development of lay leaders?

Certainly there are many legitimate styles and traditions of spiritual formation. A short tour of church history reveals this wealth ranging across monastic and mendicant, contemplative and contemporary expressions. Moreover,
the task of spiritual formation itself is a lifelong process and challenge woven into the life of every Christian. What, then, is specific and different about
the spiritual formation of lay leaders for Catholic institutions?

There are two important characteristics, in my opinion. The first pertains
to the public nature of the leadership role. The second is concerned with the
leader's responsibility to define and preserve the public identity of the institution.

The leader is, by definition, a public person. He or she plays a prescribed
role, holds an office, is entrusted with responsibility, and is invested with the
authority to speak for and act on behalf of the institution. Also, depending
on the nature of the institution, the leader will need to be sensitive to certain
kinds of expectations from the public and especially from those whom the
institution serves. Being a public person requires learning how to balance
private desires with public demands.

The leader of a church institution is a public person who represents not
only a specific institution but also often is seen as representing the church
in a more global sense. There is a sense in which we can speak of an ecclesial repositioning taking place for the lay leader. This requires that she
or he develop a certain horizon or perspective which is, at its core, a spiritual one. The spirituality that sustains a public person in the church is different from a more privately focused spirituality. The authors of these essays illumine some of the differences while, at the same time, holding to an
understanding of spirituality as basically the same project for everyone,
namely, growth into the fullness of Christ, through response to the gifts of
the Spirit.

The second characteristic of the leader is his or her responsibility for defining and maintaining the public identity of the institution. In the case of
Catholic leadership, this means, of course, a specifically Catholic identity. For
the better part of two centuries in the United States, Catholic institutions of
education, health care, and social welfare were led by clergy and religious
upon whose capable shoulders the task of maintaining Catholic identity
rested and thereby seemed assured. Patterns of decline in the past forty years
have changed that situation in dramatic ways. Catholic schooling at elementary and secondary levels relies mostly on the leadership of lay administra-

tors, not to mention lay teachers. Catholic higher education, health care, and social services are following the same pattern.

Even if Catholic institutional identity could be assured with the advent of lay leaders, in the same way that this identity was once a natural outcome of ordained and religious leadership, the challenge would not be completely addressed. This is because it has become more difficult to reach a consensus about the meaning of Catholic identity in our postmodern, religiously pluralistic culture. Volumes continue to be written on this important topic, including documents from the church's magisterium such as *Ex Corde Ecclesiae*, which addresses Catholic identity in institutions of higher education.

Therefore, integral to the spirituality of a Catholic institutional leader must be the conviction that there is something distinct about the gospel message embodied in the Catholic community and mission. There must also be an emphasis on growth in those virtues needed to articulate and defend, if necessary, that distinctive identity, as well as to inspire others to embrace it.

The essays in this collection contribute helpful, complementary pieces to a mosaic in which these two specific tasks of Catholic lay institutional leadership gradually take shape and emerge for the community to contemplate and act upon.

NOTE

1. Peter Steinfels, *A People Adrift: The Crisis of the Roman Catholic Church in America* (New York: Simon and Schuster, 2003), 14.

Preface

How does a book begin? What prompts the first pondering of what it might include? In the case of the present volume, for me, Zeni, it was the experience of teaching a course for Catholic school teachers (they were pursuing a master's in Catholic school leadership, so that they could become principals) and the larger context of teaching lay ecclesial ministers for many years. (Lay ecclesial ministers is the name given by the bishops to those lay persons providing leadership in ministry, usually in parishes.) Among the lay ecclesial ministers, there were certain ways of viewing themselves and their work; I had studied this when I conducted my first national survey, for my dissertation, subsequently reported as part of my *New Ecclesial Ministers: Lay Professionals Serving the Church*.

I noted that they understood themselves precisely as ministers (though no church document had so described them), and that they had a strong sense of having been called to their work, though existing paradigms do not have a way to name that vocation. Catholic school teachers, on the other hand, generally did not use the language of ministry and call. However, when introduced to these concepts, they quickly recognized their own experience, which for many had been, until then, inchoate.

Furthermore, for the lay ecclesial ministers, their self-understanding had motivational power, and as the Catholic school teachers claimed the traditional language of the Church to be relevant to their own experience, for many this took on real significance. My conviction is that I was experiencing with the Catholic school teachers what Karl Rahner once described as the bringing to conscious awareness of that which had already been experienced by grace. Furthermore, guided by an insight of theologian John Shea, I felt it important to try to build rope ladders between the experience

of people devoting their energies to the mission of the Church, and the received language of the tradition of the Church. This seems important both
for the individuals and for the coherence of the mission.

A second concern prompting this effort is that many people are questioning whether our Catholic institutions can maintain their Catholic identity
when they are lay led. I believe that they can, and that this task will be easier
and more fruitful for the lay leaders, and their communities, if they are con-
versant with the traditional language of the Church and more fully in touch
with their own experience of God working in their lives and institutions.

For me, Regina, agreeing to collaborate on this volume seemed a fitting
way to express my conviction that spirituality has everything to do with leadership. After serving on the leadership team of my religious congregation,
the Sisters of Charity of New York, I spent several years directing a center
where my colleagues and I explored the intersections of leadership and spirituality. Whether I worked with leaders in a college setting, with board members of not-for-profits, or with vowed women religious new to congregational leadership, the discussion inevitably moved to questions about the
spiritual meaning of their service. Again and again, I found that people
would link stories they told about themselves, whether with joy or with an-
guish, to the institutions they passionately cared about. Like Zeni, I also
found that people often did not have a way to name their personal and institutional journeys in the "received language" of the Church's tradition.

We, Zeni and Regina, worked together to develop what a book of resources for lay leaders should include, first outlining it, then developing
points for the authors of each chapter to consider. The central themes of spirituality, mission, reading the signs of the times, and so on quickly emerged.
We struggled in defining our audience. While we think that most of the volume applies to lay leaders in Catholic health care institutions, Catholic charities, and Catholic schools, colleges, and universities, we ultimately decided
to focus particularly on educational institutions, since this is the arena we
know best. Then we contacted those we wished would write each chapter,
and to our great delight, they agreed to do so.

Because we wanted to identify the language which lay leaders use to describe their experiences, we conducted three focus groups with Catholic
school principals, in the dioceses of Cincinnati, Fort Worth, and Newark, to
talk about what brought them to Catholic education and about situations in
which they felt that God was working within their schools (or forces were
working there against God's intentions). The transcripts of these conversations were made available to the authors. Michael Downey agreed to write
his essay first, so that a common understanding of spirituality, especially the
"everydayness" of it, would inform the volume. Finally, when most of the essays were received, a group of college administrators and teachers reviewed
the extent to which the language and material truly addressed our audience.

Throughout, the spirit of collaboration we encountered, and the affirmation of our hopes for this volume, gave us significant support.

The volume has four parts. We begin with a consideration of the leader as a person: chapters 1, 2, and 3 consider his/her spirituality, vocation, and core values, respectively. Each topic is developed in such a way that the reader is invited to use the discussion as a mirror, or perhaps better, as a piece of music to which the reader is a tuning fork, resonating within to the evocative themes. Part two explores the mission of the Church and her institutional ministries (those efforts to continue the teaching, healing, serving ministry of Jesus which have been developed to the point that many individuals share in the effort in a stable fashion). In chapter 4, the central biblical themes of God's reign and the ministries of the Church are presented. Chapter 5 traces the rich heritage that lies behind today's institutions and invites us to join in building the future. Chapter 6 focuses on the larger Church of which each school and college is a part, showing the international and local networks of relationships and structures that support the effort in a particular institution.

Part three presents institutions as communal realities that embody a unique spirit and spirituality. Chapter 7 takes a broad view, examining today's cultural context with its possibilities and challenges for Catholic institutions. Chapter 8 explores the concept of a spirituality of institutions that are capable of sin and open to grace, and the leader's role in fostering a community that makes room for God's Spirit. Chapter 9 reflects on the spirit-filled legacy of those who founded today's institutions and offers practical ways to honor and carry forward the gifts they have bequeathed.

Part four returns to the person of the leader, specifically to some spiritual dimensions of his/her role. Chapter 10 demonstrates that administration and holiness are not mutually exclusive. Chapter 11 asks leaders to live with the tension of "both/and," as they address complex issues that bear on relationships between educational institutions and communities of faith. Chapter 12 calls leaders to understand power in relationship to God's Spirit and so to transform their exercise of authority in that light. Chapter 13 presents stories of leaders who express a key aspect of their spirituality through their roles as mentors and formators. A glossary at the end sums up some of the most significant terms related to this subject.

Special thanks are due to the SC Ministry Foundation, Cincinnati, for a generous grant that funded this effort. We are also deeply grateful to Kathryn Ann Connelly, S.C., Marguerite Connors, S.H.Sp., and Dominica Rocchio, S.C., superintendents of Catholic schools in Cincinnati, Fort Worth, and Newark, respectively, to their staffs, and to the outstanding, articulate lay leaders whom they gathered for our focus groups. Donna Dodge, S.C., and a group of her colleagues at Sacred Heart University, Fairfield, Connecticut, thoroughly and thoughtfully reviewed most of the chapters and offered invaluable suggestions. Conversations with Dolores D'Agostino greatly helped to shape the work in its initial stages. Ewa Bracko, Cathy McGoldrick, and Pat Kelley provided secretarial and transcription assistance. Patricia Noone, S.C., not only contributed her editorial expertise but also became our valued partner in the project. We cannot thank her enough. With full hearts we thank God for each and all of our collaborators. In the words of Rumi, the thirteenth-century Persian poet: "Your lamp was lit from another lamp. All God wants is your gratitude for that."

Now that the initial germ of the book has flowered into a volume with chapters by visionary commentators, what is our hope for it? That lay leaders recognize themselves, their spirituality, their hopes for the institutions they shepherd and the individuals they serve, in the descriptions and stories here. That in a milieu that gives little support to a life of commitment, lay leaders find sustenance in these chapters as they struggle to balance life and work. That people who care deeply about God, the Church, their institutions, and those they serve be confirmed in their desire to ground their work on life-giving spiritual foundations. That lay leaders be challenged to make the language of the tradition more fully their own, to be nourished by it, and draw upon it to assist a common vision and feed the spirituality of those they lead. That this book encourages conversations about things that truly matter. Finally, we hope and trust that lay leaders claim the dignity and power of being called and chosen to carry the Church's mission . . . "forward and far" (1995 Bishops' statement).

I

THE PERSON OF THE LEADER

This section invites you as leaders to examine the challenge of leading Catholic institutions by first looking within to explore your own inner landscapes of faith. The three chapters of this first part hold a mirror before you, raising foundational questions for reflection:

1. Why do I do what I do?
2. Would it make a difference if I engaged my work as a sacred and empowering calling (vocation)?
3. What shapes the way I habitually think, choose, and act? What are my *lived* values? Where did I get them?

1

Why Did You Choose Your Work?
Reflections on Vocation

Zeni Fox

It is traditional in the Church to speak of the vocation *of those who have been called to service in the community of Christians. Can we speak of the vocation of lay leaders of Catholic institutions? Do you as a lay leader experience a vocation? Does the community see your role as a vocational one? Would the mission be better served if the answer to each of these questions were yes? The following essay proposes affirmative answers to them by exploring the experience of laity, in the context of the tradition.*

For most of us, most of the time, our days are filled with two great endeavors: loving those we love and doing our work. Sometimes—perhaps on a wedding anniversary or the birthday of a beloved friend or family member—we pause to think about the reasons we love this person, this one who is special in our eyes, in our lives. Less often, it seems, we pause to think about why we do our work, what drew us to this work, what motivates us to continue, especially in times of discouragement. In this chapter, I will invite you to ponder your own journey—what brought you to the work you do, why do you continue to do it, and what does your story have to do with God's hopes for the world. I will also invite you to put your personal reflection into dialogue with ideas about vocation, that call from God to take part in God's own work.

CALL

Since the mid-1970s, I have been paying attention to the idea of call. Then, I was teaching a graduate course for Directors of Religious Education, a role still new in the Church. My students that year were all young adults, preparing for work which did not yet have a charted path; they were also all lay people, preparing for a place in Church work that was not yet established. I learned their sense of commitment, their belief that this is something that, somehow, they should do, their inner confidence in their decision, despite their realism about the difficulties that lay ahead (and the puzzlement of their families and friends). I began to think: when I was in school, these were the young men and women who would have entered the seminary or the convent. But neither they nor I had a language to speak of their sense of call. Some years later, as part of my doctoral dissertation, I had the opportunity to learn more about these new ministers in the Church, by conducting a national survey. One finding was that the great majority of respondents affirmed that they had a sense of being called by God to do what they do. Later still, in my role as Director of Lay Ministry at a seminary, I interviewed people when they were applying to the program. Again and again I heard a refrain like, "I think this is what I should be doing now—but I do not know where it will lead." And as I listened to persons employed in ministry struggle with various issues in their work, I realized ever more fully that their sense of call, even though not fully articulated, helped them to persevere in difficult times.

In February 1989 I had a further insight into the idea of call. In three conversations with friends, I encountered again this inchoate language of call. Ann was telling me about her new job teaching English as a second language, her return to employment after being at home raising her children. She said: "It's great. I absolutely love it. I won't be doing CCD [teaching religious education classes] and vacation church school for a while. I feel this is what I should be doing now." Barbara had been involved with many volunteer activities as she raised her children; subsequently she was employed in a social service agency. She had just taken a position in the National Girl Scouts Office and said: "Everything I did before kind of prepared me for the work I'm doing now. I believe in what they are about—empowering girls, empowering women. I know it sounds silly, but I feel this is where I'm supposed to be now." Nancy and her husband had both worked for a small college; there was a change in leadership. Both of them left the school; she took a position with a museum. Nancy said, "I left because I felt I was being used to legitimize something I couldn't believe in anymore. It was hard to have us both leave, but we had to do it. At the museum, I believe in the mission; I couldn't believe in their mission anymore." In these conversations I heard the same sense of call, the same intuition of being drawn to a particular work, because of the value of the work and because of one's own gifts and experience. The convergence of these experiences attuned me to the whispers of call, which people articulated when telling stories of their lives, whether using language like "this is where I'm supposed to be," or that of belief in the value of the work itself.

Newspaper articles, especially obituaries, began to catch my attention. A few examples may serve to invite you to seek similar stories. A *New York Times* obituary of astronomer Carl Sagan included this account: "He became interested in the stars as a child, read science fiction avidly, and said that by the time he was eight he had arrived at the idea that there must be life on planets orbiting other stars. 'I didn't make a decision to pursue astronomy,' he said. 'Rather, it just grabbed me, and I had no thought of escaping.'" *Audubon* magazine's tribute to ornithologist Roger Tory Peterson reflected on obituaries which had marked his death. "A few mentioned the catalytic encounters that both direct and mark the path of a great man's life. A father who didn't quite approve. A nurturing and nature-loving seventh-grade teacher. . . . A two-dollar purse awarded for an illustration. . . . A yellow-shafted flicker, presumed dead, that exploded into life at the touch of a finger, kindling a blaze in an eleven-year-old boy's imagination that flamed for almost seventy-seven years."

Sometimes one's important work is an aspect of larger personal endeavors. John Gibbons heads a law firm in Newark, with clients such as drug companies filing patents and corporations selling stock. But his firm also files an amicus brief in almost every death penalty case in New Jersey. He said: "People in the firm have different views about whether or not there should be a death penalty, but I think that everyone agrees if we're going to have it, issues such as proportionality have to be litigated."

Sometimes a life's work emerges out of loss. The Liz Lerman Dance Exchange includes a troupe for dancers aged sixty to ninety. She explains that she began her career "doing what white modern dancers did" but that she felt out of sync with what she sensed dance was really about. "I knew it had something to do with community, but I didn't know what." The death of her mother brought her to teach at a senior center; that experience gradually led her to develop interactive, multigenerational troupes, and to the healing of her own grief. In each of these stories call was experienced in different ways: fascination with the world (the stars, or birds), a commitment to justice, or being attuned to an inner sense of how dance should be. What are the deep desires of the heart in each of these stories? A passion for knowledge, a passion for beauty, a passion for justice, and a thirst for meaning in life. The call came from without, from within, mediated by others, approved or not by others. Insistent, life giving.

VOCATION

The concept of vocation has a long history in the Church, both in stories in Scripture, including that of Jesus, and in stories of saints throughout history. In recent times in the Catholic community, both because of the work of biblical scholars and because of the teachings of the Second Vatican Council, there has been an effort to reexamine this ancient idea.[1] Let us begin this reflection at the beginning, the story of Creation as told in the opening chapters of the book of Genesis. The Bible gives a stirring account of God calling into being all that is: light and darkness, the seas and the sky, the earth and sun and moon, the birds and sea serpents, trees and plants. And on the sixth day, men and women. All that is, is called into existence, all that is, is held in being by God's loving care, God's kind regard, "It is good." And then God invites men and women to share in the ongoing process of creation, calling on them to name the creatures and to tend the garden, inviting them to share in God's work in the world. Adam and Eve, as parents of the human race, are symbolic representations of all of humanity, all called into being, all called to be partners in the work of God. This first call unites all human persons, of every faith, giving a context for the shared work which characterizes our world today, in the Church and beyond.

Pope Pius XII once said, "Spiritually we are all Semites." As Christians, we claim as our heritage the Hebrew Scriptures and the stories of the great figures in Jewish history. Abraham and Sarah, Moses and Miriam, represent a fuller expression of God's call into being and partnership, now a call to covenant, a call to a more intimate relationship with God: "I will be your God, and you will be my people." This call is to individuals and to the community as a whole; Israel is representative of all humankind, called into an interpersonal relationship with a God who reaches out to lead, to save, and to be with. Much of the Old Testament chronicles the teaching of the prophets, themselves called to a special task of reminding the Israelites that they were invited into an intimate relationship with God. Hosea uses striking imagery to remind them of their failure and God's faithfulness. He speaks of Israel as a bride, an unfaithful bride, to whom God says: "I am going to lure her and lead her out into the wilderness and speak to her heart. . . . There she will respond to me as she did when she was young, as she did when she came out of the land of Egypt" (Hos 2:16–17). Israel is a symbolic representation of all of humanity, called into a relationship of love with the Creator.

Jesus had a strong sense of his relationship with his "Abba," that affectionate term he used to speak of his Father, and a clear sense of having been sent. "I came not to do my own will, but the will of him who sent me" (Jn 6:38). And Jesus called many to join with him in his ministry, his mission. The stories of the calls of various of the Twelve are well known: Andrew and Peter, called away from their fishing boat; Matthew, called away from his tax table. The Gospel of John names various persons as disciples; Andrew is the first. In these disciple stories, John usually has a pattern: the invitation to follow, then a response of the disciple, then the disciple inviting others to follow. Some disciples whose stories he tells are the Samaritan woman, she of five husbands (and "the one you have now is not your husband"), who was the first to proclaim Jesus to a village; Joseph of Arimathea, a rich man and member of the Council, who came forward from his secret discipleship when his help, and tomb, were needed; and Martha and Mary, dear friends of Jesus, who practiced a ministry of hospitality in their own home. Men and women, rich and poor, people of high estate and low, the "good" and the "bad": Jesus called many to share in his work.[2]

An awareness of being called by God marks the stories of saints throughout the history of Christianity. St. Francis of Assisi (1182–1226), a wealthy merchant's son, while praying in a chapel heard a voice speak to him: "Francis, repair my church, which has fallen into disrepair, as you can see." At first he took this call quite literally, physically restoring the dilapidated chapel; only gradually did he grasp his mission to preach the good news to the poor, abandoning his own riches to commit himself to preaching and to poverty. Joan of Arc (1412[?]–1431), a peasant girl, heard the voices of saints, charging her with a mission to save France. Her restoration of the dauphin to the throne eventually cost her life; her holiness was grounded in a commitment to the world and engagement in the events of history. Ignatius of Loyola (1491–1556), nobleman and soldier, during a long recuperation became fascinated with the stories of saints. Drawn by their example, he determined to dedicate himself to God's service. The religious order he founded, the Jesuits, is the largest in the world; his *Spiritual Exercises* give us guidance today in the process of discerning vocation. The story of Catherine of Genoa, aristocrat and servant of the sick, is told by Dolores Leckey in chapter 10 of this volume. Like Ignatius, she combined an active life with a life of contemplation. Elizabeth Ann Seton (1774–1821), born in New York City, was a socialite in the early days of our republic. Wife, mother of five, young widow, convert, eventually foundress of a religious order, she began a school which became the nucleus of Catholic education in the United States, and left a rich spiritual legacy of letters and journals. Edith Stein (1891–1942) was born to Orthodox Jewish parents; she became a philosopher, completing her dissertation, on empathy, when she was twenty-three years old. An atheist since the age of thirteen, one day she read the life of St. Teresa of Avila and concluded, "This is the truth." Years after her conversion, she entered a Carmelite convent, seeking a life of contemplation. Arrested by the Nazis, she died at Auschwitz. Men and women, rich and poor, people of high estate and low, the call sounds down the ages, inviting many to share in God's work.

THE LANGUAGE OF CALL AND VOCATION

This chapter began with some stories of call. In none of those stories was there an explicit naming of being called by God to do the work they did;

none of them said, "This is my vocation." In the brief comments about certain saints, there is a more explicit naming of the call that shaped the lives of these men and women. However, it is helpful to note the way in which the language they used was shaped by the culture and age in which they lived.

During the time of Francis, the troubadours, with their songs and emphasis on courtly love, shaped the imagination of young people. In the Church, currents of reform were swirling, with several movements emphasizing the poverty of Jesus and the need to divest oneself of wealth. Francis speaks of his commitment to Lady Poverty and composes songs to Brother Sun, influenced certainly by the themes of his day, casting a central aspect of his vocation in the language of his time. Joan of Arc's inner call was described by her as the voices of her saints. A peasant living in a time when the role of saints was central, a time when pilgrimages to sites associated with saints and relics taken from bodies of saints were commonplace, her vocation is described in the way *she* experienced it—her saints spoke to her.

Ignatius had been drawn to a military life; when the stories of saints stirred him to want to respond more fully to God, he laid his sword and dagger on the altar and said that he would be a soldier of Christ. Those who joined his religious order went to every part of the world to preach the Gospel, as if they were soldiers sent on a mission to a foreign land. Elizabeth Seton expressed her call in terms of an intimate relationship with Christ, the language of a devoted daughter, a truly happy wife (and then quite young widow) and mother, whose life had been defined by familial relationships. Edith Stein, a philosopher, was drawn by the truth she perceived in the story of St. Teresa of Avila and so became a convert to Catholicism from Judaism. As the clouds of Nazi darkness gathered in intensity, she composed a prayer offering herself as a sacrifice of atonement for the Jewish people; when the Gestapo came to arrest her, she said to her sister, "Come, Rosa. We're going for our people." Her Jewish identity and the terrors of her time elicited the language of her heritage to describe her vocation.

We live today in a secular age; we do not expect to hear the voices of saints, as Joan did; we do not expect to kneel in a chapel and receive an audible call from God, like Francis. But Catholic belief has as a central tenet the conviction that God has revealed God's very self to us, in Jesus, and that this revelation is ongoing, that even today God is revealing the very Truth, Goodness, and Beauty of God's infinite Being to us. The God who called each of us into being reveals God's self to us, that we may enter into intimate relationship with God and through God with each other, creating community, *communio* (as Pope John Paul II stressed).

Furthermore, we are invited to take part in the mission of Jesus, the mission of preparing the way for the final coming of the reign of God. All of our lives can be part of that mission, building toward that time of a plentitude of love and understanding, of fullness and plenty, of health and well-being, of beauty and truth, of holiness and happiness, of freedom and completion, which is God's reign.[4] This vision of God's reign is derived from the promises of the Old Testament and all that Jesus did when he walked this earth. These are at once the values of the reign, God's desires for the world, and the fulfillment of the yearnings of the human heart.

In a special way our work can be a part of that mission, focused on an aspect of the reign of God, whether as a scientist seeking truth or an administrator creating a community focused on its mission, whether a parent teaching a child to share or a nurse tending a dying person, whether a social worker striving for healing in a family or a farmer growing vegetables. The stories told earlier of an astronomer and an ornithologist each represent ways in which work furthered progress toward God's reign, whether or not Sagan and Peterson were conscious of their inner call as a *vocation* and whether or not they were aware of their life's work as part of the *mission of Jesus* preparing the way for the *reign of God*. God's purpose is achieved when human persons respond to the invitation offered through the events of their lives and in the quiet of their hearts, allowing themselves to be instruments for God's desires. In that response is both the good of the community of human persons and the happiness of the individual.

In the focus groups conducted as work on this book began, there are many instances of such a response to the invitation of God. The language is more often secular than religious. But the sense of a *call* is there; listen:

> I think that the decision to leave teaching and go into administration was probably harder than deciding to get married. It was for me a very difficult, searching decision to take that step. . . . I didn't want to do this, but I knew that if Catholic education is going to continue . . . there have to be people with vision. There have to be people to make the commitment. . . . Plus my husband has been tremendously supportive.
>
> —Mary, Diocese of Cincinnati

> The principal at St. A's was leaving at the time, and the principal previous to him kept talking to me about going there and I really wasn't interested in it. Finally I decided well, you know, this was a chance. This is a chance to strike a blow for social justice. Because these people are going to grow up to be people who make decisions that are going to affect other people. So I went to St. A's and I've been there now for . . . this is my eighteenth year and I think just by looking at our website you can see that the social justice piece is really a fundamental part of the school. . . . We really work hard at it. I'm very proud of what we've done and I'm proud of our Popes, they're good. Even though it just makes me crazy sometimes, being in this job, I can't imagine doing anything else.
>
> —Clarisse, Diocese of Fort Worth

I really felt like I wanted to do something where I truly could have more of an impact on a school.

—Sharon, Diocese of Cincinnati

Our principal left two weeks before school started. . . . The pastor asked me if I would become principal. I found I loved it. I loved doing administration. Your opportunities to do so much more just open up when you're a principal . . . the opportunity to help so many more people. . . . I feel quite at home; it's where I should be.

—Joanne, Diocese of Cincinnati

Some of the faculty members came to me and said would you consider this. My answer was no. . . . You know, I like what I'm doing. And then I did begin to give serious consideration. Then the priest came to me and said, "I want you to try this. I think you would be able to handle this." You know, that little pep talk sort of thing, and with the encouragement of my husband I said okay. In the back of my mind I was called to the challenge.

—Bernie, Diocese of Cincinnati

I had a great job and I loved what I was doing. . . . And then as I looked back on it and watched all the turbulence that the school had been through I realized that I needed to step up and take that job. It wasn't really what I wanted to do because I loved working in the classroom, I loved working with the students and that's where the action was. But I knew in my heart that I could do the job and that I could get things straightened out and I could bring tranquility to the school. As I was looking back on that, I was sitting at Mass one day and the reading was from Samuel and all of a sudden it clicked and I got it. . . . That's what happened to me—like Samuel, a voice that I did not at first grasp! I hope that's what it was!

—Lynn, Diocese of Fort Worth

Teaching was something that turned me on since I was in second grade.

—John, Archdiocese of Newark

I actually started by accident. A nun fell and broke her leg and I had just come home from college. I was a math major and going to be rich. I said I would try substitute teaching and my friend at the time said I could have this job until Sister's leg healed. That was 23 years ago. . . . I fell in love with the whole thing. The people that were there, the sisters that were there. . . . The kids were great. . . . My parents were willing to put up with the fact that I wasn't going to give in any money.

—Janet, Archdiocese of Newark

I wanted to be a teacher ever since I was introduced to Sister Mary's class-room and saw what she was doing. I think I was four years old. . . . I am married to a Catholic high school administrator. A principal married to a principal. We both feel certain ideals of Catholic education that we wrote into our marriage vows. . . . So for us, this isn't just a job, this is a true vo-cation and it's the way we carry on.

—Colette, Archdiocese of Newark

There are various aspects of these stories to note. Sometimes people left what they loved to take on another role. Tradition tells us that Abraham was called out of the land of Ur and the prophet Amos was called to leave his work as a picker of sycamore trees to prophesy for the Lord; God's voice is often in places of change. Sometimes those called were very reluctant to take on the new role, as were most of the prophets. Jeremiah pleaded that he was too young and Moses that he was not eloquent. Vocational call is greater than the limitations one has, deeper than the anxieties that arise. Sometimes others played a key role, extending the invitation or providing support. In the call of Samuel, it is the priest in the Temple, Eli, who tells the young boy to go back and listen again, and if someone calls, to say, "Speak, Yahweh, your servant is listening." Sometimes there was a long attraction to the role, con-stant, marking the progress of the person's life. Only one of these stories uses the explicit language of vocation. And only one speaks of God's call—and in that case the realization that there was a *call* came long after the response to the inchoate call. In a secular age, even in a Catholic school among those who have committed themselves to an explicit sharing in the mission of the Church, the traditional language of vocation is generally not used.

CULTURAL AND ECCLESIAL UNDERSTANDINGS OF CALL

Perhaps it began with Richard Bolles's perennially popular *What Color Is Your Parachute?* first published in 1970 and now in its thirty-fourth printing. Today the language of vocation, both implicit and explicit, can be found in many contemporary books that focus on finding a job. They focus on the deeper quest, finding the *right* job, carefully discerning one's gifts and inter-ests, and seeking work that is meaningful and fits one's deeper self. The em-phasis is on such things as taking a voyage of self-discovery, breaking out of boxes, discovering the Zen of the career search. Bolles says:

The job hunt offers a chance to make some fundamental changes in our whole life. . . . It gives us a chance to ponder and reflect, to extend our mental hori-zons, to go deeper into the sub-soil of our soul. It gives us a chance to wrestle with the question, "Why am I here on Earth?" . . . We want to find that special joy, "that no one can take from us," which comes from having a sense of Mission in our life . . . the concept of Mission lands us inevitably in the lap of God.[5]

Other writers explore the inner life of one's work, the deep place where vocation is known. Parker Palmer has several titles focused on varied aspects of this theme. In *The Active Life: A Spirituality of Work, Creativity, and Caring*, he uses stories and poems from several religious traditions to invite a pondering of action and contemplation, the link between them, and the stresses of contemporary life which challenge a healthy relationship between the two. *The Courage to Teach: Exploring the Inner Landscape of a Teacher's Life* invites a deep pondering of the implications of this vocation, especially in light of the challenges teachers face. *Let Your Life Speak: Listening for the Voice of Vocation* counsels concerning ways to discern one's vocation.[6] In *Big Questions, Worthy Dreams: Mentoring Young Adults in Their Search for Meaning, Purpose and Faith*, Sharon Daloz Parks continues her incisive work focused on helping young adults discern vocation.[7] Themes of call and commitment within the corporate world are probed through myths and poetry in *The Heart Aroused*,[8] through interviews with many diverse people in *Common Fire: Leading Lives of Commitment in a Complex World*,[9] and through an analysis of the leadership of several biblical figures in *A Work of Heart: Understanding How God Shapes Spiritual Leaders*.[10] All these books use constructs which focus on human experience, on the ways in which call is heard by educated persons living in the twenty-first century and working in the professions and the world of business. All invite readers to a deeper exploration of their own experience. Such perspectives are also informing the efforts at a number of colleges, including Catholic ones, which today utilize major grants from the Lilly Foundation to explore themes of vocation with their students and faculty.

Within the Catholic Church, however, the category of vocation is often one that describes only the reality of priests and vowed religious or, sometimes, the vocations to priesthood, religious life, or married life. In many churches the Prayer of the Faithful each Sunday includes a petition for an increase of vocations—often stipulated as to the priesthood and religious life. Our history in recent centuries has shaped this view; for example, the 1912 *Catholic Encyclopedia* has a modifier to its entry on vocation, "ecclesiastical and religious,"[11] and does not have another entry. The 1967 edition adds an entry, "Vocation to Supernatural Life," which is parallel to the understanding of the universal call to holiness emphasized in the documents of the Second Vatican Council, and another, "Vocational Psychology," which outlines a developmental theory of occupational choice.[12] In the 1994 *Catechism of the Catholic Church* there are several entries for vocation; they treat either the universal call to holiness or dimensions of the contemporary understanding of vocation outlined in this chapter, drawn from the book of Genesis. None treats a vocation to one's work. It is not surprising, therefore, that for most lay Catholics there is not an adequate language available to describe their search for the *right* work, their experience of an inner drawing to *this* work, their experience of their vocation to work.

WHY "VOCATION"?

Is there any value in using the concept of vocation in reference to one's work? Contemporary works by authors like Palmer and Whyte chronicle the effect of seeking that work which one's heart calls one to—or, phrased another way, the work God calls one to. They explore the ways in which wellsprings of meaning, commitment, and creativity are tapped and the good of the world served more effectively when there is greater consciousness of vocation. In my experience, it is their sense of vocation that has strengthened lay ecclesial ministers, sustaining them in their work despite the vague contours of their place in the church, despite their struggles personally, and often financially. I believe that lay leaders of Catholic institutional ministries also have responded to God's call, first in choosing a helping profession, whether in education, health care, or social service, whether there is a conscious awareness of this or not. They have responded again to God's call when they accept roles of leadership, assisting communities of people to live their vocations more fully, to serve the reign of God more effectively, whether this language is used to describe their efforts or not. But there is a value, as theologian Karl Rahner describes it, in bringing to the level of conscious awareness that which is already present by grace, a value in the realization that *I am called, to this.*

An awareness of vocation often comes "after the fact," as described by Lynn earlier in this chapter. He heard the echo of his own experience when the story of Samuel was read at Mass, even though this was years after his response to the inchoate call. The Scripture elicited the awareness of what already existed in his life. This awareness is often helped when others note their perception of a person's vocation. Research on vocations to priesthood demonstrates that the role of someone who asks, "Have you thought about becoming a priest?" is quite important. The difficulty is that so often our Catholic communities do not think in terms of the vocations of lay people to roles in the Church, and so do not assist the development of this awareness.

However, it is not only the individual who benefits from a clearer awareness of vocation. Those who exercise leadership in the Catholic community become stewards of the heritage of the community—stewards of institutions, yes, but also of Catholic identity, and of the very mission of the Church. It is their communities, and the entire Church, which benefit when the leaders God has called forth are recognized as having a vocation. The task of creating a greater awareness of the multiplicity of vocations in our Church today has two parts. The first is work individuals need to do, the inner work which will allow the consciousness of call to grow.[13] The second is work the community needs to do—theologians,[14] bishops,[15] and communities of faith.[16] A deeper appreciation of what is unfolding in the life of the Church today, with many lay persons coming forward to serve in diverse roles, and a deeper appreciation of both our Scriptural tradition and the teachings of Vatican II, will foster the vocational awareness which is needed. At our Sunday liturgy, sometimes the response to a reading is, "If today you hear God's voice, harden not your heart." We believe that God *is* speaking, *is* calling, and individually and as a community we pray that we hear and respond.

REFLECTION QUESTIONS

1. Chart your journey to the work you do today. On a time line note significant turning points (e.g., graduation, change of job). Add the names of people who influenced you—especially your choices and your convictions about what you wanted to do with your life. Add events that had an impact on your life—external events, in the larger world or your immediate life, and internal events, such as a new realization or insight about yourself or about life. Read I Samuel, chapter 3. Does the Scriptural account give insight about your vocation? What has contributed to your vocation? Where have God's voice and providence been?
2. Which aspect of the reign of God is the particular focus of the work you do? Of the institution in which you work?
3. Most Catholic institutional ministries today are comprised of people of many, and no, faiths, both among those who serve and those who are served. Can the concept of vocation be shared by people of diverse faiths in your setting? If yes, how?

NOTES

1. The framework for this exploration of vocation is drawn from the entry by Laurence J. O'Connell, "Vocation," in *The New Dictionary of Catholic Spirituality*, ed. Michael Downey (Collegeville, MN: The Liturgical Press, 1993), 1009.

2. Reflections on discipleship are drawn from Raymond E. Brown, Joseph A. Fitzmyer, and Roland E. Murphy, eds., *The New Jerome Biblical Commentary* (Englewood Cliffs, NJ: Prentice Hall, 1990), especially 952–953, 956.

3. Perspectives on these saints were drawn from Robert Ellsberg, *All Saints: Daily Reflections on Saints, Prophets, and Witnesses for Our Time*, (New York: Crossroad, 1998).

4. Contemporary scripture scholarship recognizes the symbol of the reign or kingdom of God as the central focus of the preaching and ministerial works of Jesus. Jesus embraced the vision of Isaiah, which he took as the text for his first proclamation in the Temple: "Unrolling the scroll he found the place where it is written: 'The spirit of the Lord has been given to me, for he has anointed me. He has sent me to bring the good news to the poor, to proclaim liberty to captives and to the blind new sight, to set the downtrodden free, to proclaim the Lord's year of favor.' . . . Then he began to speak to them, 'This text is being fulfilled today even as you listen.'" A classic exploration of the biblical understanding of God's reign is found in C. H. Dodd, *The Parables of the Kingdom* (New York: Charles Scribner's Sons, 1961).

5. Richard Nelson Bolles, *The 1999 What Color Is Your Parachute: A Practical Manual for Job-Hunters and Career-Changers* (Berkeley: Ten Speed Press, 1999), 241–242.

6. Palmer, *The Active Life* (San Francisco: Jossey-Bass, 1990); *The Courage to Teach* (San Francisco: Jossey-Bass, 1998); *Let Your Life Speak* (San Francisco: Jossey-Bass, 2000).

7. Parks (San Francisco: Jossey-Bass, 2000).

8. David Whyte (New York: Doubleday, 1996).

9. Laurent A. Parks Daloz et al. (Boston: Beacon Press, 1996).

10. Reggie McNeal (San Francisco: Jossey-Bass, 2000).

11. s.v. "Vocation: Ecclesiastical and Religious," by A. Vermeersch, 1912 edition, 15:498.

12. s.v. "Vocation to Supernatural Life" and "Vocational Psychology" by W. H. Principe and J. F. Kinnane, 1967 edition, 14:736 and 738.

13. Many of the titles mentioned in the notes to this chapter could facilitate growth in awareness of one's call. Margaret Benefiel's stories of Jack Raslowsky and Jennifer Moran (see chapter 13 of this volume) illustrate ways in which religious orders such as the Jesuits and the School Sisters of Notre Dame have developed strategies for inviting lay leaders to share their stories and missions in intentional ways.

14. A helpful book outlining a theology of ministry that embraces the diverse roles of laity and clergy is Edward Hahnenberg, *Ministries: A Relational Approach* (New York: Crossroad, 2003).

15. A first step is the Report of the Subcommittee on Lay Ministry, *Lay Ecclesial Ministry: The State of the Questions* (Washington, DC: United States Catholic Conference, 1999). Individual bishops also have addressed related questions, e.g., Cardinal Roger Mahony, *A Pastoral Letter on Ministry: As I Have Done for You* (Chicago: Liturgy Training Publications, 2000).

16. Communities of vowed religious women have been at the forefront of developing a vocational awareness among those who share the leadership of institutions they have founded.

2

"Without a Vision the People Perish": Foundations for a Spirituality of Lay Leadership

Michael Downey

Christian spirituality offers a context for lay leaders to understand their role in articulating the vision and fostering the mission in their institutions. Michael Downey understands the challenge that faces leaders who must gather the fragments of a group's vision in today's complex world, in order to lead them. He directs us to Jesus' all-consuming passion for the reign of God, which undergirds the vision and gives expression to the mission of all Catholic enterprises. Lay leaders, Downey suggests, need competence, passion, and ability to communicate the Christian vision within and beyond their institutions. His essay provides conceptual tools for leaders who seek to ponder what the Spirit is doing in their midst.

Any treatment of spirituality today would do well to begin by recognizing the multiplicity of meanings associated with the term. Even within a specifically Christian or Catholic context, "spirituality" is rather slippery, a word thickly layered with significance.[1] I understand "spirituality" to refer not simply to one dimension of the Christian life such as prayer, recollection, discernment, or ascetical practice, but to the whole of one's life in response to the gift of God in Christ Jesus through the presence and power of the Holy Spirit. Christian spirituality is nothing more or less than being conformed to the person of Christ, brought into communion with God and others through the gift of the Spirit. Christian spirituality is Trinitarian spirituality, a whole way of living concerned with the quest for God the Father, through the Son who is Christ the Word, by the gift of the Holy Spirit in the whole of our lives and every dimension of our living, not just this or that part of it.[2]

With this understanding of spirituality to the fore, it is my purpose to set out the foundations of a specifically Christian spirituality for lay leadership for those lay men and women who are in leadership roles in Catholic grade and high schools, colleges and universities, Catholic hospitals and other enterprises—positions previously held by members of religious institutes or clergy. My concern is this: How do leaders of Catholic enterprises in an increasingly nonreligious milieu recognize the gift and task of their mission and the mission of their enterprises as a way of deepening their own spiritual lives and the lives of others?

I proceed in five steps. First, I begin with an understanding of the charism of leadership as the capacity to formulate and articulate a vision of an enterprise at hand. Second, I attend to some of the core elements of a specifically Christian vision. Third, I look to some of the challenges in articulating a Christian vision today, one that elicits commitment and dedication, indeed passion, on the part of constituents, coworkers, and colleagues. Fourth, I maintain that the life and work of the baptized, in this instance the lay leader, are a participation in the mission of the Word and Spirit, even if the leader has no clear sense of leadership as a vocation or ministry. Finally, in the way of practical guidance, I suggest that the lay leader grows and develops in the spiritual life and gives shape to a distinctive Christian spirituality for lay leaders, when one understands oneself as a person in whom the vision of a body becomes clearer.

THE SPIRIT'S GIFT

A Christian spirituality for lay leaders is rooted in an understanding of God's gift and giving. "Charism" is a gift given and received for the good of a body of persons and its common life, purpose, and sense of destiny. Religious orders and congregations have emerged in Christian history as a result of a charism, or gift, given to a particular person in order to respond to the needs of the Church and society at a particular time and place. The charisms of many congregations of apostolic women religious were and are often discerned in response to the needs of the poor, the uneducated, or the sick and suffering. Hence, the term "charism" is often rather narrowly associated with such congregations and orders. But the term has roots that are older and deeper.

Turning to the corpus of Saint Paul, we see that all who make up the body are gifted, no matter how insignificant the gift may seem. Just as the members are many, so are the gifts that inspire, enliven, and enlighten the body with God's own breath and brightness. In the midst of such an abundance of gift and gifting, what is it that lies at the heart of the charism of leadership?

In Paul himself we find a leader who seeks to articulate a vision amidst diverse situations. Paul struggles, sometimes a bit awkwardly, to spell out his understanding of the new community graced with God's gift of enduring love through Christ the Word by the gift of the Spirit's love. Rather than a hermetically sealed picture, Paul stitches together fragments of insight by which he builds a vision piecemeal. In addressing the Church at Corinth, his vision is of a new community that he likens to a human body. No part or member is less essential than any other. On the contrary, the lesser, weaker, or more vulnerable parts are to be given special care and attention so that the body may flourish. In such a vision, the new community's members are to relate differently to one another and to the larger human community because of a new sense of holiness moored in discipleship of Jesus Christ, rather than through strict adherence to the Law.

In this new community, holiness is not relegated to the few, to the ritually pure, or to those thought to be set apart for specifically religious activities. Holiness lies in the perfection of those elements that are the hallmarks of the new community: faith and hope and love. In the vision of the new community, holiness pertains not only to ritual and worship, but also to domestic concerns and the daily grind. It embraces every dimension of human life and living: the personal and political, the ethical and economic. It has as much to do with sexuality as it does with saving so as to tithe for the widow and the orphan. Nothing is outside the pale in the effort of the baptized to be conformed to the person of Christ, which is the core of the quest for holiness. While there may be much more to the vision, there is at least this much. Paul braids strands together, holds up and shakes out what he has come to see so that others might see it, live with and from it, carrying it forward to the next generation, putting whatever gifts each one has to the service of this understanding of the new community, the Body of Christ.

In light of a different ecclesial reality among the earliest Christian churches at Ephesus, Paul emphasizes Christ's headship, as he does with the Colossians. In the Church at Philippi, however, his emphasis is on Jesus Christ as exemplar in his self-giving. Whatever there may be in the way of coherence and consistency in the Pauline vision of a new community, it emerges from an effort to articulate vision in response to quite diverse situations.

In this schema, vision, even if it is constructed from patches of insight and intuitive hunches, comes first. Without it, in the words of the Book of Proverbs (16:9) from which the title of this essay derives, people get lost—so lost that they perish. Charisms are to be discerned in view of a vision and are to be put to its service. It is precisely the ability to articulate a vision in a persuasive and compelling way which lies at the heart of the charism of leadership.

OUR VISION: THE REIGN OF GOD

For the contours of the vision we, like Paul, look to the teaching of Christ. It is my contention that any vision which is expressed and impressed by the leader must be nurtured and sustained by the language, imagery, and narratives which disclose that which was central to the life, teaching, and mission of Jesus Christ: the reign of God.

What is the reign, or kingdom, of God? And why is the reign of God apposite in the formulation of a vision here and now? Perhaps above all it is because the reign of God conveys the sense of building, of giving shape to something in a world order wherein others share some of the concerns of Christians. In speaking of God's reign Jesus was seeking to express God's hope, desire, and intention for the world now and to come. The reign of God is a way of speaking about the world as it will be when God has God's way in the world, a world in which holiness, truth, justice, love, and peace prevail. It is the reign of God that Jesus preached and for which he died, pouring out the seeds of an enduring love for the transformation of the world in and through love.

But in such transformation, the Christian community, the Church, or the Catholic enterprise is not a freestanding entity. In every time and place, the vision must be given fresh expression in light of shifting modes of perceiving and being, with respect for diverse cultures and traditions, in view of the historical facts which shape the lives of different peoples. And in every age the question is this: What mission is inspired by this vision of the reign of God?

An understanding of the reign of God central to any Christian vision can be greatly enriched by a range of perspectives on the mystery of Christ, especially when the vision seems hazy. From among this range, it may be useful to single out John Paul II, whose horizon is shaped by the conviction that the good news is to be proclaimed in relation to what the Second Vatican Council called the "signs of the times." It is here that the Spirit of God, the Spirit of Christ, is present and active: in humanity and historicity. Human beings live at a specific time and place, within a world marked and marred by events, by what actually goes on in the world. Attentiveness to these gives us access to the deep aspirations of the human heart, as well as to its sense of failure and despair. Christians share these with the whole human family.

Two of John Paul II's writings may be particularly useful in helping to articulate a sense of mission inspired by the reign of God, as well as in laying the foundations for a spirituality of lay leadership. In the encyclical *Redemptoris Missio*, John Paul, with an eye to the reign of God, articulates the mission of Christ entrusted to the Church in light of an "overall view of the human race," maintaining that "this mission is still only beginning and that we must commit ourselves wholeheartedly to its service."[3] He looks to a changed and changing world. It is here and now that the good news of the reign of God is to take root. The vast array of cultures is both challenged and enriched by the Gospel.

Of particular import is his treatment of "the modern equivalents of the Areopagus." The Areopagus in Athens represented the cultural center for dialogue and exchange of ideas (cf. Acts 17:22–31). John Paul employs the Areopagus as a symbol of the new locales in which the good news must be proclaimed, and to which the mission of Christ is to be directed.[4] Of these various locales, the new Areopagai, John Paul singles out the worlds of communications, of culture, scientific research, and international relations, which promote dialogue and open new possibilities. Solutions to pressing problems are to be studied, discussed, and worked out precisely in these and other Areopagai, problems and concerns such as urbanization; the poor; the young; migration of non-Christians to traditionally Christian countries; peace and justice; "development and the liberation of peoples; the rights of individuals and peoples, especially those of minorities; the advancement of women and children; safeguarding the created world."[5] John Paul also takes stock of the desperate search for meaning, the need for an inner life, and a desire to learn new forms and methods of meditation and prayer.[6] The mission is to take up these and the other pressing concerns amidst the new Areopagai, bringing the gospel of Christ to bear even and especially there. In so doing, the Christian community is at the service of "furthering human freedom by proclaiming Jesus Christ."[7]

In all these Areopagai, the reign of God is coming into being. And given the increasingly secularist ambience of the Catholic institutional ministries, communities, and enterprises in which the mission of Christ and the Church must now take effect, it is precisely the laity, and particularly lay leaders, who have a crucial role to play.

In his Post-Synodal Apostolic Exhortation on the Vocation and the Mission of the Lay Faithful in the Church and in the World, *Christifideles Laici*, John Paul grounds in baptism the participation of all in the Church in the mission of Christ.[8] He looks to the particular role of the lay person in the realization of mission, emphasizing that the distinctive character of lay life is to be a sign of the reign of God in the world.[9] He understands the lay state not just in anthropological and sociological terms, but also as a theological and ecclesiological reality.[10] It is the laity who, in seeking the reign of God by engaging in temporal affairs and ordering them according to the plan of God, are the presence of God's reign in the world.[11] But, again, this vision must constantly be formulated and reformulated in diverse communities in light of shifting modes of perceiving and being.

THE BEAUTY OF BRICOLAGE

In times of cultural transition and social upheaval, vision may be hard to cultivate. But it is never more necessary. We find ourselves within a world context marked on many fronts by disillusionment and disappointment. Efforts in the bygone century to present a coherent big picture against which we can see a future filled with promise have failed. Ours is a time marked by interruption and disorientation wherein the center no longer seems to hold, and where there is increasing doubt about the trustworthiness of claims to any objective or absolute truth.[12] The Church's position in the current world order is not as secure as it once was. The recent sexual abuse scandals, and the seemingly incomprehensible decisions of Church leaders in the face of the sexual misconduct of its members, have not helped to secure the Church's place as an authentic voice of good news. Even as the Church continues unabated in an effort to convey a coherent, all-encompassing global vision into which everything fits, there is widespread recognition that it is foolhardy to try to establish a solution that is perennially valid, self-evidently true, intelligible to any reasonable person.

Drawing from the French, some contemporary thinkers use the word bricolage in describing how to face complex matters in a chaotic, fragmented world marked by plurality and ambiguity. Bricolage conveys a sense of lining up whatever is at hand, gathering bits and pieces, pulling together strands from here and there in the way that one would stitch a patchwork quilt or construct figurines from pieces of scrap metal found in a junk heap. The term describes an approach to an issue or concern that gathers insight from whatever is at hand, assembling insights in the way of a conceptual beggar in order to provide some small perspective, recognizing that this is necessarily partial and limited. Bricolage is best done not in strict adherence to a plan set in granite, but to the creative dynamism as it unfolds and gives direction in interaction with the materials at hand.

The notion of bricolage may be helpful in coming to terms with the concern regarding lay leaders to carry on the mission of Catholic higher education. In an instructive paper presented at a conference on "Lay Leadership and the Age of the Laity: Emerging Patterns of Catholic Higher Education,"[13] a gathering of Catholic lay leaders earnestly exploring how they might carry forward the mission and identity of the Catholic institutes entrusted to them, Melanie Morey and Dennis Holtschneider have offered the following observations: "Whatever the reasons for the personal optimism [of lay presidents], the data clearly indicate that lay presidents lack significant preparation for leadership in the areas of mission and identity and, at least in general terms, identify this gap as a serious problem for the future of Catholic education, but not for themselves individually."[14] Further: "With little or no formal preparation, formation, or study, lay men and women enter Catholic college and university presidencies with a distinct leadership disadvantage. It would seem this lack of religious education and formation could have a negative impact on the enterprise of Catholic higher education. Presidents, however, do not seem so convinced, nor do the institutions they serve."[15] So, while recognizing the problem, the presidents see it in everyone else's proverbial backyard but their own: "Catholic college and university presidents have an uncanny ability to see the splinter in another's eye while missing the plank in their own."[16]

The work of Morey and Holtschneider is extremely useful in pointing to some of the challenges of lay leadership. Three observations: First, the "leadership disadvantage" does not pertain to Catholic college and university presidents alone, but is likely the case with lay leaders in the whole range of enterprises once led by vowed religious or clergy. Second, while the Morey and Holtschneider research focused on lay leaders, it is my contention that many clergy and religious today are likewise inadequately prepared and formed in the theological and spiritual foundations to support the mission and identity of a Catholic enterprise. The highly pragmatic and utilitarian mind-set of many who claim to be more pastoral and "hands on"—often at the expense of sound theological and spiritual education and formation—has contributed to the theological and spiritual illiteracy of religious and clergy, as well as of the laity.

My third observation takes the form of a question: Is it possible that what leaders lack is an understanding of mission and identity more in line with a comprehensive world view in which everything has its place in a tightly knit order? If this is what is lacking, is there cause here for lamentation or for hope? If we lament it as a costly loss, is there also reason for hope? Is something being offered amidst the loss? I answer in the affirmative. But it will come only in the hard work of bricolage, fashioning a vision around the governing image of the reign of God in order to give people a clearer sense of what they are doing in this or that enterprise and why, without being altogether certain about where all the pieces fit.

Central to any Christian vision must be the reign of God, in which truth, holiness, justice, love, and peace will prevail. This is brought about as one works in the here and now to safeguard and promote the dignity of the human person, the rights of workers, the person in relationship and community, opting for the poor, building solidarity among persons, nations, races, and classes, and caring for creation. To this must be added an ongoing commitment to forgiveness as a basis for a new world order. In his message to the world's diplomats for World Peace Day 2002, John Paul sums up his main point in the lapidary phrase: no peace without justice, no justice without forgiveness.[17]

With the vision sometimes still in the making, not knowing how the details of a specific Catholic enterprise relate to the vision, the leader must be able to discern the movements of the life and breath of God, i.e., the Spirit, amidst the new Areopagai, so as to further the reign. Aware that a Catholic enterprise can no longer be understood as standing alone as a separate entity, but as a small part of a larger world, be it the world of education, or health care, or the effort to secure peace and justice, the leader must have the knack for seizing the moment, knowing when and how to move in response to the Spirit amidst the larger human project, helping those one leads to find their way and articulate their concerns in the new Areopagai, always bringing the elements of the vision to bear.

But there is more. Not only must the leader have the wherewithal to articulate the vision for those one leads; the leader must also spell out the vision for others in the Areopagai who adhere to different visions, but whose efforts are nonetheless directed to the service of human freedom and dignity.

What does the lay leader seek to promote? When the teacher asks, What am I educating to? how does the lay leader respond? How does the leader deal with questions of life and death in hospital ministry? How does she or he guide others to help the sick wrestle with questions of God?

The answer seemed clearer when religious and clergy were in charge of Catholic enterprises. For example, the first Sisters of Mercy, following the lead of their foundress, Catherine McAuley, looked after the material needs of the poor, sick, and ignorant on Dublin's Baggot Street. Throughout the world, Mercy hospitals, schools, and colleges—all with a particular mission to the poor, the sick, and the unlettered—were fueled by the example of one woman and her vision. McAuley's Sisters have lived by the life-orienting conviction that her approach to nursing, health care, and education really does make a difference.

Perhaps much too late, religious and clergy are making valiant efforts to train lay leaders to live from a vision that guided the foundation and growth of the enterprise. But we will not soon be rid of the questions: What is distinctive about a Catholic health care system? Or a Catholic university? What are we educating to? Finally, what will become of these enterprises in the next generation? How will the mission of Catholic education and health care continue when there are few, if any, Catholic schools and hospitals as we now know them? Who will then be poised to lead those seeking new ways and new means of presence in order to continue the mission of Christ the Teacher and Healer? It is now upon the shoulders of lay leaders to begin to craft the vision of a new community of presence and mission amidst the new Areopagai, a new mode of interaction with those who inhabit different worlds, just as Paul did. Even if we do not know all the elements of such a vision in service of the reign of God, as we work toward it in the manner of bricolage we share in the mission of Word and Spirit.

ONE MISSION: OF WORD AND SPIRIT

As various Catholic enterprises grapple with the question of mission and identity, there is often a tendency to rely on the language of the founding religious institute or clerical body. Traces of this are often found in the open-ing lines of mission statements of schools, universities, hospitals, and other Catholic bodies. Whatever the specific mission statement, working toward the reign of God is always the one mission of any Catholic body. And this, in turn, is a share in the mission of Word and Spirit, indeed a participation in the divine life. Even if one does not have any clear sense of lay leadership as a vocation or a ministry in the Church, it is nonetheless a share in the mis-sion of Word and Spirit, which is a mission to make manifest the magnitude of God's love in the world.

Word is God's love heard and seen. *Spirit* is the principle of God's cre-ativity and bonding. Love expressed and bonding take many different forms. To participate in the mission of Word and Spirit is to see and to share in the manifold manifestations of human expressivity and creativity as they disclose the divine reality. The gift and task is to cultivate, nurture, and sustain the great variety of the manifestations of the magnitude of God's love in all forms of expressivity and creativity: education, health care, work for human rights, promotion of the dignity of women, safeguarding the integrity of all creation, respecting the last, littlest, and least in our midst. All these creative expres-sions of love lead to a fuller communion in God's love: the reign of God.

We need only to look at the expressivity of the artist, the poet, the musi-cian, the gardener, the dancer, and the architect, indeed of all who are en-gaged in creative endeavor. They bring together a wide range of elements—textures, colors, sounds, movements—into the creative act, inviting us to a realization of the magnitude of love. This is no less true of the work of the scientist or health care worker, of parenting, educating, or caring for the vul-nerable, sick, and dying. All activities which help build the reign of God, amidst the many worlds we inhabit, are a share in the mission of Word and Spirit, which is the mission of Christ, the mission of the Church, the mission of any Catholic enterprise.

A SPIRITUALITY OF PONDERING

Rooted in the common ground of a baptismal spirituality, what is the partic-ular way in which the lay leader—in everyday life and work—is conformed to the person of Christ, brought into communion with God and others in the gift of the Spirit?

The leader of any of the various institutes once led by members of reli-gious institutes or the clergy must have three ineluctably related strengths. First, there is the comprehensive grasp of the enterprise, be it school, hos-pital, parish, or convalescent home, together with the ability to formulate and articulate the vision of that enterprise. Second, there is the sense of the human person, a certain savoir faire in the dynamics of human freedom and responsibility. Third, the leader must be able to spell out the vision and what is distinctive to the enterprise for others who inhabit different worlds of meaning and value, but who are vital participants in the new Areopagai where the mission is to take effect.

The lay leader often struggles day by day with heavy administrative responsibilities, programming tasks, and fiscal constraints that are part and parcel of the enterprise. The interpersonal may or may not be the leader's strong suit, so at times such matters are delegated to another. But a Christian spirituality for the lay leader demands that leaders live out their daily lives on a field on which at least these three poles are always in view: (1) the enterprise at hand; (2) the care of the persons in one's charge, both those who serve the enterprise (employees) and those who are served by it (clients); and (3) the larger worlds of which the enterprise is a part. All three are to be informed through and through by a vision which the leader holds on to, holds out, and holds up so that others may live freely with, in, and from it, working effectively for its realization. Much more is called for from a leader than being an effective administrator, or a human resources "manager"—and more still if one is to bring the vision to the new Areopagai in a way that is both respectful in dialogue and persuasive in the face of ambiguity.

It is my suggestion that these three poles constitute the matter for the discipline—dare I say asceticism?—at the heart of the spirituality of lay leaders. Holding these three poles together in a noble tension while working for the reign is no easy task. It is only possible for those who are given the charism of leadership for the good of the body.

Central to this gift is the ability to sustain the tension, resisting the tendency to reduce everything to pragmatics, assessments, effective programming. While holding these three poles in a noble tension, the leader's gift is to ponder the emergent contours of the vision still coming to be, cobbling together a vision of the reign in the way of bricolage so as to invite others to live from it in the Areopagai of our own time and place. How will we continue this mission of health care when we have even fewer, if any, Catholic hospitals? How will we care for our aged and dying faithful, religious and clergy, when there are no more Catholic convalescent homes?

What is the spirituality proper to the lay leader? Consider an icon. Classic renderings of the Christian mysteries such as Rublev's icon of the Trinity, or the Vladimir Madonna, or the Descent of Christ into Hell open a whole world of meaning, purpose, and value through a single image. As I use the term in this context, when a person serves as an icon in a group or body, something of the nature of the whole is disclosed. Elsewhere I have suggested that priests are an *icon of the community's pondering heart* and lay ecclesial ministers are an *icon of the Church adventing*.[18] Cardinal Roger Mahony has developed the notion of the deacon as *icon of Christ the servant*.[19] Although she does not rely on the notion of icon, Sandra Schneiders develops the notion of the commitment to the God-quest in a way which precludes any other life commitment as the distinguishing feature of consecrated religious life.[20] I suggest that a spirituality proper to lay leaders, but most certainly not exclusive to them, may be discerned in terms of the leader as *icon of the pondering body*.

Consider Mary, the woman with the pondering heart. She heard the Word and responded to the Spirit without knowing how everything would work out, unsure of how all the pieces fit together. She simply lived with the realization that all comes from God and is to be returned to God. Thereby she shared in the mission of Word and Spirit. And pondering was no small part of it.

To ponder does not mean reflecting on abstract concepts, or probing deep Greek philosophical thoughts. Pondering conveys, rather, a sense of mulling over, considering, of weighing, of trying to balance things that seem to be at odds with one another. In so doing, transformation can take place. By pondering, something gestates into new life.

Central to this spirituality for lay leaders is the realization that the leader is first and finally part of the body, and in service of its enterprise. Collaboration among the various members is a necessary part of effectiveness in mission. Pondering on the part of the leader thus entails calling forth the wisdom and insight, gathering fragments of intuition, listening long and lovingly to all the members of one's body, learning about the enterprise from those who seem last, littlest, and least in the body—and then considering, mulling over, balancing it all, cobbling together what has come forth from the body, in an effort to fashion a clearer sense of how the mission might be more effectively realized in service of the reign of God.

Pondering is not too far afield of contemplation, a specific approach to prayer with its own disciplines and rhythms. Contemplation is not the sole provenance of cloistered monks and nuns. It requires a particular asceticism, at the core of which is setting aside time and giving oneself over to what really matters. Contemplation is not about doing. It requires disciplined focus. In the Christian tradition, the contemplative is "all eyes"—paying attention, being alert, keeping vigil, learning again and again how to read human life and events as they disclose God's presence. Above all, contemplation, like pondering, is about receiving something that is yet coming to be. The one who is truly contemplative has learned to be contemplative not only in prayer but likewise in action.[21] So too the one whose gift and task is to cultivate, nurture, and sustain the discipline of pondering.

In the midst of the confusion, as we struggle to find our way in the world of health care, or of education, if we ponder in humility, with gentleness and patience, something comes to life that is not of our own making. By gracefully bearing it all, the tension is transformed so that pieces of the vision fall into place. We begin small, weaving strands of a vision while carrying the tension brought on by misunderstanding and incomprehension, waiting in hope until it gestates into a living, breathing incarnation of God's love—in and through us. And the reign of God advents in our midst.

We will not soon be rid of the confusion and lack of certainty. The leader must sustain these tensions, even while inviting others to begin again to sing a new song of God's goodness and fidelity. In their turn others carry the tune to new forums and in new keys. In carrying these tensions forward the leader will come to a fresh and deep understanding of what it means to live anew from the deepest hope for the life of a new community, transformed by the love that will prevail over all evil, even as our Catholic enterprises and institutions struggle for survival.

In sum: The lay leader must have (1) *competence* in the enterprise at hand; (2) a deep *passion* for the enterprise and the persons served by it, as well as for those who, together with the leader, serve it; and (3) a facility for *communication* of a specific Christian vision to one's colleagues and collaborators, as well as to constituents of the other worlds of meaning, purpose, and value of which one's enterprise is a part. This is the Spirit's gift, enlightening, enlivening, and guiding the leader to ponder long and lovingly, giving shape to a vision of the reign of God at this time and in this place, thereby participating in the mission of Word and Spirit for the transformation of the whole world and all the living in and through love.

This is the lay leader's gift and task, preparing the way for the next generation, and the next, to find fresh modes of presence and mission from which will emerge new leaders to carry forward the vision in their own time and place.

REFLECTION QUESTIONS

1. In St. Paul's vision of the new community or Body of Christ, all are gifted by the Spirit. What are some of the unique gifts that you bring to the community of your institution?
2. Holiness is the mark of every believer; it "pertains not only to ritual and worship, but to domestic concerns and the daily grind." Go through the hours of a typical day. How is the Spirit of God present in your "daily grind"? How might you grow in awareness of God's presence and activity through the day?
3. Downey, quoting Pope John Paul II, states that laypersons' distinctive way of sharing in the mission of Christ is "to be a sign of the reign of God in the world." What does the reign of God look like through your eyes, in your specific situation? How are you a sign of good news in the public forums ("Areopagai") of your world?

NOTES

1. For a sample of the various meanings of Christian spirituality see Lawrence Cunningham and Keith Egan, *Christian Spirituality: Themes from the Tradition* (New York and Mahwah, NJ: Paulist Press, 1996), 22–28.

2. For a fuller treatment of a Christian spirituality that is Trinitarian through and through, see my *Altogether Gift: A Trinitarian Spirituality* (Maryknoll, NY: Orbis Books, 2000).

3. John Paul II, *Redemptoris Missio*, no. 1: Encyclical on the Permanent Validity of the Church's Missionary Mandate. December 7, 1990.

4. John Paul II, *Redemptoris Missio*, no. 37.

5. John Paul II, *Redemptoris Missio*, no. 37.

6. John Paul II, *Redemptoris Missio*, no. 37.

7. John Paul II, *Redemptoris Missio*, no. 39.

8. John Paul II, *Christifideles Laici*: Post-Synodal Exhortation on the Vocation and the Mission of the Lay Faithful in the Church and in the World. December 30, 1988, no. 15.

9. John Paul II, *Christifideles Laici*, no. 23, citing Paul VI, *Evangelii Nuntiandi* 70. *Acta Apostolicae Sedis* 68 (1976): 60.

10. John Paul II, *Christifideles Laici*, no. 15.

11. John Paul II, *Christifideles Laici*, no. 9.

12. Although I avoid using the term, I have in mind here what is described as the postmodern condition. See Jean-Francois Lyotard, *The Postmodern Condition: A Report on Knowledge* (Minneapolis: University of Minnesota Press, 1984).

13. Melanie M. Morey and Dennis H. Holtschneider, *Leadership and the Age of the Laity: Emerging Patterns in Catholic Higher Education*, (paper delivered at conference on "Lay Leaders in Catholic Higher Education: An Emerging Paradigm for the Twenty-first Century," Sacred Heart University, Fairfield, CT, June 13–15, 2003).

14. Morey and Holtschneider, "Leadership," 10

15. Morey and Holtschneider, "Leadership," 11.

16. Morey and Holtschneider, "Leadership," 10.

17. John Paul II, "Message for World Day of Peace," January 1, 2002: *Origins* 31, no. 28 (December 20, 2001): 461–66.

18. Michael Downey, "Ministerial Identity: A Question of Common Foundations," in *Ordering the Baptismal Priesthood: Theologies of Ordained and Lay Ministries*, ed. Susan K. Wood (Collegeville, MN: Liturgical Press, 2003), 3–25, see 20–23.

19. Roger Cardinal Mahony, "Gather Faithfully Together: Worship, Eucharist, Ministry" (paper presented at the National Catholic Deacon Conference, Saint Mary's College, Moraga, CA, June 23, 2000), p. 5 ff.

20. Sandra M. Schneiders, *Finding the Treasure: Locating Catholic Religious Life in a New Ecclesial and Cultural Context* (New York: Paulist Press: 2000), 32–38.

21. For a superb treatment of the notion of being "contemplative in prayer, likewise in action," see Joseph F. Conwell, *Walking in the Spirit* (Saint Louis: Institute of Jesuit Sources, 2003).

3

"Hints and Guesses": Discerning Values

Msgr. Richard M. Liddy

"Hints and Guesses"—why? Because when we plumb the depths of human experience, we discern, even though dimly, our groundedness in the divine. Richard Liddy leads us through this inner journey, inviting us to claim our experience and to understand it in light of God's self-communication to us through Jesus and the Church. He then explores ways in which all members of the Church can grow in being part of the mission of Jesus by "habits of our hearts," oriented toward a lifestyle focused on goodness, responsive to the promptings of the Spirit within our daily lives.

According to Michael Downey, Christian lay leaders need a vision, for "without a vision the people perish" (Prv 16:9). That vision, of course, is Trinitarian, for we are brought within the Father's tender embrace of his Son in the Holy Spirit. That vision is also of the kingdom coming among us, as in each historical situation the Christian leader discerns through the bricolage of fragmentary insights and hunches the next step in the coming of the kingdom. T. S. Eliot in his *Four Quartets* writes of this as the "hints and guesses" by which we discern the hand of God.

In this chapter I specify these insights by reflecting on our Christian growth in virtue, and I do so by pointing to a vocabulary that can help us link our faith statements with our own human experience. Such a vocabulary is an instance of *fides quaerens intellectum,* the ancient goal of Christian theology, "faith seeking understanding." For as Christian leaders we are called upon not only to repeat faith statements, but also "to give a reason for the faith that is in us" (I Pt 3:15); that is, to explain how the realities of faith fit in with the rest of our human living. Our own leadership and the mission of our Catholic institutions depend on it.

In other words, our topic is "discerning value," that is, the Spirit-laden values that build up our selves and our communities. In order to talk about the habits of the heart needed for this discernment, it is important to call attention to the human dynamics by which we "search" at all—that is, the "heuristic" character of the human spirit as it searches for being and for value. Before talking about the concrete human habits we need to develop in our discernment, it is important to point to a language about our human searching as such. Since, to my mind, no one has made these connections so clearly as the Canadian philosopher-theologian Bernard Lonergan (1904–1984), I will be drawing on his writings in this essay.[1] Our topics then are: our infinite human quest; the fulfillment of our quest; discernment; community; conversion; and habits of the heart.

OUR INFINITE HUMAN QUEST

In an essay entitled "Mission and Spirit," Bernard Lonergan refers to "the passionateness of being." What could he possibly have meant by such a phrase? After all, for the most part one thinks of "being" as a cold and lifeless philosophical concept. What possible meaning could "being" have for a Catholic hospital administrator? A teacher? A principal? And what could "being" have to do with passion? With desire? With a desire so intense one would suffer for it?

Unless, of course, "being" is the totality, all there is, the totally true, the good, the beautiful, the universe in all its concreteness—everything about everything. Being is what the teacher in the classroom is introducing her students into: the world with all its contours and challenges and vastness. Being is the background against which administrators and principals make their decisions and lead their institutions. It is the "call of being" that keeps us all searching, seeking, questioning, wondering. And it is the notion of being in our very spirits that enables us to say occasionally, "Yes, that's what I have been looking for!" or "No, that's not it," or "That's partially correct—a hint, perhaps, but there is more to it."

This notion of being is what I have referred to as the "heuristic" character of our human spirit, that is, the shadowy anticipation of what answers will have to live up to if we are to recognize them as answers and say, "Eureka! I've found it." As Plato in his dialogues makes clear, our human spirits have this character of openness to being—otherwise we would not recognize an answer when we found one. It is this that the teacher can count on in the classroom: that, besides her own efforts, there is in the child the notion of being which invites him to discover the universe.

We begin to get a handle on being, therefore, by asking and answering questions. By the child's incessant "What is this?" and "What is that?" By the insights and correct judgments the child makes as he or she grows up. By the scientist's careful and methodical questioning as he penetrates the secrets of the universe. By the historian's searching out our human roots. And by the administrator's questions about how to motivate diverse human beings.

But the notion of being also prompts the question of God: the searcher's questions, "Is there a person behind all this? A mind here? A heart?" "Is being ultimately on my side?" "Is being personal?" For the notion of being that is our spirit is ultimately open-ended. There is no limit to our questioning and so there is nothing to prevent us from asking the question of God.

The notion of being is also the notion of value, for we are not only knowers but also "doers." To the extent that we are not only knowers, but also deciders and doers, the notion of being is transformed into the notion of value: that is, all that is truly worthwhile—that is worth our while, our time, our effort, our striving. Value is the "passionate" dimension of being as it draws us more and more to choose the truly good and not just what satisfies—not just the maximum of pleasure and the minimum of pain. For the truly valuable we will sacrifice ourselves.

Such is "the passionateness of being," the value of the truly real as it attracts us. Such attraction can penetrate even our sensuous, experiential being—our dreams.

THE FULFILLMENT OF OUR QUEST

Saint Thomas Aquinas once described the human person as *capax Dei*, that is, capable of God. Because our spirits are basically open to being, to all that is, even the infinite, we are capable of receiving God: we are capable of receiving "grace," that is, the created participation in divine Trinitarian life itself. Because we are capable of being, because there is no limit to our spirits—though our achievement is always finite—we are capable of receiving the Spirit within us.

Where is our desire for being and value ultimately headed? Our desire can be to learn more and more about this world, and to seek more and more the values of this world—but ultimately our desire is for what transcends this world: the "Beauty ever ancient, ever new," worth seeking with all that is in us. As Christians, we believe that the universe itself participates in "such striving and groaning."

> Creation waits with eager longing for the revealing of the children of God. . . .
> We know that the whole creation has been groaning in labor pains until now;
> and not only the creation, but we ourselves, who have the first fruits of the Spirit,
> groan inwardly while we wait for adoption, the redemption of our bodies. . . .

Likewise the Spirit helps us in our weakness; for we do not know how to pray as
we ought, but that very Spirit intercedes with sighs too deep for words. (Rom
8:19, 22–23, 26)

The Christian message responds to such desire for knowledge and love,
the desire that is written into our human hearts. Such a message proclaims
the Trinitarian love life of Father, Son, and Holy Spirit, and the sharing of that
life with humanity. We believe that even now the depths of our being are in-
serted into the life of God and we are being invited to live accordingly. We
are capax Dei, capable of God, and that capacity finds fulfillment through
the love of God poured into our hearts through the Holy Spirit.

That love life would have a communal expression. Beyond all the horizontal aims of human life—prosperity, progress, etc.—there is also Jesus' call
to form the new community that in spite of all detours and dead ends will
bring together scattered humanity. This level is totally beyond what humanity could ever bring about by its own resources; nevertheless, it is in continuity with the infinite desire of our human minds for "being" and with the infinite desire of our human hearts for the truly valuable. It is beyond the
human, but the human can be and has been raised to participate in this
higher level through which we enter into the Trinitarian life itself.

DISCERNMENT

Certainly, as with all things that are "in process," when the process has not
been completed, its final end is obscure. Saint John's Gospel speaks of the
work of the Spirit as like the wind: you hear the sound of it, but you do not
know where it is coming from or where it is going (Jn 3:8). Nevertheless, by
the gift of the Spirit cooperating with our spirit, we can discern an outline of
the kingdom that is coming into our midst.

This Spirit-filled infinite longing plays itself out in the day-to-day, moment-
to-moment "calls" of everyday life. It is what the upward thrust of our questioning seeks and what in us prompts us to say, "Yes, that's it! That's the answer! That's what I must do!" or conversely, to say, "No, that's not it—I must
continue to seek." Or, "That's partially the answer—that's a hint I must follow further. Let me take a further guess." And, as we noted, such shadowy
anticipations can invade our sensuous and experiential being, and they can
even invade the fabric of our dreams.

The criterion of our discernment is the coherence of our spirit with the
Holy Spirit moving within us. Saint Ignatius of Loyola spoke of "consolation
without an external cause" as the criterion of our decision making—that is,
"the peace that the world cannot give." Reason or "figuring" is not enough.
Our spirits need the Lord's Spirit.

COMMUNITY

Thus, the passionateness of being works "from below," in "the springs of thought" where images emerge that can provide "hints" as to what we are looking for, what we are afraid of, and what we truly want. The Spirit works in and through our own spirits as we seek out the "hints and guesses" by which we find our way in the world.

At the same time, the passionateness of being works "from above" through the loves we experience in community. This is the dynamism that "by inter-subjectivity prepares, by solidarity entices, by falling in love establishes us as members of community."[2] Within each individual person, consciousness heads for self-transcendence, and in a community of self-transcending persons there can emerge "the new creation," God's design for the human family.

As Christians, we believe that the visibly sent Son of God bequeathed to us through his Body a vision that is beyond us, that is, God's vision for our lives and our world. At the same time, that vision is in continuity with our native desire for being and for value, the truly good. Because he was not only God, but also one of us, Jesus was able to communicate to us the way to the Father. In the images, symbols, meanings, and truths mediated to us through the Body of Christ, the Church, we encounter Christ as the Way, the Truth, and the Life. He is the sacrament of our encounter with God.

To realize, appreciate, and respond to this visible mission of the Son, there is within our hearts the invisible mission of the Holy Spirit, who teaches us the meaning of Jesus' life and words. Besides the faith infused into our hearts by the Holy Spirit, there is also the faith that comes from hearing the Word of God in the community of the church. Without the visible mission of the Word, the gift of the Spirit is a being-in-love that is "anonymous," that remains simply an orientation to mystery awaiting interpretation. And without the invisible mission of the Spirit working within our hearts, "the Word enters into his own, but his own receive him not" (Jn 1:11).

Consequently, just as the Father sent the Son, so the Son sends us on a mission to our particular parishes, schools, hospitals, communities. As the Father and the Son sent the Spirit to the disciples, so they continue to bestow the Spirit on the ever new members of the Body of Christ.

But all of this can be obscure—for being and the direction of the universe are obscure. Because we are talking about the ways of God, we have at best analogical knowledge—hints and guesses—of what we are talking about. We do not know unequivocally all that we mean. And so besides doctrine, which defines the limits of our belief, we also use poetry and music, song and ritual, to express our longings and to translate Jesus' own words and symbols into our own minds and hearts. Furthermore, the decisions of our hearts and lives can open us to ever new depths of meaning: as Pascal put it, "the heart has reasons that reason knows not of."

CONVERSION

One day, as I hurried from meeting to meeting at Seton Hall University, where I teach, I realized that not only was I rushing around—sometimes frantically!—but I was also "being drawn" by the meanings and values discussed in those meetings and penetrating the life of the university. For such meanings and values emerge in the midst of community, and in the midst of conflicts in community—conflicts that can make both us and our communities better.

> The school of virtue is the community in which one finds oneself. We are life or death for each other. From others we learn honesty. Their presence invites us to live for something greater than ourselves. They are, in fact, the abiding sacrament of Christ. So I must listen humbly to what they say, to what God tells me through them, and then put their message into practice.[3]

Through the presence of others who challenge and refine our own thinking, we grasp more fully the intentions of the Spirit working in our time. The Spirit works within us to give us the desire for the hints and guesses that presage the emerging vision of "what needs to be done" to build up the Body of Christ. At the same time, the Word works through our human words and our human communities, as we try to build communities that are truly healing of the wounds of the human family.

Of course, things do not work out in a smooth line. When we sit down and think about it, the motive of fundamental love can take over our lives and help us make concrete decisions in line with that motive. But in practice things can turn out quite differently. We can be surprised by situations and re-act according to our spontaneities: our need to protect ourselves, our desire for pleasure or for power. We can think we are doing good, and at the same time what the Scriptures call "our hidden faults" can smudge our undertakings. We can talk a good game, but our hearts can be far from the Lord. This is "original sin"—our personal and social inability for sustained development, our inability to keep responding according to our better nature.[4]

And so we are involved in a war, and the stakes are big. On the one hand, there are all the forces, both around us and within us, that would lead us to throw in the towel and take the easy way out, so that our human situation spirals more and more into incoherence. On the other hand, there is within us the passionateness of being: our innate desire for all that is meaningful, loving, and beautiful. It is that innate desire that is stoked by the gift of the Spirit, and that by the gift of the Spirit is not only brought within the embrace of the divine Trinity, but is also healed of its listlessness and its impotence. A life of seeking a maximum of pleasure and a minimum of pain is transformed into a life focused on value—whatever the cost.

But it is one thing to move beyond ourselves in fits and starts. It is another thing to do this regularly, easily, spontaneously. It is only by reaching the sustained self-transcendence of the virtuous person that one becomes a good judge, not only of this or that human act, but also of the whole range of human goodness. And throughout this development we are continually stopped by the disenchantment that asks whether what we are doing is truly worthwhile.

In the light of the Spirit influencing our quest for being and value, we make decisions that not only affect the world around us, but also affect ourselves. Every intentional act makes it easier to perform that act in the future—and less necessary to persuade ourselves to do it the next time. It becomes habitual, a "second nature." And such habits constitute our character. If we have not developed good habits, if we have not become accustomed to doing good, all our good intentions will tend to go out the window when we are caught by surprise.

On the other hand, every good action makes it easier for us to repeat that action in the future. What in the beginning was a definite *agere contra*, an acting against, a difficult resistance to a bad habit, becomes eventually easier and even more filled with peace. Our ultimate aim is a total openness to being: to all that is beautiful and good and true. Our aim is to respond immediately to the Spirit-given hints and guesses by which we can be led to love and transform our world.

The philosopher Alfred North Whitehead once remarked that moral education is impossible without the constant vision of greatness—stories of those who have lived well before us. Moral education communicates that vision in many unnoticed ways. The vision gathers the way dust gathers, not through any massive action but through the continuous addition of particles that remain.[5]

Such is the process of moral conversion, and it eventually leads to choosing the highest value, that is, the value of falling in love with and being in love with God.

> At the summit of the ascent from the initial infantile bundle of needs and clamors and gratifications, there are to be found the deep-set joy and solid peace, the power and the vigor, of being in love with God. In the measure that that summit is reached, then the supreme value is God, and other values are God's expression of his love in this world, in its aspirations, and in its goal. In the measure that one's love of God is complete, then values are whatever one loves, and evils are whatever one hates so that, in Augustine's phrase, if one loves God, one may do as one pleases, *Ama Deum et fac quod vis* [Love God and do what you will]. Then affectivity is of a single piece. Further developments only fill out previous achievement. Lapses from grace are rarer and more quickly amended.[6]

Our human and religious development, then, is of a piece. Whether we are priests, vowed religious, or lay people, the experience of "grace" is as large as the Christian experience of life. It is experience of our capacity to go beyond ourselves, of our unrestricted openness to being. And it is experience of a twofold frustration of that capacity, in the objective frustration of life in a world distorted by sin and in the subjective frustration of our own incapacity to break with our evil ways. It is the experience of a transformation, a conversion, that we did not bring about ourselves but rather underwent.[7] It involves many elements, including "letting evil take its course," so that the tension of life is heightened, our circumstances shift, our dispositions change, new encounters occur, and our hearts are touched.

HABITS OF THE HEART

Some years ago I made a weekend *Cursillo*, literally "a short course" in Christianity—part of an influential movement of that name that came to the United States from Spain in the 1960s. Although priests were spiritual directors on Cursillo weekends, the real power of the movement came from lay persons talking to one another about their spiritual lives. One of the first talks on the Cursillo weekend was called "Ideals," and it basically asked the question, "What is your ideal in life?" In other words, "What turns you on?" And, the talk suggested, one of the ways we might figure out our ideal is to ask ourselves a few questions: "Where do our free thoughts go?" "Where do we spend our free time?" "Where do we spend our extra money?"

In other words, what we think about and what we do with our time and money can give us a clue, a hint, as to our "ideal," that is, our values and our priorities. As we can trace the movement of the wind by seeing where it takes a kite in the sky, so we can trace our own values by answering questions about how we use our freedom. The Cursillo talk went on to suggest that "grace," or God's gift of love, can indeed be our ideal. As a prayer by Pedro Arrupe, former superior of the Jesuits, suggests, "falling in love with God" can be an ideal for human life:

Nothing is more practical than finding God, that is, than falling in love in a quite absolute, final way. What you are in love with, what seizes your imagination, will affect everything. It will decide

- what will get you out of bed in the morning,
- what you will do with your evenings,
- how you spend your weekends,
- what you read,
- who you know,

- what breaks your heart,
- and what amazes you with joy and gratitude.

Fall in love, stay in love, and it will decide everything.

This is why we pray—to get in touch with that basic fire within us, our basic capacity for love and the gift that fulfills that capacity, the gift of the Holy Spirit. This is why we take time out to think, to meditate, to read, to converse with wise people: so that we can get in touch with our basic desire for being and value and the basic fulfillment of that desire, the experience of "being in love with God." We pray and we seek the good, we develop a lifestyle focused on goodness, so that we can allow the Spirit to help us make concrete decisions that will incarnate the Spirit's promptings in our world today.

The genius of Saint Benedict and his monastic rule is that they ordered time and space so that this Spirit-stoked desire could find an orderly expression in human life. Besides the orderly celebration of the times of the day and of the year, the monastic rule also ordered the spaces in which one lived.[8] A regular ordering of space and time is a "habit of the heart" that follows from our being material beings—rooted in the space and time of the universe, but stretching beyond. Following Benedict's direction, we need to order our lives so that our praying and working, our eating and sleeping, can all be for the glory of God and the good of our neighbor. Just finding regular times and places for prayer—and keeping to it—can make a great difference in our lives, in what we value, how we treat people, etc. If we do this, our very dreams can cooperate—as they did in the Scriptures—with the passionateness of being, so that the lower levels of our being can cooperate in the wise decisions we need to make.

Joseph Pieper once wrote a book called *Leisure: The Basis of Culture.* The idea of the book is that unless we take time out to learn, time to allow the Spirit's promptings to take shape in our lives, we will not experience the freedom and creativity to undertake the projects that our world needs so much. These are the projects that need to be initiated and completed in our parishes, our schools, our universities, our health care facilities, or wherever we may be. Every human situation needs to be redeemed from the surd of meaninglessness and the lack of love. Every human situation needs the light of the Holy Spirit to be shed upon it—and that light shines through our own human eyes. We need to take time to smell the flowers and to allow the dream to be born in us of the world God wants to create.

This is how the magnificent Trinitarian vision that Michael Downey spelled out in his chapter, "Without a Vision the People Perish," takes place in our concrete universe. Our universe, our great world with its billion-year history and teeming nebulae, is within the Trinitarian embrace. And that

embrace touches us through our very bodies, our physical, chemical, bio-
logical, and psychological being, just as we recapitulate in our own lives the
whole history of the human family.

There is a sense in which we can be clear about the meaning of the Word
of God, and that is what we mean by Christian doctrine. But there is also a
sense in which that meaning is shrouded in darkness: so beyond us that, in
Aristotle's phrase, our minds are "like owls' eyes in daylight"—unequal to
the depths of the meaning of the Word of God. And so we squint, and
with the eyes of our hearts we try to discern the meaning of the Word, especially the Word in the Areopagus of contemporary culture, as it sheds light
on our contemporary situation.

Michael Downey talks about it as the bricolage of insights and guesses by
which we grasp the needed vision. "In this schema, vision, even if it is constructed from patches of insight and intuitive hunches, comes first."[9] And the
vision has to do with such things as "building community" and "discerning
the signs of the times"—discerning in the midst of the complexities of contemporary life where creative solutions to contemporary problems can be
sought. The reason why the vision for approaching these problems comes
only in "hints and guesses" is that the Lord is communicating to us a plan that
is beyond us and beyond anything that we could figure out for ourselves,
and yet, in some strange way, it is a plan that is in conformity with the deepest longings of our human hearts and minds.

God's understanding of the universe does not interfere with his having a
plan for my own particular life, as having endowed me personally—"from
the gene pool"—with specific talents, abilities, and charisms. As the great
nineteenth-century English figure, John Henry Newman, wrote:

> God has created all things for good; all things for their greatest good; everything
> for its own good. What is the good of one is not the good of another; what
> makes one man happy would make another unhappy. God has determined, un-
> less I interfere with his plan, that I should reach that which will be my greatest
> happiness. He looks to me individually, he calls me by my name, he knows
> what I can do, what I can best be, what is my greatest happiness, and means to
> give it to me. God knows what is my greatest happiness, but I do not. There is
> no rule about what is happy and good; what suits one would not suit another.
> And the ways by which perfection is reached vary very much; the medicines
> necessary for our souls are very different from each other. Thus God leads us by
> strange ways; we know he wills our happiness, but we neither know what our
> happiness is, nor the way. We are blind; left to ourselves we should take the
> wrong way; we must leave it to him. Let us put ourselves into his hands, and not
> be startled though he leads us by a strange way, a *mirabilis via* [miraculous
> way], as the Church speaks. Let us be sure he will lead us right, that he will bring
> us to that which is, not indeed what we think best, nor what is best for another,
> but what is best for us.[10]

In this chapter I have linked the transforming life of the Trinity with our natural openness to all of being and our spirit's anticipation of what it seeks. The Spirit works within us, in the hints and guesses given even in our dreams, so that we can discern the Word of God leading us to participate in building up the Body of Christ in history. This process is real. It is the process of being converted and of concretely forming the habits of the heart whereby we play our personal part in bringing about this grand vision.

And so, when we speak of God's gift of himself in the Word made flesh, when we speak of the gift of the Spirit by which we become temples of the Holy Spirit and adopted children of the Father, when we speak of our destiny to know the Father even as we are known, we are speaking of a plan for which we were created, a plan that is absolutely beyond us, but which God in his goodness and mercy wants us actively to participate in even now.

REFLECTION QUESTIONS

1. Remember an experience you have had of "going beyond yourself," an experience of "unrestricted openness to being" (perhaps in nature, or with your child). Recall everything you can of that moment. Savor it.

2. As you think about the community of persons with whom you work, how does God invite you, through them, to recognize God's presence more fully in our time and place? How does God invite you, through them, to grow in virtue?

3. Which two or three "habits of the heart" or virtues particularly define you as a person? As a leader? What habit do you most desire to grow in at this time?

4. What habits particularly characterize your work community? How can you and your community articulate and celebrate these positive virtues?

NOTES

1. I am particularly indebted here to an article by Bernard Lonergan, "Mission and Spirit," which appears in *A Third Collection: Papers by Bernard Lonergan* (Mahwah, NJ: Paulist Press, 1985), 23–34. In that article Lonergan was responding to an article by Karl Rahner entitled "Christology within an Evolutionary Framework." Lonergan's aim was to ask how we might conceive of the emergence of the supernatural, the emergence of "grace," within the context of the evolutionary emergence of higher levels of being.

2. Lonergan, *A Third Collection*, 30. Of course, this falling in love with God occurs in the context of a particular life and its emotional commitments. The "Poem of St. Francis of Assisi" illustrates this poignantly:

> I love the sun, I love the stars, I love Clare and the sisters
> I love the human heart and everything beautiful.
> O Lord forgive me,
> It is you alone that I am meant to love.
> But the Lord was smiling when he said in reply:
> I love the sun, I love the stars, I love Clare and the sisters.
> I love the human heart and everything beautiful.
> O Francis, what can I forgive?
> I love the same things as you.

3. Hugh Feiss, O.S.B., *Essential Monastic Wisdom* (San Francisco: Harper, 1999), 66.

4. Tatha Wiley, *Original Sin: Origins, Developments, Contemporary Meanings* (New York: Paulist Press, 2002).

5. Referred to in Bernard Lonergan, *Topics in Education: Collected Works of Bernard Lonergan* (Toronto: University of Toronto Press, 1990), 10:102.

6. Bernard Lonergan, *Method in Theology* (Toronto: University of Toronto Press, 1996), 39.

7. Lonergan, *A Third Collection*, 32–33.

8. Feiss, *Essential Monastic Wisdom*, 5–6.

9. See Michael Downey in chapter 2 of this book.

10. John Henry Newman, "Putting Ourselves in Christ's Hands," in *Prayers, Verses, and Devotions* (Ft. Collins, CO: Ignatius Press, 1989). Copied from *Magnificat* 5, no. 13 (February 2004): 174–75.

II

THE MISSION OF THE CHURCH AND INSTITUTIONAL MINISTRIES

In part two, our focus broadens from the leader to the mission, as we attempt to see the big picture of Catholic institutional ministries through which the Church continues the teaching, healing, and serving ministry of Jesus. Chapter 4 presents the central biblical themes of God's reign, Jesus' mission, and the ministries of the Church as foundations for the mission of Catholic institutions. Chapter 5 traces the rich heritage bequeathed by those who founded these institutions, and invites us to claim and continue their legacy. Chapter 6 focuses on the larger Church within which individual institutions exist, showing the international and local network of relationships and structures which supports the effort in a particular institution.

4

"The Reign of God Is among You": Biblical and Theological Themes for Lay Leadership

Monika K. Hellwig

What themes of Catholic belief are most central to understanding the role of Catholic institutions and their leaders in the life of the Church and in the plan of salvation? Monika Hellwig explores several of these, especially as they are related to the role of the laity in the Church. She also examines themes relative to a spirituality of the laity. Her rich theological framework is presented in a style eminently accessible to leaders educated in disciplines other than that of theology.

Jesus proclaimed the immediacy of God's reign, and he proclaimed it as startling good news. He proclaimed it by the whole tenor of his presence to people, by his works of healing, his banishing of evil spirits, his inspiring of hope, and his bringing of reconciliation. He proclaimed it also in words of instruction, exhortation, invitation, encouragement, and challenge. He proclaimed the good news to all who would listen, calling for a profound change of heart, and therefore of relationships, values, and expectations in life. But while he proclaimed the good news to all, he invited a chosen few individually to share both his life and his mission intimately as disciples, as apprentices working with him.

This is really the calling of all the baptized. We are not called to passivity while clergy and vowed religious engage in the works of Jesus enumerated in the first paragraph. In our baptism, confirmation, and Eucharist, we have been initiated into the life and death and resurrection and apostolate of the redeemer. We have been called to turn the world around in a Godward direction by a peaceful revolution changing the structure of relationships in all situations.[1] Yet, it is a fact of life that as the centuries have gone by, as the number of Christians has grown exponentially, it has become all too easy to take for granted that our society and culture as such are Christian, and that the Church exists for worship rather than to be a mission of transformation of the world.[2]

Nevertheless, the Second Vatican Council has brought Catholics back to their biblical roots, and with the return to the New Testament mandate to the followers of Jesus, the call for lay leadership has become obvious once again. Even a casual reading of the Acts of the Apostles makes it obvious that the early church, still possessing personal memories of Jesus, did not know of a distinction between laity and clergy, much less of a distinction between vowed religious and other baptized persons. What they did recognize and speak and write about is the variety of callings that make up the one body of the Risen Christ, acting in the world to redeem it. Those callings included some that we would not immediately think of, such as the calling of Apostles who were founders of local churches, and the calling of prophets and people who spoke in tongues. But these lists and stories also include many callings to ministry that we would recognize today, such as that of teacher, of healer and comforter, of missionary sent to new places, of provider of hospitality to the community and to strangers, of leader in prayer, and so forth. Paul in his letters is insistent on the importance and dignity of many different functions, all prompted and sustained by the same Spirit.[3]

That prompting and sustaining of the divine Spirit, which is the Spirit of Jesus, is the inner reality of what we mean when we speak about Christian spirituality, and when we speak of the spirituality of lay leadership. To emphasize this, the Church has spoken of the "indwelling" of the Holy Spirit. It is the breath of God that is described in Genesis as bringing human beings to life in the first place, and it is by a new reception of the divine spirit that our lives are enhanced and lifted beyond our ordinary, natural selves, to a greater vision, hope, and commitment. Like falling in love, it empowers people to reach for greater things with steadiness of purpose and courage and peace of mind. The church needs many people to respond to the call and to undertake leadership roles that are ministries for the church and for the coming of the reign of God in human society.

In our long tradition, while honoring all these ministries, we have come to distinguish between those that belong to the baptized by virtue of their membership in the Church, and those ministries that have been assigned to the ordained by virtue of their ordination. Essentially these latter are particular sacramental functions. In the church, all leadership functions are ministries, which means that they are ways of serving the community and its members. Leadership functions in the church do not exist to confer honor, power, or status on those who perform them but to provide for the needs of the community and its members. For many centuries in the Catholic Church all the governing and community organizing functions, as well as the work of biblical and theological reflection and explanation, had for the most part been left to the clergy. At the same time, works of teaching and caring for all kinds of needy people had largely been left to the vowed religious. It was good that so many generous people came forward and devoted their lives entirely to good works, but it was not good that, with notable exceptions, the rest of us assumed that the call to these works was not directed to us.

In the decades since the Second Vatican Council, there have been two complementary developments: a sharp reduction in the numbers of clergy and vowed religious, and a rising understanding and expectation of the vocation of the lay baptized to assume the tasks that keep the church alive as community and as transforming force in the world.[4] The increasingly active and responsible leadership roles that lay people have been called on to undertake have included many roles within the church itself, even within its formal worship and governance, and many roles that look outward into the society at large, to support what is good and transform what is destructive in private and public life. It is largely through the expertise of lay people, both scholars and people of experience in the professions and in public life, that the Church has formulated a comprehensive social teaching by which Catholics and others can judge what is happening in their societies.

How does this process of formulating the Church's social teaching work in practice? It is a complex process of bringing the vision of human life that Jesus proposes in the Gospels into conversation with the changing experience and the growing body of knowledge of our world. The purpose of this conversation is to discern what we can do to bring our world step by step closer to welcoming God's reign in human affairs, as Jesus shows us that vision of the coming reign (kingdom) of God. The realization of this has large consequences for the spiritual lives of all who exercise leadership roles. In the first place, it is a constant learning experience, because we can never say we have understood the gospel exhaustively, and we need both to deepen and to extend our knowledge and understanding of the Church's teaching. We need especially to continue to study the Church's social teaching because it is constantly developing as we know more about how the world works.[5]

Clearly, while the spiritual life of lay leaders needs to be a constant learning experience, it also needs to be a constant conversion experience. When most leadership roles were exercised by clergy and religious, these leaders had a long and intense Christian formation. It was a formation in personal spirituality, in community living, and in apostolate. It was understood that all these strands contributed to shaping a life that was one of continuing conversion at progressively deeper levels, and that both head and heart, intellect and will, were constantly involved. The church has many traditions of spiritual formation, maintained and developed by the religious congregations. Lay people have often found it possible to adapt for themselves traditions such as the Benedictine, the Franciscan, or the Ignatian. What is not so well developed is a properly lay tradition of spirituality, though there have been efforts at this by the late medieval guilds, by St. Francis de Sales, and by modern movements such as that of the Focolarini.

In the formation of lay leaders, besides the learning and conversion aspects, there needs to be, as with the vowed religious, a community aspect that gives support, encouragement, and guidance. This should, of course, be the parish. But again, it is a fact of life that the vast majority of Catholics are in parishes that are far from giving the kind of community support that lay leaders in the church and in the world need. There is a certain circularity in this. Effective lay leadership is required to build this kind of parish, but this kind of parish is required to produce and support effective lay leaders. A common solution in Catholic life has been the forming of small Christian communities that give the support the members do not find in their parishes. That, of course, is a second-best solution in a less than perfect church, and the effort of these small Christian communities should ideally be directed not only to sustaining the life and apostolate of the members, but also to the building of more solid parishes. If the small Christian communities take dedicated Christians away from parish life, then in the long run the contribution of these communities to the church is self-defeating.

This centrality of the parish as the building block of the church is important because of the very nature of the redemption. All that we do as disciples of Jesus has to do with reconciliation, rebuilding broken relationships, and ultimately, the solidarity of the human race in its relationship with God and the many and complex relationships that human beings have with one another. Jesus himself preached to ordinary, politically insignificant peasant people. He spoke largely about two concerns: in the first place, a trusting and responsive relationship to God the creator and savior, and in the second place, a generous, trusting, and inclusively welcoming relationship of people with one another.

The wisdom that Jesus taught about human relationships included the following. People are always more important than things. When enemies are treated as friends it makes it very difficult for them to keep behaving as enemies. There is no progress in human relationships without forgiveness, and forgiveness rests in a compassionate understanding of the social and psychological traps that hold people in destructive behavior. It is not as important to preach to people as to act in order to meet their needs. What God asks of us consists not so much of ritual observances and careful orthodoxies, though these have their role, as of simple justice and kindness. All of this, of course, has been reflected and explained in much more detail in the course of the centuries of Christian experience, reflection on experience, and formal Catholic teaching.

Careful reflection on the words of Jesus and the subsequent development of the moral, spiritual, and social teaching of the Church show that redemption is essentially a community work. Redemption is certainly a divine work, and human collaboration in it is certainly the work of Jesus. But it is not Jesus in isolation who accomplishes the work of redemption. It is the whole Christ, present in those reborn in baptism and living by the Spirit of Christ. That is what Paul in the New Testament and the Church in its official teaching have not hesitated to call the Mystical Body of Christ.

But as Paul also pointed out, it is in the unity of the community, celebrated and realized especially in the Eucharist, that the gathering of the faithful becomes effective as the presence of the risen Christ active in the world. For all these reasons, it is especially in the parish, the place where the community comes together to celebrate its Sunday Eucharist, that church is constantly being brought into existence so that the work of redemption may go on. There are many good books on the centrality of the Eucharist in Christian life.[6]

What has been shown so far, therefore, from Scripture and tradition about the foundations and formation of spirituality for lay leadership includes three aspects: continuous learning, continuous conversion, and continuous community building within the traditional structure of the church. There is, of course, a fourth, which most people would mention first, namely, response to the call for ministry. Discerning what we are called to do and responding is a more delicate process than people commonly believe. To most people, their calling does not come with a trumpet blast from heaven. It comes from a combination of what attracts them, what they are capable of doing, what others call on them to do, and where they are accepted. No one has a "right" to a particular ministry or task. It is not a privilege or a right, but a service.

In theory this is straightforward, while in practice it can be complex and difficult. Many lay leaders find, for instance, that even when they have been called to an office or role in the church, they are not so well accepted by the particular clergy with whom they have to work. Or it may be that they are in work such as promotion of social justice where they have a difficult prophetic task and are vehemently rejected by the Catholic community, accused of stirring up controversy, reducing the faith to political action, and so forth. There is also a much more difficult situation in which someone in prayerfulness and peace before God sees what must be done, but has no endorsement from the hierarchical Church or from the Catholic community. A great deal of patience, discernment and consultation are needed. It is always good to be guided by authority, and tradition, but if no one ever did something new and unauthorized, many human needs would go untended. Catholic history is sprinkled with lives of pioneers in compassionate works who met considerable opposition in the beginning, and much later were canonized as saints.[7]

There are, of course, some ministries internal to the church community which are open only to those called by church authority. There may be restrictive categories, and these often change in the course of time. Usually there are channels for questioning the restrictions and influencing change, but change in the structures of the church tends to happen in centuries, while individuals do not live for centuries. It would be a waste of energy, if not actually an obstruction of the ongoing work of redemption, to become bitter or argumentatively angry, or even to engage in subversive activity over restrictive categories of those officially permitted to serve in certain ministries. As no one has a personal right to serve in any particular capacity, while the community is always entitled to call forth service from its members, we can assume that the need will eventually assert itself. The community will be the channel by which that need is made known, and eventually hierarchical authority will lift or ease the restriction. However, it will not usually be in the same time frame, but rather later than the need is felt.

We are all called to active leadership in the church and in the world. That call to leadership is rooted in our baptism into the church. The particular roles that we are called to play differ, and we know them through circumstances, direct call, or painstaking discernment. Some never really wake up to their calling, because they have been taught to think of themselves as quite passive in relation to salvation and in relation to the church. Others worship with the church for a long span of years, keeping the commandments, accepting the beliefs of the church, and generally being good people, before they realize they are called to take an active role in the parish that is their local church and in the world. Yet others blossom quickly into lay leaders wherever they are. The church has room for everyone. As long as they keep coming, they can be invited continuously into active participation. Meanwhile, what is truly important is that those who are actively engaged as lay leaders know themselves as servants of the community, not bosses, and see their role as integral to the whole life of the church, and not as setting them apart as a superior rank of Christians.

REFLECTION QUESTIONS

1. In a group with others, if possible, consider how you see your work in relation to the saving work of Christ and in relation to your baptism.
2. Reflect on, and if possible share with others, how your understanding of what it means to be Christian, and your role in the church, have grown through your lifetime.
3. In the setting of your own institution, how can spirituality be nourished and fostered?

NOTES

1. A continuous reading of Luke's Gospel and the Acts of the Apostles makes this abundantly clear.

2. For further reading see Yves Congars, *Christians Active in the World* (New York: Herder and Herder, 1968); it is a classic, worth making great efforts to find.

3. See, for instance, I Corinthians 12, about the variety of gifts of the Spirit, conferred on the believers for service in creating a very different kind of society from the one taken for granted in the Corinth of their time.

4. The Council itself set an agenda for this in the document *Apostolicam Actuositatem,* The Decree on the Apostolate of Lay People, which can be found, for instance, in Austin Flannery, O.P., ed. *Vatican Council II* (Wilmington, DE: Scholarly Resources, 1965). It can also be bought as a pamphlet from a Catholic bookstore or downloaded from the Vatican's website.

5. Catholic social teaching is constantly in progress, because conditions of human life in the world change. While the social teaching goes back to the earliest centuries, during the last century and a quarter it has been summarized and focused in a series of papal letters known as encyclicals. A book that collects the encyclicals of Popes John XXIII and Paul VI and gives an excellent introduction explaining the whole process of the Church's modern social teaching is Joseph Gremillion, *The Gospel of Peace and Justice* (Maryknoll, NY: Orbis Books, 1976).

6. For a focus on the aspect just mentioned here, see Monika K. Hellwig, *The Eucharist and the Hunger of the World*, 2nd ed. (Franklin, WI: Sheed & Ward, 1992).

7. This includes almost all the foundresses of religious communities of women, as well as some of the founders of men's communities, such as Francis of Assisi and Ignatius of Loyola. Obviously, they all began as laypersons when they took their various apostolic and prophetic initiatives.

5

Catholic Institutional Ministries: Their History and Legacy

Doris Gottemoeller, R.S.M.

Where do Catholic institutions fit in the big picture of Jesus' continuing mission in the Church? Doris Gottemoeller, R.S.M., saliently summarizes the history of educational and health care institutions, a "distinctive and enduring" feature of American Catholicism for over two centuries. She places these institutions in historical context against the backdrop of four major influences: demographics, the role of religious congregations, the role of the laity, and the question of blending into the culture versus keeping a critical distance from it. Gottemoeller reminds us that the Church's preeminent stance is to be turned outward in mission, evoking ever-new responses to people's changing material and spiritual needs. Catholic institutions offer a distinctive way of being Catholic, of living the Church's mission and influencing social systems in a pluralistic culture. They leave an enduring legacy of continuous presence and standards of excellence.

The tendency to create our own educational, health care, and social service institutions is one of the most distinctive and enduring characteristics of the American Catholic community. Since the birth of the republic, thousands of Catholic schools, colleges, seminaries, residences for orphans, the handicapped, and the elderly, hospitals, clinics, and sanitaria have borne witness to the Church's concern for the well-being of its members and to its desire to serve its neighbors. The vision of Matthew 25 is given power and continuity in countless institutions: "For I was hungry and you gave me food, I was thirsty and you gave me something to drink. . . . Just as you did it to one of the least of these who are members of my family, you did it to me" (NRSV). Making sense of the long and complicated history of institutional ministry requires us to recognize four significant factors: the impact of

changing demographics within the Catholic community, the role of religious congregations, the role of the laity, and the tension between assimilation and prophetic distance.

In 1785 Catholics in the thirteen states numbered twenty-five thousand in
a population of four million. Most were concentrated in the two states
known for their religious toleration, Maryland and Pennsylvania. Today
there are over 66 million Catholics in a population of 290 million Americans,
23 percent of the total. Catholics are still proportionally more numerous in
the urban centers of the Northeast and Midwest, but the numbers in the
South, the Southwest, and the far West—e.g., the city of Los Angeles—have
grown at a faster pace since World War II. The size, ethnic composition, and
location of the Catholic population have been tremendously influenced by
immigration and, to a lesser extent, by internal migration. Conditions in Europe, such as famine in Ireland and the *Kulturkampf* in Germany, drove tens
of millions to our shores between 1840 and 1920. More recently, civil wars
and poverty in Latin America and the Caribbean prompted millions more to
seek safety, freedom, and opportunity in the United States. Similarly,
refugees from Viet Nam, Korea, Laos, and other Asian countries have aug-
mented the Catholic population in recent decades. As the descendants of
earlier immigrants achieved prosperity in the second half of the twentieth
century, they tended to migrate from city centers to suburbs, from the Northeast to the South and Southwest. In every era of our nation's history these de-
mographic realities influenced the real or perceived need for distinctive
Catholic institutions.

The second factor is the history of religious congregations. Every congregation is founded to respond to some need in the Church or broader community. Each has its own specific mission, spelled out in its constitution,
whether teaching, catechesis, health care, care of orphans or prisoners, etc.
These congregational missions may be as general as "the works of mercy" or
as specific as the care of the mentally ill. In the vast majority of cases congregations have founded institutions, or committed to staffing those founded
by parishes or dioceses, to carry out these works. Congregations from Germany, Ireland, Poland, Italy, and other countries accompanied their compa-
triots here and helped them put down roots in American soil. Other congregations that were expelled from Europe by hostile governments found a
scope for their missions in the United States. Still others were founded in
America to minister to the growing needs of the church community. In many
ways, the history of the congregations provides insight into the development
of Catholic institutions.

The twentieth century witnessed several movements of lay leadership in
Europe and the United States, grouped under the heading of "Catholic Action"—the participation of the laity in the apostolate of the bishops. This
earlier form of lay participation was superseded by the Second Vatican

Council's affirmation of the universal call to holiness and the responsibility all the people of God share for the mission of the Church. As the laity gradually moved into responsibility for the leadership of institutional ministries, this was seen as an expression of their own vocation, rather than as a concession to the diminishing numbers of clergy or religious. More recently, new canonical structures have been approved in which laypersons serve as sponsors of institutions, that is, as the persons ultimately accountable to the Church for the institution's fidelity to its Catholic identity and mission. Finally, the advent of "lay ecclesial ministers"—baptized persons who are professionally prepared and officially authorized to perform a ministry— has raised the question of whether lay sponsors of institutions belong in this category.

A final factor, less quantifiable than the previous ones, but perhaps even more important because of its underlying implications, is the tension between an unquestioning assimilation into American culture and the maintenance of a critical distance. Adoption of English versus preservation of another language is the most obvious example of the tension. Is provision of schools (and liturgy) in one's language of origin a temporary pastoral accommodation or is it essential to the preservation of the community of faith? Language aside, is it essential to Catholic identity to maintain separate Catholic associations for professional groups such as doctors, nurses, lawyers, teachers, librarians, etc., or separate institutions for elementary, secondary, and higher education or for the care of the sick and infirm? According to one's perception of the hostility of the environment, the answer may differ. Is a Catholic institution first and foremost a ministry by and for Catholics, or is it an expression of the Catholic mission to the larger needs of society? Is it possible that an institution founded in one era for one purpose may find another focus in a later, more secularized, pluralistic, and ecumenically sensitive era? These are some of the questions that form a backdrop to a review of the history of the Church's institutions. In the pages that follow, we focus on three categories of institutions: elementary and secondary schools, higher education (including seminaries), and hospitals, as they developed over the past 225 years.

THE EARLY REPUBLIC: 1776–1840

The Church's early institutions were shaped by the reality of its minority status in a Protestant milieu, as well as by the tolerance enshrined in the constitutional separation of church and state. The emerging public school system was Protestant in its culture and piety, but there were no legal barriers to founding separate schools. The dependence on immigrant clergy made the founding of boys' schools imperative to cultivate a generation of potential American seminarians. Early hospitals were little more than refuges for the indigent; those with means were cared for in their homes. It was during this period that the first hospitals devoted to treatment were founded, and the doctors who founded them turned to women religious to staff them. After about 1824 a nativist spirit began to rise in some large cities, prompting immigrant Catholics to desire their own schools and hospitals. A brief discussion of each category of institutions follows.

Bishop John Carroll founded the first boys' school at Georgetown in 1791 and assigned it to the care of the Jesuits. Gabriel Richard, a Sulpician priest working in the Northwest Territory, founded a girls' school in 1804 at what would later be Detroit. Catholic schools really began to multiply, however, with the formation of indigenous communities of religious sisters. The Sisters of Charity founded a school at Emmitsburg, Maryland, in 1810 and eight more by 1828. The Sisters of Charity of Nazareth and Sisters of Loretto (both founded in 1812) continued the movement. In 1830, most Catholic parishes in New York City, Philadelphia, and other eastern cities had some type of school. In 1840, there were at least two hundred Catholic schools in the United States, about half west of the Alleghenies.

The founding of Catholic colleges was a major concern of bishops during this period, as they looked for sources of vocations and places where clerical prospects could begin their training. In fact, the distinction between secondary and baccalaureate education was not what it is today. The Jesuits, who founded or took over many of the colleges, looked on them as similar to a German *gymnasium* or a French *lycée*—a school that offered in a unified program of about six years the same course content that English and American educators divided between two institutions, a four-year secondary school and the first two years of college. Aside from the Jesuits, the Sulpicians, the Dominicans (briefly, in Kentucky), and the Vincentians (in Missouri) were the only orders to establish colleges before 1840. The Sulpicians began St. Mary's Seminary, Baltimore, in 1791 and Mount St. Mary's Seminary in Emmitsburg in 1808.

The first extant Catholic hospital was founded in St. Louis, Missouri, in 1828 by four Sisters of Charity from Emmitsburg, at the invitation of Bishop Joseph Rosati, C.M. The Sisters of Charity had earlier founded the first Catholic mental hospital in the United States, near Baltimore, and the first Catholic orphan home, in Philadelphia. During this period, sisters of many congregations were invited to nurse in hospitals started by physicians in mining communities, railroad towns, and new cities. They tended victims of cholera, yellow fever, and typhoid in hospitals and in their homes. These efforts, shaped by commitment to the vision of the Gospel, helped qualify religious to assume responsibility for health care institutions in the years to come.

YEARS OF IMMIGRATION AND CIVIL WAR: 1840-1879

During the middle third of the nineteenth century, the Catholic Church in America grew enormously in size and assumed new characteristics. In 1849 the Catholic population was approximately 663,000, or 4 percent of the total population; by 1870 it was 4,500,000, or 11 percent of the total. Descendants of the original English and French settlers were vastly outnumbered by immigrants from Ireland, Germany, and a dozen other countries. These new arrivals tended to congregate in the port and industrial cities of the North. The steady stream of Catholic immigrants led to a rekindling of nativist sentiments under the new name of Know-Nothingism. Anticlerical violence peaked between 1854 and 1855 and only came to an end with the Civil War.

Church officials had never taken an unequivocal stand in the controversy over slavery, generally tolerating it in the South, as long as it was humane, and repudiating it in the North. Overall, the Church chose a posture of political neutrality during the Civil War, and its members fought in both armies. However, its standing was enhanced by the charitable activities of its clergy and women religious in both the Confederate and Union states. Also, the Church was the only major denomination that did not split into two churches during the War. Sadly, however, the Church failed to meet the pastoral needs of the millions of newly emancipated blacks, and the ongoing separation of the races within the Church went unchallenged.

During this period there were a number of authoritative pronouncements on the necessity of parochial schools and on the obligation of pastors and parents to support them. For instance, the First Plenary Council of Baltimore in 1852 insisted that Catholic schools were indispensable for the security of faith and morals among Catholic children. The Second Provincial Council of Cincinnati decreed in 1858 that the establishment of parish schools was a serious moral duty of pastors. In 1866 the Plenary Council of Baltimore cited this decree when it recommended that a parochial school be built next to each and every parish church. As insistent as these statements were, implementation varied widely. On the one extreme were dioceses like New York and Cincinnati, where Archbishops John Hughes and John Purcell made the building of schools a personal crusade. In contrast, the dioceses of New England neither totally implemented nor totally ignored the teaching. Fewer than 40 percent of their parishes ever built schools during the nineteenth century. Some of the factors that influenced local choices were the availability of public funding, the resources of the parishioners, the perceptions of the Protestant bias of public schools, and the leadership of bishops and pastors.

This was a period of significant expansion in Catholic higher education. Forty-two Catholic colleges were founded in the 1850s, many by religious congregations new to the American scene. Examples are the University of Notre Dame by the Congregation of the Holy Cross in 1842, Manhattan College by the Christian Brothers in 1853, St. Bonaventure University by the Franciscans in 1856, and the University of Dayton by the Marianists in 1859. The Jesuits added to the number of their schools (e.g., Santa Clara University in 1851), and the Vincentians added Niagara University in 1856, while the Augustinians opened Villanova in 1842. St. Louis University and Georgetown launched medical schools before the Civil War, although the former was short lived. Notre Dame and Georgetown established law schools after the war. Seminaries founded during this period were under diocesan auspices, with the mission of serving several dioceses, or under the auspices of religious congregations, for the benefit of their own members and diocesan clergy. Examples of the former are St. Charles Borromeo Seminary in Philadelphia (1838), Mt. St. Mary Seminary of the West in Cincinnati (1851), and St. Francis de Sales Seminary in Milwaukee (1856). The latter include the seminaries under Benedictine sponsorship at St. Vincent Archabbey, Latrobe, Pennsylvania (1846), St. Meinrad Archabbey, Indiana (1854), and St. John's Abbey, Collegeville, Minnesota (1857).

Of the sixteen congregations of women religious in the United States in 1849, five nursed in hospitals. The Sisters of Charity were in several cities, the Sisters of Charity of Nazareth in Kentucky, the Sisters of Mercy in Pittsburgh, the Sisters of St. Joseph in Philadelphia, and the Oblate Sisters of Providence in Baltimore. Their institutions could accommodate anywhere from a handful of patients to many hundreds. In every case they were committed to provide access to any clergyman a patient might request, whether Catholic or Protestant. This was in contrast to many other private and public hospitals where priests were not welcome to minister to Catholic patients.

PASTORAL ACCOMMODATIONS DURING THE INDUSTRIAL AGE: 1870–1914

By 1900 there were twelve million Catholics in the country, more than 15 percent of the total population. Increased heterogeneity in the immigrant population (especially increased numbers of Southern and Eastern Europeans), the multiplication of ethnic parishes, and greater social and geographic mobility all contributed to the pastoral challenge. Up until this time the tendency of Catholics to remain in denominational ghettoes and to prefer their own institutions whenever possible had effectively preserved their Catholic identity while distancing them from the center of American life. During this period, some of the Catholic intellectual elite came to favor another vision, called Americanism, which held that American democratic institutions were especially compatible with Catholic tradition. The challenge of entering the mainstream without compromising core identity was encountered in different ways in each area of institutional life.

The choice of parochial versus public schools continued to be a bellwether of Catholic identity. In 1884 the Third Plenary Council of Baltimore mandated the establishment of a grammar school in each parish within two years. In several dioceses, synods were held that reinforced the mandate by threatening the removal of pastors who failed to comply. As in earlier decades, compliance was mixed. In addition to the factors identified in the last period, ethnicity played a role. Chicago's Poles outnumbered Italians by two to one in 1900, but had thirteen times as many schools—undoubtedly a reflection of cultural values and traditions. Yet another factor was that some parents saw public schools as a vehicle of upward mobility for their children.

A more fundamental issue was epitomized by the "School Controversy" of 1890–1893, triggered by a speech given by Archbishop John Ireland to the National Education Association in 1890. In terms of extent, intensity, and bitterness of feeling, the dispute was unprecedented in American Catholic history at that time. Briefly, Ireland (a leading voice in the Americanist movement) asserted the necessity and desirability of state schools, but stated that they were not reaching their potential because they were eliminating religion from the minds and hearts of youth. Hence parochial schools were necessary only because of the present irreligious character of public schools. The remedy, the archbishop said, was either to divide tax monies between denominational and nondenominational schools (which would both be, in effect, "public") or to allow religious instruction on released time in the public school. He also approved something like the latter arrangement in the small towns of Faribault and Stillwater, Minnesota. So divided was the hierarchy over the issue, and so intense was the debate, that it was ultimately referred to Rome. Vatican officials issued a decree that allowed Ireland's experiment to continue but forbade its duplication in other dioceses.

In succeeding decades Catholic education continued to grow and become more professionalized. The Catholic Educational Association was founded in 1904, and diocesan offices exercised greater administrative control over schools. Following the lead of public schools, the Catholic community added more and more secondary schools to the educational continuum.

The most significant event relative to higher education in this period was the founding of the Catholic University of America in 1887. The Third Plenary Council of Baltimore had called for its establishment in response to the concerns of those who felt that the Catholic colleges were not meeting the intellectual and religious challenges of the day. For the first ten years of its existence, Catholic University was deeply embroiled in the controversies over Americanism. Both this movement and the later (mainly European) crisis of Modernism grew out of Catholic efforts to respond to social change and new currents of thought in the natural sciences, biblical scholarship, and philosophy. The "liberal" responses championed by the Americanists and Modernists were decisively rejected by Church authorities, and neoscholasticism was prescribed as the official Church answer to the philosophical and theological problems of the age.

The establishment of a Catholic university oriented toward graduate education and research did have the positive effect of stimulating postbaccalaureate programs at other Catholic institutions—first, professional programs such as medicine, law, engineering, education, etc., and then graduate degrees in the arts and sciences. This period also saw the establishment of Catholic women's colleges. Notre Dame of Maryland was chartered in 1876 and Trinity College in Washington, D.C., in 1900. By 1926 twenty-five colleges for women constituted more than a third of the institutions accredited by the Catholic Education Association. Existing seminaries and new ones started during the period struggled with the need to develop curricula in tune with the needs of the age without falling prey to accusations of Americanism or Modernism.

The number of Catholic hospitals grew from 75 in 1872 to nearly 400 in 1910. This phenomenal growth paralleled the increase in hospitals in general, prompted by advances in medical science and the development of whole new medical and surgical specialties. The sisters who founded and staffed these hospitals also established nursing schools in conjunction with many of them, thus influencing the preparation of countless caregivers.

INTO THE MAINSTREAM: 1914–1964

The election of a Catholic president near the end of this period marked the triumph of a kind of assimilation to American culture. By 1964 the Catholic population had increased to 44,874,000, or 24 percent of the total. Most Catholic voters supported John F. Kennedy, as did many others, no doubt reassured by his public statements that his religion would not be a factor in his conduct of the public's business. The Church gradually lost its immigrant status, and the wholehearted participation of the Catholic community in two World Wars solidified their personal sense, and the public's perception, of their American identity. Catholics had indeed entered the mainstream of American life. And as part of this mainstream, Catholics and their institutions shared one of the greatest challenges for all Americans in this period: the persistence of racial prejudice.

The schools grew in number and size throughout this period, peaking in the late 1950s and early 1960s with the postwar baby boom. In 1914 there were 5,403 parochial schools, enrolling 1,429,000 children; in 1964, 10,452 parish elementary schools enrolled 4,471,000 children, and 450 private schools enrolled another 85,000. In 1964 more than a million young people were registered in 1,557 parish and diocesan high schools and 901 private secondary schools conducted by religious communities. Religious vocations also peaked in the mid-1960s and then began a decline that has never been reversed. The educational needs of black Catholics in the South were met by the Sisters of the Blessed Sacrament for Indians and Colored People with the founding of elementary and secondary schools and of Xavier University in New Orleans. By mid-century, however, the de facto segregation of most Catholic schools had become a matter of conscience. Despite the objections of some parents, a few bishops led the way in ending segregation in their school systems prior to the Supreme Court decision of 1954, e.g., Archbishop Joseph E. Ritter in St. Louis in 1947 and Archbishop Patrick A. O'Boyle in Washington, D.C., in 1948.

By 1964, 366,172 students were enrolled in 295 Catholic colleges and universities. By the late 1960s nine Catholic universities had graduate schools awarding doctoral degrees, and many had professional school faculties in areas such as law, medicine, business, finance, engineering, architecture, nursing, education, dentistry, pharmacy, music, social service, industrial relations, diplomacy, and physical education. In contrast to Catholic elementary and secondary schools, institutions of higher education received state and federal funds in the form of veterans' benefits, aid for construction of buildings, research grants, and scholarships supported by the National Defense Education Act of 1958. As the number of seminaries continued to grow, their leadership concerned itself with administrative reforms and improved academic standards. By the 1960s seminaries began to seek and obtain accreditation, with resulting recognition of their credits and degrees. It seems safe to assume that the recipients of American Catholic higher education during these years became some of the laity and clergy who anticipated the Second Vatican Council through movements of social and liturgical reform, and who were in the forefront of its early implementation.

Catholic institutions for health care also grew apace over these years. The formation of the Catholic Hospital Association (now the Catholic Health Association) in 1915 provided a venue for ongoing national discussion of key issues of Catholic identity and professional practice. Until mid-century, however, Catholic hospitals were almost entirely segregated. The first hospital established as an integrated facility with black physicians on the staff was St. Vincent's in Kansas City in 1953.

POST-CONCILIAR ERA: 1964–2000

Women religious were among the first groups to feel the impact of the Second Vatican Council. They were mandated to renew every aspect of their lives and mission in light of their founding charisms and the needs of the present day. Sisters had benefited from the Sister Formation Movement, an effort begun in the late 1940s, to upgrade their educational, professional, and spiritual preparation for religious life and ministry. Armed with insights from this experience, they took the Council's mandate to heart and set about a wholesale self-examination and experimentation with new expressions of lifestyle and ministry. One result was a diminished visibility in their institutions, as they abandoned medieval dress and took on new (often noninstitutional) initiatives in ministry.

Beginning in the mid-1970s, sisters inaugurated the concept of sponsorship of their ministries, the purposeful influence over the mission and culture of organizations. The rate of increase in the Catholic population declined in these years, as Catholics reduced their family size. Upward social mobility saw Catholics moving from urban to suburban parishes, and many inner city parishes and schools closed. While some categories of institutions declined numerically, others grew, and those that survived strove for higher standards of excellence than heretofore.

Catholic elementary and secondary school enrollment declined from its peak in the 1960s to the current 2.6 million, due partly to a decline in the school age population and the migration of Catholics from older parishes to the suburbs, where public schooling was of a high quality. There may be a shift in process, however. Between 1988 and 1998 the Catholic school population actually increased 3.8 percent in the West and Far West. Between 1985 and 1999, 230 new Catholic schools opened. Current interest in charter schools and voucher plans among the public indicate that people are willing to make choices for quality schools, and Catholic schools are regarded as an attractive choice, even for some non-Catholics who view religious instruction as a plus.

Dozens of financially weaker colleges have closed over the past forty years, and the 235 that remain are generally stronger academically and organizationally than at mid-century. Virtually all institutions created lay boards of trustees, in some cases reserving key powers to the sponsoring religious congregations. As the colleges and universities assumed more autonomy from the founding congregations, questions of academic freedom arose. Was the mission of higher education compatible with external ecclesiastical authority? The Vatican's Congregation for Education answered the question in 1991 with the promulgation of *Ex Corde Ecclesiae*, an instruction on the preservation of Catholic identity and theological orthodoxy in higher education. Norms for its implementation on the American scene were promulgated by the American bishops. Enrollments in seminaries decreased precipitously during this period, and there have been numerous closings. Most seminaries have added ministry training programs, including the master of divinity degree, for laypersons wishing to minister in the Church.

Health care is the area of institutional presence that has undergone the greatest growth and change in recent decades. With the advent of Medicare in 1965, hospital care became affordable for all older Americans. Rising levels of prosperity throughout most of this period, as well as dramatic advances in surgery, medical technology, and pharmacology, fueled the public's appetite for bigger, costlier, technologically more sophisticated hospitals. Catholic hospitals grew in number and size along with all the others. More recently, under the pressure of managed care, hospitals have consolidated into regional and national systems. Catholic hospitals have not been slow to follow. Beginning in the early 1980s, sponsoring congregations realized that the continuance of their health care mission required them to unite their many institutions into systems under central management, with common financing. Gradually, separate congregations combined their institutions or smaller systems into cosponsored systems. Today, over 70 percent of Catholic health care is organized into about ten large systems. A National Coalition on Catholic Health Care Ministry regularly brings together representatives from the bishops, the sponsoring religious congregations, and the hospitals and health systems to guide the future directions of the ministry. One project of the Coalition is the New Covenant Initiative, an effort to create a shared vision of the caring and healing ministries in order to collaborate more fruitfully in a common mission. Its stakeholders are drawn from health, education, and human service ministries, parishes, and dioceses. Examples of effective projects are parish nursing programs and low income housing initiatives that incorporate health and social services.

CARRYING THE LEGACY INTO THE FUTURE

The Church's institutional presence has been a constant factor in her American experience for over two centuries. As we move into the new millennium, we can single out five characteristics of the present situation that carry promise for the future. The first is that Catholic institutions represent a *continuity of response* to the pastoral and social needs of people. In season and out, the Church has continued a ministry to the poor, the sick, the handicapped, the uneducated, and those experiencing the gamut of human needs. Catholic institutions have come to embody *standards of excellence* that witness to the importance they place on their work as an expression of Christian mission. Catholic institutions no longer promote a separatist Catholicism; rather, they represent the *inculturation of the faith in a pluralistic environment*. This institutional commitment is often a tool for the Church's *systemic influence* in American society. Because of the extent of our commitment to the alleviation of social ills, our longevity, and the quality of our services, we have earned the right to be heard in the chambers in which public policies are crafted. Finally, the responsibility for Church institutions has largely passed into the hands of *lay leaders*, a sign of their maturing role in the Church. We can look forward to the further evolution of the Church's institutional ministries under their leadership, with gratitude for what has been and with hope for the future.

REFLECTION QUESTIONS

1. What was the mission of your institution when it began? What and whose needs was it founded to meet? If those needs have changed over the years, how has the mission evolved in response?
2. Gottemoeller cites four factors that have influenced the history of Catholic institutional ministries: changing demographics; the role of religious congregations; the role of the laity; and tensions between assimilation and prophetic distance. Which of these has had the most significant impact on your institution? From your experience as a leader, can you give a concrete example of the "assimilation versus prophetic distance" tension?
3. The essay asks, "Is a Catholic institution first and foremost a ministry by and for Catholics, or is it an expression of the Catholic mission to the larger needs of society?" What do you think?

REFERENCES

Adrianyl-Quintin, Gabriel, et al. *The Church in the Modern Age*, translated by Anselm Biggs. New York: Crossroad, 1981.

Aubert, Roger, et al. *The Church between Revolution and Restoration*, translated by Peter Becker. New York: Crossroad, 1989.

———. *The Church in the Age of Liberalism*, translated by Peter Becker. New York: Crossroad, 1989.

———. *The Church in the Industrial Age*, translated by Margit Resch. New York: Crossroad, 1981.

Crews, Clyde F. "American Catholics: 1965–1995." In *The Encyclopedia of American Catholic History [ACH]*, ed. Michael Glazier and Thomas J. Shelley, 83–86. Collegeville, MN: Liturgical Press, 1997.

Dolan, Jay P. *The American Catholic Experience*. New York: Doubleday, 1985.

Fogarty, Gerald P. "American Catholics: 1865–1908." In *ACH*, 73–78.

Gleason, Philip. "Catholic Education, Higher." In *ACH*, 249–54.

Hennessey, James. *American Catholics: A History of the Roman Catholic Community in the United States*. New York: Oxford University Press, 1981.

Kauffman, Christopher J. *Ministry and Meaning: A Religious History of Catholic Health Care in the United States*. New York: Crossroad, 1995.

O'Toole, James M. "American Catholics: 1908–1965." In *ACH*, 78–83.

Perko, F. Michael. "Catholic Education, Parochial." In *ACH*, 254–59.

Shelley, Thomas J. "American Catholics: 1815–1865." In *ACH*, 69–73.

6

Catholic Education as Part of an Ecclesial System: Structures, Mission, Vision

Elinor Ford

As Richard McCord noted in the foreword, one dimension of the Church is that it is an institution. Therefore, each Catholic school is part of a larger reality—a diocese, the Church in the United States, and the Church of Rome. In this chapter, Elinor Ford sketches the system of Roman Catholic education in the United States, with attention to the ways the different parts relate. At the same time, she outlines a vision that embraces the parts, posing a challenge to leaders to embody the fullness of what Catholic schools and universities are called to be.

> The Catholic teacher, therefore, cannot be content simply to present Christian values as a set of abstract objectives to be admired, even if this be done positively and with imagination; they must be presented as values which generate human attitudes, and these attitudes must be encouraged in the students. Examples of such attitudes would be these: a freedom which includes respect for others; conscientious responsibility; a sincere and constant search for truth; a calm and peaceful critical spirit; a spirit of solidarity with and service toward all persons; a sensitivity for justice; a special awareness of being called to be positive agents of change in a society that is undergoing continuous transformation.
>
> *—Lay Catholics in Schools: Witnesses to Faith*[1]

This quotation conveys the essence of what it means to be truly a *Catholic* teacher. It not only echoes Jesus' last command to each disciple to go forth to continue his life and mission by teaching *all* people, but it also embodies the beatitudinal spirit with which this must be done—to all, for all, and of all. But if this explains the vocation of the teacher, how much more does it describe the layperson called to the ministry of Catholic educational leadership—to be the teacher of teachers, the passionate witness to witnesses.

Lay leaders live out this leadership when they create among those who serve and those served a genuine community. Such a community is one that celebrates and gives thanks for, not just tolerates, each other's differences. The members journey daily together, supporting each other's faith and professional growth. The Catholics within this community use a regular "faith alive" participation in Eucharist as the engine that powers and grows their own and others' spirituality and ministry.

This educational community is dedicated to *educare,* to calling out both from ourselves and from those we serve what Thomas Merton termed the song God placed in our hearts. This song keeps aching to escape so that we can be fully human, fully alive. Graduates of Catholic schools sing well if the educational institution enables them to become adults who have the will and the skill to learn, to think, to pray about their thoughts, to live what they believe, and to proclaim the good news in their homes, churches, and marketplaces by writing and speaking persuasively.

THE VISION AND MISSION

In chapter 2 Michael Downey reminds the reader that "without a vision the people perish." This is just as true for institutions. Organizational theory[2] related to both the secular and the ecclesial worlds demonstrates that the leader is the determining factor in whether there even is a vision, its quality, and, more important, if the vision ever emerges from the realm of rhetoric to become a lived reality. The same theory explains that the vision has to be a communal one. In fact, true collaborative thought and deed within any organization depend on each member having internalized and made a commitment to the stated vision. There will and must exist differences in the implementation of the vision, but it must always be the unifying force in the midst of the community's rich diversity.

The vision must be the result of a prayerful and collaborative discernment by the servers and the served. As such, it will reflect the virtues and values of the communal members and be a long-range view of why the institution should and does exist. The vision created must be able to serve as the mirror that reflects whether the workings, the structures, and the results achieved by the institution are of God, rather than of one or more pressure points within or without the institution.

ECCLESIAL STRUCTURES

The complexity of the modern world makes it all the more necessary to increase awareness of the ecclesial identity of the Catholic school. It is from its Catholic identity that the school derives its original characteristics and its "structure" as a genuine instrument of the Church, a place of real and specific pastoral ministry. The Catholic school participates in the evangelizing mission of the Church and is the privileged environment in which Christian education is carried out.

—*The Catholic School on the Threshold of the Third Millennium*[3]

Catholic Elementary and Secondary Schools

Each Catholic school is part of the larger structure of the Catholic Church. The Congregation for Catholic Education, which is part of the Curia, has responsibility for all Catholic schools. Various documents of the Congregation provide a vision and guidelines for dioceses and schools throughout the world. The Code of Canon Law, the law of the universal Church, treats matters relevant to schools as such, as well as related topics such as norms for the sacraments. In addition, each diocese has guidelines and regulations governing schools.

Therefore, to understand the particular ecclesial structures that affect Catholic educational institutions and programs, lay leaders should have in their personal libraries and be well acquainted with the following materials: *The Code of Canon Law: A Text and Commentary*;[4] diocesan administrative manuals and leadership materials for a given educational level or program; *A Primer on Educational Governance in the Catholic Church*;[5] *Formation and Development for Catholic School Leaders*,[6] and select resources from the Sacred Congregation for Catholic Education.

Since Catholic educational institutions are established under local, state, and federal laws, the lay leader must also be familiar with these secular mandates. The National Catholic Educational Association (NCEA) has several legal publications to assist those who work in Catholic education.[7]

The Diocese and the School

The Ordinary of the diocese is the appointed arch/bishop, whose power of governance in the diocese is legislative, executive, and judicial. Since the Ordinary may not delegate his legislative power, boards, commissions, councils, and committees associated with diocesan and parish Catholic educational institutions and programs are consultative or advisory. At most, they may have limited jurisdiction, which is carefully described in their articles of incorporation and other written materials (Canons 134, 135, 466).

The Ordinary may delegate his executive power (Canon 137). Oversight of the Catholic elementary and secondary schools and all other educational ministries in the diocese is often delegated to the Vicar/Secretary for Education, who, in turn, delegates executive responsibility for the Catholic schools to the Superintendent of Schools. The Superintendent is responsible for ensuring that each Catholic school observes the diocese's educational policies and guidelines with respect to the school's governance and Catholicity, and that it provides the best possible religious education and faith formation programs for the students and families served. The Superintendent also sees that the schools provide quality academic education in compliance with local, state, and federal mandates that apply to Catholic schools.

All schools within a given diocese, whether parish, diocesan, religious community, or other private schools, must have the written consent of the competent ecclesial authority, if they are to be established as Catholic. The Ordinary is responsible for the religious education and faith formation programs within any Catholic institution in his diocese (Canons 803, 808). Policies and guidelines with respect to these are described in appropriate diocesan manuals and other materials. These same materials also describe the specific line and staff relationships and responsibilities between and among diocesan officials and any diocesan boards and the leaders and boards of a Catholic school in the diocese.

Since there is a variety of Catholic educational institutions, the ecclesial governance structures described here are of their very nature general. Each diocese creates the specifics of its own governance policies and guidelines in conformity with the Ordinary's legislative mandates and the Code of Canon Law. Lay leaders should, therefore, compare the descriptions in this chapter with the written policies for the diocese and schools with which they are associated. The first descriptions given are for elementary schools (PK–8) and secondary schools (9–12). A brief discussion of the governance structures of colleges and universities within a diocese follows.

Catholic School (PK–12) Statistics and Financing

A 2004 report[8] notes that there are almost two and a half million students served by almost 8,000 elementary and secondary Catholic schools in the United States. Minority school enrollment is 26.5 percent of this population, and non-Catholics 13.5 percent. The report states that the mean elementary annual tuition is $2,178, with a per pupil cost of $3,505. For the secondary school the mean is $4,289, with a per pupil cost of $5,571. (Based on the average public school per pupil cost of $7,284, it has been estimated that Catholic schools save the citizenry *$18.6 billion* annually.)

Currently, most PK–12 Catholic schools are primarily financed by the parents through tuition, fund-raising, and development efforts. State and/or federal grants provide minimal support in areas such as bus transportation, school nurses, guidance counselors, secular textbooks and other teaching materials, technology support, remedial tutoring for the economically disadvantaged, special education students, drug prevention, and school safety. There are also voucher programs for low income students in some states. Information with respect to all these is available from the Superintendent of Schools, the Education Department of the United States Conference of Catholic Bishops, state Catholic conferences, and the National Catholic Educational Association.

If the school is a parish/diocesan one, it may also receive a parish/diocesan financial subsidy. When vowed religious staffed these schools for a very minimal stipend, most of the parish schools were tuition-free. The parish subsidy was almost 100 percent, with the difference being made up by fund-raising. A recent report[9] states that today over 85 percent of Catholic elementary schools have a parish subsidy, but it is well below the former 100 percent. Of these schools, only 45 percent received a parish subsidy greater than 20 percent of the cost of running the school. The report also noted that schools in parishes with stewardship programs received larger subsidies than those without.

Most dioceses contribute in some fashion to Catholic schools serving the very poor. Schools sponsored/owned by religious communities also make significant contributions to this population, such as staffing by community members, the use of community-owned buildings, and direct financial contributions.

Elementary Schools (PK–8)

In the earliest years of our country, before religious communities assumed the principalship and major staffing of the schools, most parish elementary schools were governed by lay boards of trustees who established and maintained the school building, the curriculum, and finances and hired and fired the lay staff. The trustees were supposed to be directly responsible to the pastor, but history demonstrates that there were constant tensions between many trustees and their pastors, since the latter's parish governance powers were not recognized.

From the late 1700s until the 1960s, parish elementary schools grew exponentially, primarily because of the heroic work and sacrifices of vowed religious. Today the dominant staffing pattern for the elementary school is mostly lay. The laity, too, serves with dedication, competence, and sacrifice, as their financial remuneration is usually much less than that of their public school counterparts.

To ensure that Catholic schools not only survive but also prosper, despite the ever rising costs, there have been ongoing creative and unique strategic planning and development efforts in dioceses among diocesan staff, local clergy, principals, school staff, parents, and parishioners. The result is a myriad of Catholic elementary school organizational designs. For this discussion these shall be classified as parish elementary schools, interparish elementary schools, diocesan/regional schools, religious community schools, and other private schools.

Parish Elementary Schools

Much of what is described here for the single parish school will be applicable to all the different types of Catholic elementary schools. Exceptions will be noted in the descriptions of each of the other types of schools, presented below.

As the canonically appointed leader of the parish, the pastor is responsible for all parish Catholic education and faith formation efforts "from womb to tomb" (Canon 519). He is required by canon law to establish a parish finance committee to assist him in the proper and effective management of the parish's resources, including the parish Catholic school (Canon 537). Canon law also suggests that every parish have a pastoral council to advise the pastor in his "teaching, sanctifying and governing" role "with the cooperation of other presbyters or deacons and the assistance of lay members of the Christian faithful" (Canons 519, 536). This pastoral council usually establishes an education committee concerned with the effective and efficient administration of all parish educational programs. This includes the school and all parish religious education and faith formation programs for children, youth, and adults.

The parish elementary school usually maintains the traditional PK–8 grades for the children of parishioners, youngsters from other parishes, and non-Catholic children. The pastor hires the principal and is responsible for the principal's reappointment or termination. When a new principal is needed, many pastors have the parish school board create a search committee made up of board members, parents, and school staff. The search committee follows the diocesan guidelines for principal selection, and, if the Office of the Superintendent of Schools has already prescreened applicants for principalship within the diocese, makes its recommendations to the pastor from this list.

The pastor and principal serve as ex officio members of the parish school board/council/committee, with the principal working most closely with the board and keeping it informed on pertinent school matters. In addition to assisting in the selection and evaluation of the principal, the consultative role of the board also includes creating policies for the discretionary action of the school's administration; developing long-range strategic school plans; ensuring that the annual budget coheres to this plan; and establishing and participating in school development, fund-raising, marketing, and public relations projects. Because of the different duties that the board has, its members should be selected not only because they are deeply committed to the school's vision and mission, but also because they possess various experiences and talents that will enable the board to achieve its multiple tasks successfully. The diocese usually has guidelines for parish school boards that are used to create local school board manuals.

While the pastor is the canonical administrator of all parish programs and activities, including the school, the principal is the chief day-to-day administrator of the school, reporting directly to the pastor. Of particular importance to the pastor is the principal's selection of faculty who are not just qualified and proficient in teaching assigned subjects, but also committed to promoting the Catholic identity and mission of the school. This is critical if there is to be a nurturing gospel-based school ethos that will inspire and support staff, students, and their families to live out their vocations to build up the reign of God. The pastor-principal relationship must, therefore, be a prayerful, energized, and cohesive one.

The principal also meets regularly with other principals and the staff of the Office of the Superintendent of Schools. These meetings are designed to keep the principal updated on current ecclesial matters, federal, state, and local educational mandates, projects and monies/services available to Catholic schools; to create principal to principal to superintendent problem-solving networks; to discuss and share ideas and efforts toward faith formation and quality education; to support the principal's spiritual leadership role; and to provide opportunities for the principal's own personal faith formation and growth.

Interparish/Consolidated Parish Elementary Schools

The interparish school is often the result of making more efficient use of the best physical plants for Catholic elementary education, by closing less efficient ones and in effect consolidating the Catholic schools of several parishes. One building within a given parish may serve as the interparish school, or the school buildings in several parishes may be chosen, with each one assigned specific grade levels, such as early childhood, middle school, or junior high.

The interparish school is governed by the pastors of the parishes served by it, with one pastor being appointed by the diocese or selected by the other interparish pastors to be the "contact pastor" to whom the principal reports directly. This contact pastor is responsible for communicating school matters to the other pastors, encouraging them to participate in given school activities, and seeking their consent to proceed with matters that require the pastors' joint permission. Usually there are guidelines that describe the ecclesial governance of interparish elementary schools.

Diocesan/Regional Elementary Schools

This is a relatively new concept in Catholic elementary education. The term "regional" is sometimes given to the interparish network described above. But lately this type of school is the result of an inspired diocesan plan to ensure that Catholic elementary education is available for as many as possible. The diocesan/regional school serves the needs of a given geographic region. It is under the direct supervision of the Superintendent of Schools as the bishop's school executive. The pastors in whose parishes the school building(s) exist, and/or whose children are served by the diocesan/regional school, often have consultative roles, such as being members of the school board and/or participating in the superintendent's selection of the principal.

Religious Community Elementary Schools

These are private schools established, owned, and/or sponsored by a religious community, with the written permission of the Ordinary, to serve a given population of elementary age children. These include Montessori schools, schools for the physically and mentally challenged, schools for the more affluent, and schools established for minority students and the economically disadvantaged. Among the latter are those more recently created with extended day and Saturday schedules and with provision for meals, special tutoring, and extra sports and other activities.

The principal is appointed by and is responsible to the religious community and/or school board/trustees. This board may be consultative, as are the parish boards. Here the board advises the designated religious community administrator. Some of these schools have a board with limited jurisdiction. Such a board governs the school except in matters that are the purview of the religious community and the Ordinary of the diocese. The latter is particularly concerned for the Catholicity of the school and its faith formation and religious education programs and activities. Published guidelines describe the precise role of a board with limited jurisdiction.

The gift that religious congregations have been and continue to be for American Catholic education at all levels is a priceless one. Many of these congregations are currently in a transition period. Given their smaller membership, they are reshaping their ministerial directions and priorities. Their sponsorship and/or governance of their own private elementary and secondary schools is taking new forms. Brother Frederick C. Mueller, F.S.C., points out what their continued presence means to the future of Catholic education:

> The social capital provided by the religious congregation for a school has been and still can be a source of institutional strength. Religious community sponsorship of Catholic elementary and secondary schools . . . would appear to be the best hope for the continuance of the unique Catholic school that has been traditionally associated with religious congregations of women and men in the United States.[10]

His article provides an excellent analysis and synthesis of today's complex sponsorship and governance structures in religious community schools.

Other Private Elementary Schools

These are schools established by parents and/or other laity for a given purpose, with the written permission of the Ordinary, and incorporated following state laws. Usually the school has a corporate board that has complete governing power for the school except for those issues reserved to the Ordinary of the diocese by canon law (Canons 803–806).

Secondary Schools

Catholic secondary schools may be classified as parish, diocesan/regional, religious community, and other private schools. Unity among these different types of Catholic secondary schools is maintained and enriched through the Office of the Superintendent of Schools. This office has one or more qualified professionals with experience at the Catholic secondary school level who are available to review, consult, and support all the principals' and school boards' efforts to achieve their mission by providing the best possible faith formation, religious education, and academic education in a financially effective and efficient way.

Parish Secondary Schools

There are fewer parish high schools today, most having been either closed or subsumed into diocesan/regional high schools. The governance of parish high schools is similar to that of the parish elementary school, with the pastor the canonical administrator of the parish and the principal the administrator of the school reporting directly to him.

Diocesan/Regional High Schools

The diocesan/regional Catholic high school is operated directly by the principal or a president-principal team, with the president as the school's chief executive and the principal overseeing the day-to-day operations. The principal/president is responsible to the diocese/superintendent and works closely with the board. In some cases this is the arch/diocesan board itself, or one established for the particular school. All board policies for the school must be approved by the bishop and/or the superintendent.

Working with the school's board, the president/principal creates a budget that is approved by the superintendent and/or the diocesan board or other diocesan financial officers. A balanced budget must be maintained by the president/principal. In some dioceses the tuition and any subsidies from the diocese and/or parishes are established diocesan-wide rather than on a school-to-school basis.

The superintendent is usually in charge of the principal/president selection process, following diocesan guidelines for such appointments. Usually the school board is involved in creating a search committee and making recommendations. In some dioceses, if a diocesan priest is to be named as either president or principal of the school, this appointment is made directly by the Ordinary. Processes for the selection, reappointment, and termination of diocesan/regional high school principals and presidents, as well as the line and staff relationships between and among the school administration, diocesan officials, and boards, are described in detail in diocesan manuals and other materials.

Religious Community and Other Private Catholic Secondary Schools

The sponsorship, governance and financing of these schools is similar to that described for religious community and other private Catholic elementary schools and is detailed in specific published materials. These are derived from the diocesan statement of agreement to establish the school as Catholic in the diocese; diocesan policies and guidelines for such schools; the articles of incorporation; local, state, and federal mandates that apply to a Catholic school; and, in the case of religious community schools, the community's vision and mission statements and other documents that describe its reasons for sponsoring/owning such schools.

Catholic Colleges and Universities

Although colleges and universities are part of the Catholic school system and part of the ecclesial structure, they are quite different in their focus, internal structures, and mode of relationship with the Church. We consider them here in order to give a picture of the continuity in Catholic education endeavors.

As of 2004 there were 222 Catholic colleges and universities in the United States. The first, Georgetown University, was established in 1789 by America's first bishop, the Jesuit-educated John Carroll, as the "Academy at George-town" open to "every class of citizens" and students of "every religious profession." Bishop Carroll's intent was to create a distinguished school of Catholic higher education so as to promote respect for Catholicism in the United States. Today, Georgetown University's general mission statement reflects well the ministry of Catholic higher education in America:

An academic community dedicated to creating and communicating knowledge, Georgetown provides excellent undergraduate, graduate and professional education in the Jesuit tradition—for the glory of God and the well-being of humankind. Georgetown educates men and women to be reflective lifelong learners, to be responsible and active participants in civic life, and to live generously in the service of others.[11]

To achieve this, Catholic colleges and universities must be places where adults are motivated to ask the ultimate *personal* questions, "Who am *I*?" and "Whose am *I*?" followed by the ultimate *communal* questions, "Who are *we*?" and "Whose are *we*?" It is the responsibility of the leadership to listen very carefully to the answers to these transcendent questions. Only then can the campus teaching, inquiry, and ethos be shaped to support individual and communal lifelong journeys.

The work of Dean R. Hoge et al.[12] is a "must-read" for leaders of Catholic higher education who wish to ensure that their institutions strive to do this. This research not only describes what today's young adult Catholics are really like, but also suggests what they need to become fully human and fully alive. The volume is especially informative in defining both what Catholic identity means for the individual student and what in Catholicism attracts and motivates young adults to become passionate witnesses and evangelizers.

Types of Catholic Colleges and Universities

The Catholic University of America, Washington, D.C., is the only national one. It was established by Pope Leo XIII and the bishops of the United States in 1887 as a graduate and research center, but today includes undergraduate education. Catholic University is governed by a self-perpetuating board with arch/bishops of dioceses being a majority of the membership. The University is supported by contributions from all the dioceses in the United States and by tuition, grants, scholarships, fund-raising, and development projects.

Diocesan Universities

As the name implies, these are established by a diocese. They are governed either by a board of trustees with some powers reserved to the diocese or by an independent board with no power reserved to the diocese.[13] Seton Hall University, the oldest diocesan university in the United States, was established by the first bishop of the Archdiocese of Newark, New Jersey, in 1856, to provide "a home for the mind, the heart, and the spirit." Today the Archbishop serves as president of both governing boards; members include laymen and women, diocesan priests, and bishops of the dioceses of the state of New

Jersey. Like the other four diocesan universities, Seton Hall is subject to state and federal education laws and mandates and voluntarily seeks and obtains accreditation by the appropriate secular educational agency.

Religious Community Colleges and Universities

Most of America's Catholic colleges and universities were first established by religious communities such as the Jesuits, who have twenty-eight in the United States today. But a great number of colleges founded by religious communities were begun as normal schools for the sole purpose of training their own religious membership for the teaching profession. When these became two- and four-year colleges and in some cases universities, the institutions were opened to everyone.

These institutions are governed either by a board of trustees with some power reserved to the religious community or by an independent board with no power reserved to the religious community.[14] Religious community members are usually represented on the board to maintain its founding charism, the particular vision and gift which gave rise to the school. Their participation also allows them to share the community's gifts with the critical work they had started.

Other Ecclesial or Lay Initiative Colleges and Universities

Sacred Heart University in Fairfield, Connecticut, was the first Catholic university in the United States to be led and staffed by laity. It was established in 1963 by Bishop Walter Curtis, the second bishop of Bridgeport, who envisioned the need for lay leadership and governance in Catholic higher education.

One college that was founded, as well as governed and staffed, by lay people is Magdalen College in New Hampshire. In 1973 three lay men, influenced by Vatican II and especially its document, the *Declaration on Christian Education*,[15] established a college for the purpose of training young people to become true lay apostles in the world. As all such institutions must, the college received ecclesial permission to call the school Catholic from its bishop in Manchester, New Hampshire. In recent years some other Catholic colleges have been started by laity; they are still in the early stages of their lives.

The laity today, in the same spirit as those laymen of 1973, have certainly become a tremendous leadership force in Catholic higher education. Standing on the shoulders of their predecessors, especially members of religious communities, lay people now are in the majority as presidents of Catholic colleges and universities, with 116 of the 222 presidents being lay men or women.

Ecclesial Relationships

To understand the relationship of Catholic colleges and universities to the ecclesial system, the lay leader must be well acquainted with four critical documents. These are the Code of Canon Law,[16] *Ex Corde Ecclesiae, The Apostolic Constitution of the Supreme Pontiff John Paul II on Catholic Universities;*[17] *Ex Corde Ecclesiae, The Application to the United States* (commonly called the *Application* document);[18] and *Guidelines Concerning the Academic Mandatum in Catholic Universities (Canon 812).*[19]

Pope John Paul II's document *Ex Corde Ecclesiae* ("born from the heart of the Church") states, "The basic mission of a University is a continuous quest for truth through its research, and the preservation and communication of knowledge for the good of society. A Catholic University participates in this mission with its own specific characteristics and purposes."[20] This document also states that the general norms described in this section "are based on, and are a further development of, the Code of Canon Law and the complementary Church legislation, without prejudice to the right of the Holy See to intervene should this become necessary."[21]

The *Application* document that details how *Ex Corde Ecclesiae* is to be applied in the United States cogently explains that a Catholic university demonstrates its Catholicity, in the spirit of *Ex Corde Ecclesiae,* by a "public acknowledgement in its mission statement and/or its other official documentation of its canonical status and its commitment to the practical implications of its Catholic identity."[22] The document then says that the membership of the board, to the extent possible, should have a majority of Catholics committed to the Church, and that each board member "must be committed to the practical implications of the university's Catholic identity as set forth in its mission statement or equivalent document."[23] The *Application* also instructs the board to have a mechanism for relating to the local bishop and other diocesan agencies for "matters of mutual concern," and to regularly evaluate the coherence of the university to the "ideals, principles and norms expressed in *Ex Corde Ecclesiae.*"[24]

In another section the *Application* document declares that "Catholics who teach the theological disciplines in a Catholic university are required to have a mandatum granted by competent ecclesiastical authority."[25] To clarify the mandatum requirement, the United States Conference of Catholic Bishops (USCCB) published *Guidelines Concerning the Academic Mandatum in Catholic Universities (Canon 812).*[26] It is the individual professor's and not the institution's responsibility to obtain this mandatum, and these guidelines spell out the who, why, and how of this process.

These documents also describe the importance of the bishop's role in promoting the great work of Catholic higher education. Bishops fulfill their roles individually and through the higher education and campus ministry divisions of the USCCB. The bishops meet twice yearly with representatives of the higher education presidents to promote the Catholic identity of their institutions and to discuss topics of mutual concern. The USCCB has a publications office that makes available pertinent Vatican documents, bishops' statements, and other materials concerned with Catholic higher education.

The Catholic higher education leader also network with one another through the Association of Catholic Colleges and Universities (ACCU). This Association serves as the voice of Catholic higher education in the United States.

Campus Ministry

Campus ministry is one of the most powerful forces that Catholic higher education has on campuses to live out its Catholic identity. As such, the university leadership must ensure that this ministry is not an "add-on" but is integral to campus life. This ministry is so important to the ecclesial church that the USCCB and every diocesan office has a division devoted to it. These serve not only Catholic university campus ministries, but also the diocesan-created campus ministries at state-sponsored and other secular colleges and universities.

Campus ministries are critical because they provide a spiritual and social anchor for young Catholic people at a time in their lives when, away from home, they are bombarded by a plethora of cultural choices and influences. An active and energized campus ministry gives these young people a first-hand experience of what it means to live faith as an adult in a deeply spiritual and life-giving way.

CATHOLIC EDUCATION HALLMARK: UNITY, NOT FRAGMENTATION

This chapter has dealt primarily with formal Catholic institutions, PK through university. The leaders of these institutions must always remember that their own critical ministry is but one part of the broad-based educational mission given by Christ to his Church. In every parish there are religious education programs that include adults as well as young people. There are also many parish and diocesan programs and activities for teens, young adults, the married, singles, and seniors. This list goes on and on as courageous, creative, and visionary clergy, vowed religious, and lay persons see educational and faith formation needs and meet them.

The Church is one, holy, catholic, and apostolic. When any one educational ministry dominates or tries to dominate, then the whole church suffers from fragmentation, rather than the oneness, the unity, that should be its hallmark.

Even the science of modern quantum physics tells us this. In the British quantum physicist David Bohm's wholeness theory,[27] one can find a quantum-like explanation of why humanity does not live as a global village. Humans fail to understand and live out the quantum principle that the totality of existence is enfolded in every fragment of space and time. Everything in the universe affects everything else because each is part of the same unbroken whole. Everything in the universe must also be more than interdependent; the universe must reach wholeness. Wholeness is achieved when there is a *generative* order in which each and every animate and inanimate being participates in how reality unfolds, by finding commitment and meaning in its role and being attuned to everything else in the universe.

Such generativeness occurs for educators when they are deeply committed to the vocation and ministry to which they are called, and when they stay attuned to one another so that wholeness and not fragmentation of ministry prevails.

How much more true must the quantum wholeness theory be for those called to leadership in the name of Christ! Those who lead Catholic educational institutions must be well versed and passionately engaged in their own specific educational endeavors. But they have an obligation to stay *attuned* to all other ministries and support them so that they too flourish. Then, to use Bohm's quantum theory, the totality of all existence strains toward its Omega point in Christ Jesus, when it will be enfolded in every fragment, every ministry, every person in our Church and world. Or perhaps, as Jesus, the ultimate teacher, told us so simply and yet so profoundly, "I am the vine. You are the branches" (Jn 15:5).

REFLECTION QUESTIONS

1. What challenge is presented to you as a leader as you reflect on the place within the whole system that you and your school occupy?
2. What documents of the universal Church and your diocese will you use to better understand the part your school plays in the larger enterprise of Catholic education and of the mission of the Church in proclaiming the reign of God? Which will be helpful to the faculty of your school?
3. How is connection with the larger community of the Church fostered in your school, among students? Faculty? Parents? Board members?

NOTES

1. The Sacred Congregation for Catholic Education, *Lay Catholics in Schools: Witnesses to Faith,* October 15, 1982, n. 30.

2. Danah Zohar, *Rewiring the Corporate Brain: Using the New Science to Rethink How We Structure and Lead Organizations* (San Francisco: Berrett-Koehler, 1997), 128–130.

3. The Sacred Congregation for Catholic Education, *The Catholic School on the Threshold of the Third Millennium,* December 28, 1997, n. 11.

4. James A. Coriden, Thomas J. Green, and Donald E. Heintschel, eds., *The Code of Canon Law: A Text and Commentary* (Mahwah, NJ: Paulist Press, 1985). Book III, *The Teaching Office of the Church,* is especially important for Catholic educational leaders. Specific canons have been cited throughout this chapter.

5. J. Stephen O'Brien, ed., *A Primer on Educational Governance in the Catholic Church* (Washington, DC: National Catholic Educational Association, 1987). This gives more detail on the governance of the many different types of Catholic schools. Charts provide clarity on the various line and staff relationships.

6. Maria J. Ciriello, O.P., ed., *Formation and Development for Catholic School Leaders,* 2d ed., 3 vols. (Washington, DC: United States Catholic Conference, 1998). This is an excellent and complete reference for PK–12 educational leaders. The first volume is concerned with the leader's role in leadership, curriculum, and instruction. The second describes the spiritual leadership role and the third the principal's managerial role, with a section on governance.

7. Sr. Mary Angela Shaughnessy, *A Primer on Law for Administrators and Boards, Commissions and Councils of Catholic Education* (Washington, DC: National Catholic Educational Association, 2000). The author does an excellent job making the law accessible to the nonattorney leader. Some of her other legal publications for NCEA are written for schools, preschools, extended day care, teachers, volunteers, special education, parish religious education programs, and campus ministries.

8. Dale McDonald, P.B.V.M., *United States Catholic Elementary and Secondary Schools 2003–2004: The Annual Statistical Report on Schools, Enrollment and Staffing* (Washington DC: National Catholic Educational Association, 2004), ix, 16.

9. Robert J. Kealey, *Balance Sheet for Catholic Elementary Schools: 2001 Income and Expenses* (Washington DC: National Catholic Educational Association, 2001), 14.

10. Frederick C. Mueller, F.S.C., "Sponsorship of Catholic Schools: Preserving the Tradition," in *The Catholic Character of Catholic Schools,* ed. James Youniss, John J. Convey, and Jeffrey A. McLellan (Notre Dame, IN: University of Notre Dame Press, 2000), 59, 38–61.

11. Office of the President, "Georgetown University Mission Statement," http://data.Georgetown.edu/president/mission_statement.html (February 13, 2004).

12. Dean R. Hoge et al., *Young Adult Catholics: Religion in the Culture of Choice* (Notre Dame, IN: University of Notre Dame Press, 2001). See especially chapters 8 and 9, helpful in defining Catholic identity.

13. Bishop John Leibrecht, "Draft Ordinances for the NCCB Committee to Implement the Apostolic Constitution, *Ex Corde Ecclesiae,*" memorandum sent to archbishops and bishops and presidents of Catholic colleges and universities, May 4, 1993, Appendix, Category 3 a, b. Bishop Leibrecht was chair of this NCCB committee

of the United States bishops. In the appendix he lists the descriptive categories of Catholic colleges and universities and their types of boards.

14. Leibrecht, "Draft Ordinances," Appendix, Category 4 a, b.

15. Vatican Council II, *Gravissimum Educationis*, Declaration on Christian Education, October 28, 1965.

16. *Code of Canon Law*, Book III, Title III: *Catholic Education*, Chapter II, Canons 807–814.

17. Pope John Paul II, *Ex Corde Ecclesiae, The Apostolic Constitution of the Supreme Pontiff John Paul II on Catholic Universities [ECE]*, August 15, 1990.

18. United States Conference of Catholic Bishops, *Ex Corde Ecclesiae, The Application to the United States* (Washington, DC: United States Conference of Catholic Bishops, 2001).

19. United States Conference of Catholic Bishops, *Guidelines Concerning the Academic Mandatum in Catholic Universities* (Washington, DC: United States Conference of Catholic Bishops, 2001).

20. *ECE*, Part I B., n. 30.

21. *ECE*, Part II, Article 1, n. 1.

22. *Application*, Part II, Article 2, n. 5.

23. *Application*, Part II, Article 4, n. 2 a–b.

24. *Application*, Part II, Article 4, n. 2 c, e

25. *Application*, Part II, Article 4, n. 4 e.

26. U.S. Conference of Catholic Bishops, *Guidelines*.

27. David Bohm, *Wholeness and the Implicate Order* (London: Routledge, 1980), 1–19, 140–157, 172–207, a scientific explanation of Bohm's wholeness theory that has implications for leaders. This should be related to Danah Zohar's work described in note 2.

III

THE SPIRITUAL LIFE
OF INSTITUTIONS

The essays in this section explore the meaning of institutions as communal entities, as bodies in their own right. Chapter 7 discusses institutions as embedded in and shaped by a larger culture that, reciprocally, they also influence. Chapter 8 presents institutions as embodied spirits and enspirited bodies, complete with their own spirituality. Chapter 9 develops them as carriers and tenders of a multileveled legacy from their founders and suggests ways that the legacy might penetrate the entire organizational structure.

Catholic tradition both supports and enriches this understanding of institutions as communities: together, in our various communal incarnations, we are mysteriously growing into the Body of Christ and serving the reign of God.

7

Reading the Signs of the Times: Some Present Cultural Realities

Brian O. McDermott, S.J.

As leaders seek to receive and shape an institution's culture, they do so as part of larger webs of cultural patterns, symbols, and meanings. Brian Mc-Dermott, S.J., situates Catholic institutions in dialogue with the signs of the times in contemporary United States and world culture. He identifies several features of special import. One is diversity in its many faces, including religious, ethnic, economic, and generational; another is commodification, a bottom-line business mind-set. Both confront leaders with serious issues of power and access, as they test real-life, real-time commitment of institutions to fundamental principles of Catholic social doctrine.

Lay leaders, that is, those lay people who take up formal authority in a school, health care institution, or social service agency, are called to provide two kinds of service: to offer good management and to provide good leadership. By management I mean all those activities that help the group to respond to often complex challenges that, by their nature, do not call the group beyond its present level of competence. This kind of work we can call technical work.

"Leadership," on the other hand, names all those activities that assist the group to do difficult work, what others and I would call adaptive work. Adaptive work involves some degree of loss, some measure of serious unlearning for the sake of new learning, work that will involve a change of behaviors and attitudes, and thus will provoke disequilibrium, anxiety, and other painful feelings because people feel they are being pushed beyond their present competence. For those who manage and those who provide leadership (as I understand these terms), it is imperative to move, again and again, from the "dance floor" of immediate interaction to the "balcony," where they can notice the larger patterns of the system they indwell and its relationship to its wider context.[1]

When we move to the balcony, we begin to notice cultural realities. "Culture" embraces both the inner life of an organization and multiple dimensions of its surrounding context. Culture is that web of expressions of the human spirit consisting of behavior patterns, beliefs, institutions, art, rituals, symbols, and narratives, a web which, once it has been expressed, turns around to shape both those who have expressed the culture and those who inherit it.

Human beings are "interdividuals," are laced into each other, and their individual identities emerge from a social network, beginning with their parents. The other is within the self and not simply juxtaposed to the self. The culture we indwell shapes us from within and not simply from without. Indeed, distinguishing one's personal identity from its cultural "surround" poses an interesting challenge. As we try to strip away the cultural dimensions of ourselves, we seem to arrive at a progressively *thinner* sense of our nameable self.[2]

The Bible has a complex view of human culture. The first eleven chapters of Genesis offer a narrative of creation, beginning with the divine production of the subhuman world, then of the first humans, and then the cultural realities produced by humans. For the biblical writer, the created world is a combination of God's good creation, divine blessing or favor ("grace"), and sin. This mix is what human culture is all about, theologically speaking. Culture is human-made, and it partakes of the "stuff" which constitutes humankind: coming from God's creative hand as good, being graced and elevated by God's self-giving love, and being marred by willful deviation from what is authentically human.[3]

Culture expresses the deep aspirations and longings of a people as well as the fears, distrust, and destructive competitiveness that block or distort their best aspirations and longings. Because culture conveys a powerful sense of givenness, and provides important components of an individual's or group's identity, it shows a certain amount of resistance to change. Habitual behavior ensures that culture will last over time and be able to be passed down through time. Changing cultural patterns can feel like losing part of one's self, and so resistance arises to prevent the anxiety and disequilibrium such loss will promote.

In this chapter I examine, in a very selective way, some of the cultural realities that form the "surround" of a lay leader in a Catholic organization in the United States today. First I consider various forms of diversity that challenge these lay leaders, then I examine a powerful dynamic in present-day culture which I call "commodification," and then, from another angle of vision, I name some of the cultural factors in our world in relation to various services lay leaders need to provide to their organizations.

DIVERSITY AND THE LAY LEADER'S TASK

U.S. Catholic institutions have changed markedly in the past few decades, even as they have shown deep continuity. As a recently published portrait of the Catholic Church in the United States shows, all the major Catholic organizations have become more diverse in their leadership, their employees, and the constituencies they serve.[4] Catholic higher education is home to administrators, faculty, and staff belonging to many faiths (and none). The student bodies are increasingly non-Catholic, while international students form a significant segment of those profiting from this education. Catholic elementary education serves more and more non-Catholics, especially in the cities. Catholic social service organizations seek support from governmental agencies and partner with non-Catholic groups to serve all those in need, regardless of their religious affiliations. The same can be said of Catholic health care systems, which seek to preserve their identity and the religious and ethical sensitivity that guides them, while extending health care to the general population. Catholic academic medical centers carry on important biomedical research, often of a cutting-edge sort, while making every effort to be guided by the U.S. Bishops' Ethical and Religious Directives and not by the prevailing norms of secular academic medical centers.[5] One consequence of this kind of complexity is that it can put the medical center in the position of needing to educate the hierarchy and ordinary Catholics about sophisticated scientific and procedural issues.

The growing Latino-Hispanic population in the United States constitutes an enrichment of Catholic culture, even though not all Latinos and Hispanics belong to the Catholic Church. In 2000, 16 percent of American Catholics were Hispanics. While the number of U.S. Hispanics who identify themselves as Catholics is decreasing, still the cultures of Latinos/Hispanics as they encounter the largely European-derived culture of white U.S. Catholics challenge leaders of Catholic organizations to include them in the authority structure and to address their needs. Asian Catholics from places like China, Vietnam, and the Philippines represent another set of challenges as they seek both to incorporate themselves into the United States and to preserve distinctive cultural features they bring with them into this country.

The growing disparity between the rich and the poor and the powerful financial squeeze put on the middle class in terms of educational and health care expenses provide another, painful example of diversity. Catholic institutions have historically been inclusive, often performing well with limited resources. In today's climate, many people are in danger of being completely bypassed by the information culture, and the number of the medically uninsured is staggering for a nation as prosperous as ours. Unemployment seems to resist solutions, and a growing "underclass" requires both schooling and health benefits; both are beyond its reach.

On the positive side, the Catholic population includes numerous financially successful Americans. Many of them are very grateful for their Catholic education and are now stepping up to the plate and contributing handsomely. A culture of giving supports the Georgetowns and Notre Dames, the high schools and middle schools, Catholic hospitals around the country, and enterprises such as the Catholic Campaign for Human Development.

The clerical-lay distinction is another serious form of diversity in the Catholic world. The increasing number of lay Catholics in authority roles in education, social service, and health care institutions in our country has encouraged a new level of collaboration between lay people and clergy and religious involved in these organizations, as well as conflict and unresolved issues. The Roman Catholic Church is a culture in which ordination and jurisdiction are closely allied. In other words, being ordained is coupled with possessing formal authority in the Church, so that lay people are accountable to the ordained. The result is that clergy can tend to think of themselves as the core of the church, or the "owners," even if they might not explicitly express it this way.

The Church hierarchy does not have direct control over lay leaders, as it does over those who are clerics. It does have the power to declare an organization Catholic or not, and it can decide the criteria by which this is determined. A hospital that does not follow the Ethical and Religious Directives would be challenged by the local ordinary. Bishops may offer or withhold official recognition (or "mandatum") that a college professor at a Catholic institution who is a member of a theology or religious studies department is teaching in accordance with church doctrine. Many bishops chose to implement the policy of granting the mandatum in a discreet and nonpublic way.

Sponsorship, a dimension of Catholic institutional life that for a long time was taken for granted, is nowadays a question of intentional reflection and decision on the part of lay-run organizations which want to preserve in appropriate ways the legacy of the founding religious institute even as the numbers of religious working there have seriously diminished. The authorities in the sponsoring religious institutes can withhold use of their congregation's name if they find the school or hospital wanting in its fidelity to the inherited mission and identity.

Another striking form of diversity is in the types of young people in the United States. Generalizations are dangerous, but some writers see at least two important cohorts—the so-called Generation X and the so-called Millennials. These young people differ in their ways of relating to institutions.

Generation X folks were born roughly between the early sixties and late seventies. Their lives have been marked by economic uncertainty, the Vietnam War, deep distrust of institutions, including religious ones, strange behaviors such as self-mutilation, and a far-ranging irreverence. They have not been able to identify with their parents' values and are profoundly shaped by a popular culture, which their seniors can at times find incomprehensible. They mock large narratives (including monikers like "Gen-X"). They cobble together pieces of meaning (bricolage, as Michael Downey reminded us) as best they can. Tom Beaudoin, in his study of Generation X, finds theological significance in the popular culture emanating from and in turn influencing this cohort.[6]

The generation of Americans born in 1982 or later bears the name "Millennials" because it is not a yet more pronounced version of Generation X (if it were, it would be called Gen-Y), but a real departure from it. Neil Howe and William Strauss portray these young people as taking technology fully for granted, quite willing to be known as intelligent, feeling they have made their parents' values their own and sensing a closeness to their parents, and liking teamwork and group activities.[7] They believe selfishness is the root of most of the problems in the United States and have a concern for rules and regulations. They believe that they are destined to have a huge, positive impact on American society. If these descriptions have any merit, it is apparent that facile identification of young people as individualistic and self-centered is off the mark. This kind of person will be more apt to work in institutions rather than against them, and will be likely to want to be loyal to some institutions, while hoping that the institutions to which they commit will, in turn, show loyalty to them.

Managing diversity forms part of the portfolio of lay leaders because the services of formal authority are all about managing various kinds of boundaries. The potential richness of this diversity needs fostering, while the negative forces of racism, sexism, and ethnocentrism need to be recognized and worked against.

COMMODIFICATION: CONTEMPORARY CULTURE'S SCARY FACE

In contemporary life, institutions must either grow or die, or at times merge with another institution to continue to exist in some fashion. A dominant culture all around us here in the United States is corporate culture, which usually gives maximum value to efficiency and to the "bottom line" of profitability. All efforts by corporations to balance the bottom line with the human well-being of the various stakeholders (employees, customers, etc.) must work against a more monolithic understanding of corporate life and purpose. Catholic organizations, whether educational, health care related, or social service oriented, direct their activities to the flourishing of persons and communities, and efficiency and financial stability are ordered to that deeper purpose. There is a temptation for these institutions to turn to technological solutions in an unbalanced way to protect themselves from the difficult work of encouraging deep unlearning and learning (a major task of schools), confronting the mortality and vulnerability of the human condition (a major task of health care), or dealing with the chaos of human society (a major task of social services). Some social psychologists point out that a major reason for serious conflict in work situations is that those engaged in the work of the group feel (unconsciously at least) that they must avoid the inherent difficulty of the work to which their group's mission calls them.[8]

Lay leaders need to ask themselves whether their organizations exhibit a culture of engagement or a culture of avoidance vis-à-vis the tough challenges facing them. Do they mimic those entities beyond themselves that turn every task into a technical one, that is to say, a task that calls on only presently possessed competence? Or are they organizations that engage challenges on their own terms, and are willing to enter that zone of (relative) incompetence that certain types of challenges call a group to, even though this will mean managing very difficult feelings?

The impulse in institutions to make their work as technical as possible, on the model of certain kinds of business practices, shows up in a school when the lay leaders begin to view the students as customers, and where faculty are expected to bring in revenue through outside consultation to cover the expenses of their office space and office supplies. This dynamic is intensified when contact time between faculty members and students is completely rationalized: for example, one-to-one meetings being limited to fifteen-minute periods. This same commodification can happen in a hospital or social service agency, when cost analysis and streamlining bring financial stability at the price of the mission of the group.

The bottom-line business mind-set, as distinguished from the best business practices, can lead an organization down a destructive path, but a path that is tempting in times of relative scarcity, competition, and pressure to perform coming from the board of directors. The commodity culture views everything as a means, people included, and considers the end, the goal, as being what is recorded on the bottom line, to the detriment of the life and activity of the institution. Lay leaders are under pressure to "commodify" and they will need to resist mightily this cultural pressure if they are to be faithful stewards of the bodies for which they are responsible. The task is made all the more difficult because they are accountable to their boards of directors for making the best use of their (limited) resources and for doing the technical work as competently as possible.

Globalization, itself a mushrooming culture of cultures, extends commodification to the dimensions of our planet. It is not simply a matter of the impact of globalization on institutional life in America, but the role American institutions play in increasing the impact of globalization on others. Individually and collectively, we Americans live off of the Third World. The appliances we use, the clothes we wear, the communication capacity we take for granted happen because people in other parts of the world live at a very different economic level of existence. These faceless people acquire countenances when they are hired in our schools, hospitals, and social service-oriented institutions, but for the most part they remain anonymous. We would hope that the positive face of globalization increases, so that the increasing interaction of peoples around the globe brings greater intercultural and interreligious understanding, but this can happen only if the human dimension always remains in the forefront of this worldwide dynamic. Fidelity to identity and mission on the part of Catholic schools, hospitals, and social service agencies represents to the larger world this rightful sense of priorities.

CULTURAL FACTORS AND THE SERVICES LAY LEADERS NEED TO PROVIDE

It is risky to generalize about large populations of persons, but it is tempting, as well. The brief descriptions of Generation X and the Millennials made clear that the generations differ from each other and cannot be placed on one template. But certain features of contemporary American culture do stand out. Young people multitask; many of them seem to need to do several things at the same time, and focused attention can be a challenge. The media offer all manner of entertainment and engagement; popular songs are larded with immense amounts of sex and violence, interspersed with heart-rending cries for help and expressions of grief in the face of the human condition. All kinds of boundaries are traversed, and traditional sources of meaning are treated with the utmost irony, if not witheringly savaged. Keeping disciplined attention on the real issues during "white water" times comes very hard to multitasking folks. The upside is that some of these folks may well be able to handle complexity better than some of their seniors.

We live, as well, in an analgesic society, one in which there is no delay tolerated when it comes to pain relief. Television promises every form of lawful "fix" where discomfort is concerned. The impact of this is very significant for those engaged in formal authority roles who try to exercise leadership, because one of the principal services formal authority figures can offer a group during difficult times is to provide a container both for themselves and for the members of the group. A good image for this is that of a pressure cooker, which is strong enough to hold the pressure of water as it builds up, but which also has an escape valve so that the pressure does not become excessive or dangerous. The anxiety cannot be eliminated, because it is a sign of the true dimensions of the challenge facing the group. But the anxiety needs to be managed, paced, so that people will continue to participate in the difficult process of unlearning and new learning. If people grow up believing that every form of discomfort or pain ought to be eliminated at the first sign of its emergence, then the group will have immense difficulty holding steady in the transition zone—"groan zone"—that the challenges call the group to remain in.[9]

A major contribution persons in formal authority positions in a school, hospital, or social agency make to the ongoing lives of their organizations consists of reminding the members of their mission. They need to do this reminding day in and day out, finding various ways to paraphrase—without changing—the formulation of the mission. When the going gets tough during difficult work and people are feeling anxious and want technical fixes to step in and make things better, it is imperative that people reconnect with the deep purpose of the organization, its reason for being, the mission that makes the tough going acceptable if not enjoyable. In any organization at any time tasks can drown out the sense of mission, the connectedness to deep purpose, but in the cultural context we are living in right now, it is particularly difficult for lots of folks to stay connected with the mission. Many people do not experience anchors in their lives; many people grow up in families in which there is only one parent, or families that have moved around frequently, where parents have migrated from one job to another. Can the people in authority name the mission in a way that is attractive, indeed compelling, in a way that calls forth reserves in those members of the organization who do not experience strong anchors in their lives?

As I mentioned earlier, another service authority provides during difficult times is managing external and internal boundaries. Some examples: on a very large scale, this can take the form of the authority people merging their hospital into a consortium of hospitals to ensure continued life for the enterprise. Obviously this is an instance of major management of an external boundary. Management of an internal boundary would be inviting doctors in that same hospital to relate to their patients in a more personal, compassionate way, so that responsibility for this way of interacting does not devolve exclusively on the nurses. We live in a time when there is extraordinary shifting of boundaries, in family life (the divorce rate, for instance), in business (the closure of industries or their move to overseas locations), in the military (their need to learn not only how to fight wars but also how to rebuild devastated nations), and in the professions (doctors needing to learn how to be business people because of managed care and teachers needing to learn not only how to teach but also how to manage student violence). The Internet has redefined personal boundaries so that much that used to be private is now publicly available (e.g., camcording people in their homes and then showing it on the Web).

People need healthy boundaries even as they rebel against them. (We used to say this about adolescents but it applies to many who are chronologically adult, as well.) The Millennial generation may well cooperate with boundaries more than Generation X would, but people relate to boundaries on both the conscious and unconscious levels and it is only human to be ambivalent about the boundaries in our lives.

Safety is yet another contribution lay leaders offer and represent in their institutions. In normal times, the safety level can be fairly high when the organization is dealing with challenges that lie within its present competencies. When the challenges call for really difficult work, lay leaders must offer a certain degree of safety so that personnel will continue to be present and active in face of the challenges, but the safety cannot be so great that the folks become disconnected from the "heat" of the challenges. Being in a space of (relative) incompetence because of the challenges facing the group creates a feeling of unsafety. Unconsciously if not consciously, people will want the authority figures to deliver them from this unsafety.

So far I have been referring to "normal" times. But we do not live in normal times. We have witnessed the terrors of the Cold War replaced by the terrors of terrorism. On a regular basis newspapers report not only the attacks of insurgents on coalition forces in Iraq but also the sale of nuclear materials to maverick nations and terrorist efforts to poison prominent Washington politicians. The boundary between combatants and noncombatants has pretty much disappeared.

Within the Church, the clergy sex abuse scandal has imprinted itself on the consciousness of most U.S. Catholics. Bishops and priests, heretofore symbols of protection and safety, have in some terrible instances functioned as the very opposite of those two values. All Catholic institutions are feeling the impact of this huge loss. The role lay leaders in Catholic institutions play at this particular point in our history as representatives of safety and protection is enormous. The expectations directed to them will be larger than life. It will be all-important that they be credible, trustworthy men and women of integrity who have the courage, even in these difficult times, to pace the degree of safety in their organizations. By this I mean that they must not protect their folks from the difficult, unsettling challenges facing them, while offering enough safety so that their personnel are able to "stay in the fray" and not abandon the mission, either physically or psychologically.

As authority figures, lay leaders are also called to protect vulnerable voices of minority dissent within the organization who may hold important pieces of truth for it. Some dissenting voices will be in the culture surrounding the organization, and lay leaders will need to listen to them, as well.

"Dissent" is a loaded word in Catholic circles these days, because of the rather technical meaning it has been given by the hierarchy. For some church leaders, dissent refers to public disagreement with church teachings, disagreement that finds its way into the secular press. For others, this is an extremely limited definition, and they want to affirm the right of theologians respectfully and critically to examine church doctrines and their presuppositions, for the sake of deepening the church's understanding of its own teaching.

In the practical world of institutional decision making, forms of partnering with what at times may seem to be unlikely outside groups in ways that fit the mission of the school, hospital, or social agency are an important aspect of the work, and not an instance of infidelity. At times the surrounding culture holds significant information for the group, even if its values and perspectives seem truly alien to the lay leader and his or her institution. A striking example of this is the situation where students at a Catholic medical school need to go to a non-Catholic hospital to learn abortion procedures even if they do not intend ever to perform an abortion; they do this because they must have this knowledge both to attain licensing as a doctor and to know how to help a woman who is suffering from complications of an abortion.

CONCLUSION

Lay leaders work in a world of dizzying diversity, of powerful forces such as commodification, and an array of other cultural realities which provide both resources and challenges for them in their efforts to exercise management and leadership from a position of formal authority. Other chapters in this volume address the spirituality of organizations and of leaders. The modest aim of this chapter has been to delineate some of the principal features of the cultural landscape within which the leader must operate. The constant touchstone for the lay leader must be the mission of the institution, with its priority given to human flourishing. An internal organization culture that keeps its priorities straight and combines a strong faith commitment with delivery of excellent services to its constituencies holds something essential for the culture beyond itself: it proclaims, in its daily activities, that it is possible to be religious and a servant of the wider culture and its needs, to be faith-oriented and competent. Only passion for the mission will justify taking on the "risks of leadership" I have indicated. And only the eyes of faith are able to discern in times of organizational disequilibrium that the mission contributes modestly yet significantly to *the* mission, *the* project, in our world, which is God bringing about God's reign, through Christ, in the power of the Holy Spirit.

REFLECTION QUESTIONS

1. McDermott identifies diversity as a key cultural factor. Which of diversity's faces—religious, ethnic, economic, generational, clerical/lay—does your institution actively engage? Which does it avoid? Why?
2. How does pressure for a technical, bottom-line approach (commodification) touch you and your institution?

3. How does the culture of globalization affect your institution? How do you respond?
4. The essay asserts that in today's anchorless culture, leaders must manage internal and external boundaries and keep institutions clearly connected to their missions. How do you do this? Where do you find emotional and spiritual support for your efforts?
5. Where do you find your greatest area of challenge as a leader in relation to the wider culture? What are some of the culture's positive aspects that spark your hope and creativity?

NOTES

1. I am indebted to Ronald A. Heifetz and Marty Linsky for these understandings of management and leadership and technical and adaptive work. See their *Leadership on the Line: Staying Alive through the Dangers of Leading* (Boston: Harvard Business School Press, 2002). This volume can be a wonderful resource for lay leaders in many different kinds of organizations.

2. See James Alison, *The Joy of Being Wrong: Original Sin through Easter Eyes* (New York: Crossroad, 1998), 22–23.

3. See Claus Westermann, *Creation* (Philadelphia: Fortress Press, 1974).

4. Bryan T. Froehle and Mary L. Gautier, *Catholicism USA: A Portrait of the Catholic Church in the United States* (Maryknoll, NY: Orbis Books, 2000).

5. *Ethical and Religious Directives for Catholic Health Care Services,* 4th ed. (Washington, DC: NCCB/USCC, 2001).

6. Beaudoin, *Virtual Faith: The Irreverent Spiritual Quest of Generation X* (San Francisco: Jossey-Bass, 1998).

7. Neil Howe and William Strauss, *Millennials Rising: The Next Great Generation* (New York: Vintage Press, 2000).

8. A fascinating study of this dynamic is offered by Anton Obholzer and Vega Zagier Roberts, eds., *The Unconscious at Work: Individual and Organizational Stress in the Human Services* (London and New York: Routledge, 1994).

9. For this section I am drawing on Ronald A. Heifetz, *Leadership without Easy Answers* (Cambridge, MA: Harvard University Press, 1994).

8

Giving the Spirit a Home: Reflections on the Spirituality of Institutions

Regina Bechtle, S.C.

Institutions do indeed take on lives of their own. Regina Bechtle, S.C., invites us to consider Catholic institutional life as a place of grace amid its struggles and sinfulness, a place where God's Spirit chooses to abide. Drawing on the central Christian themes of community and incarnation, she explores the concept of a spirituality of institutions. For leaders open to this vision, leadership is about making room for the Spirit to move freely, as a community follows its own spiritual path of resistance, self-emptying, and transformation. Leaders can find much wisdom in their own journeys of faith as they seek to serve the Spirit at the heart of their communities.

"I'll really miss those students. That was one dynamite class!" Or, "I can't wait till those seniors graduate. It seems as though they have an attitude that pulls down the whole school." Or, "Working with this staff is one of the best experiences I've ever had as a leader. The way all of us challenge and support each other is incredible." Who among us hasn't sensed that indefinable but unmistakable "spirit" that can inhabit a whole group, to the delight or despair of all? Organizational consultants and religious writers alike affirm that institutions do have a collective spirit, a spirituality that is more than the sum of the individual spiritualities of persons affiliated with them.

This chapter seeks to unpack this assertion. Against the backdrop of contemporary cultural attitudes towards institutions, we will first look through the lens of the Catholic theological principles of incarnation and community to find solid foundations for a spirituality of institutions. Next we will explore institutions as *spirit-filled bodies*—living entities open to grace and sinfulness—and as *embodied spirits*—on a journey of growth and transformation, en route to becoming incarnate expressions of the Body of Christ. Lastly, we will reflect on some facets of the leader's role in fostering an organization's awareness of the spirit it embodies.

INSTITUTIONS AND THEIR SPIRIT

We live in a society profoundly suspicious of its institutions. Reports tirelessly trumpet the bad news: once-trusted corporations and executives facing lawsuits and criminal charges; sports, even the Olympics, tainted by corruption; media in thrall to special interests; politicians locked in partisan maneuvering; health care, social services, and education snared in bureaucratic tangles or gasping for survival, their not-for-profit missions dependent on the bottom line. Not even the Church, once the presumed pinnacle of blameless conduct, has escaped the shame of scandal.

The sociologist Robert Bellah and his colleagues have examined the distrust of institutions that stems from individualism and leads to a diminished sense of common life in contemporary North America.[1] Many of us can empathize with this skeptical attitude. After a day of meetings mired in red tape and turf wars, it is easy to conclude in frustration that we cannot live *with* institutions a moment longer. But in truth we know we cannot live *without* them.

In his analysis of the contemporary Church, Peter Steinfels underscores this point: "Even Jesus relied on institutions to announce his message and propel it into the world. . . . There is simply no church that is not an *institutional* church." A people is not a homogeneous mass, he writes, "but a group with a sense of itself, a collective memory, a solidarity, an anticipated destiny—all of which must be preserved in formulas, rituals, written or recited epics, lines of authority, prescribed and proscribed behaviors."[2] The life of a group such as the Church must find concrete, tangible, institutional form or it dies.

Our religious heritage orients us to view institutions as spirits embodied, as places of graced possibility. Whether on the micro level of the local school, parish, sports team, college, or neighborhood organization, or in macro terms—school systems, diocesan structures, professional societies, churches—institutions, much as the persons who constitute them, give and receive energy, power, spirit. They are open to the action of grace and of evil. They act, for good or ill, with more or less freedom, to influence the world around them. By words and deeds, policies and behaviors, institutions translate their deepest dreams and desires into real time and space. By what they do and fail to do, they can evoke blessing or blame.

THEOLOGICAL FOUNDATIONS:
COMMUNITY—GOD ENGAGES US AS A PEOPLE

In its teachings on community and incarnation, Catholic theology offers solid foundations for what can be described as a "spirituality of institutions." Fundamental to the Christian worldview is the belief that God's Spirit abides in groups as truly as in individuals, that our Catholicness is embodied in people and embedded in communities. St. Paul appealed in the name of the one Spirit to the Christians of Philippi: "If our life in Christ means anything to you, if love can persuade at all, or the Spirit that we have in common, . . . then be united in your convictions and united in your love, with a common purpose and a common mind" (Phil 2:1–2).

Implicit in the Catholic worldview is the belief that our God engages us as a people. Each person, to be sure, is created unique by a loving God, given freedom, knowledge, and responsibility, destined for fullness of life. Yet God's dealings with humankind reveal a definite divine bias for groups.

God's way with humans always leads through community, though not easily or automatically. The great narratives of Scripture recount how men and women, created to be in loving relationship with each other, soon allow envy, greed, pride, and fear to drive a wedge into the community of living things. As Eden crumbles into Babel, partnership becomes domination, mutuality and cooperation become competition. Famine drives a motley crew of nomads into Egypt, oppression kindles their passion, and the glory and drudgery of deliverance forge them into a people. The covenant is made with the community, the Law is entrusted to the community, and the prophets' words are directed toward the community, the whole people of Israel, or persons who stand for the whole.

Hebrew and Christian Scriptures alike tell the story of communities as well as individuals who share in the ongoing drama of being created by God, falling from grace, and being redeemed. The mission and message of Jesus Christ modeled a new order of relationship that overturned distinctions between "Jew and Greek, slave and free, male and female" (Gal 3:28), in favor of building a community of persons restored to communion with God, each other, and all creation. In chapter 4 Monika Hellwig speaks of the "startling good news" of the "immediacy of God's reign" proclaimed by Jesus, who summoned disciples to share his work of reconciliation.[3]

The Trinitarian God who is a community loves community. Our God is a God of the group. Organizations have a privileged role to play as partners in God's creative action in the world. Through them, God's dream of wholeness and right relationship for all creation can come closer to reality.

THEOLOGICAL FOUNDATIONS:
INCARNATION—SPIRIT IS INCARNATE IN BODIES

To appreciate institutions as living, organic bodies, we need to explore our sense of being incarnate, flesh and blood creatures. Being embodied is something all humans have in common. Beneath all our differences of skin color, facial features, or body type, we share flesh, formed from the clay of earth. Though in some eras religion has viewed the body with suspicion, Christian faith believes otherwise. It teaches that our human bodies are holy ground, created good by God. The Word of God dignified our bodies by becoming one of us, fully human, in our flesh. God's Spirit moves and works in the world through our bodies, which will share in Christ's glory and be raised on the last day.

The physical body we share links all humans, indeed the whole created universe, at a fundamental level. The body incarnates—gives flesh to—Spirit. An institution, too, is a "body of bodies," an organic, living Body. Though composed of many members and many parts, an institution has one life, one spirit. As we learn to treat the body/Body with care, reverence, and appreciation, we develop a kind of consciousness of the "corporate" (the term in the broad sense referring to any group united as a body, from the Latin *corpus*).

Believers profess that the Spirit inhabits and dwells within us in our lives as a Body, in our corporate, communal, institutional life, no less than deep within our individual hearts. In the image of the Body of Christ, Catholic faith finds the end-point of our corporate life and community-building work. We are all growing into the Body of Christ. One of my favorite descriptions of the Church is "a body of bodies becoming the Body of Christ."[4] Communities, groups, organizations, and institutions within the Church are living bodies that give structure to the Spirit. Their purpose is to build up the Body of Christ in service of human wholeness and creation's flourishing.

What does our experience tell us about incarnate life, about living as a body, and as the Body of Christ? First, the Body is eternally becoming, constantly evolving/changing. The Body we are now is not the Body we once were. We know this all too well each morning as we get out of bed. The Church knows it, too: who could have foreseen the sweeping changes that have summoned lay men and women to roles of leadership in some arenas, even as other doors of ministry remain firmly closed to them? Yet the Body is constantly evolving; the Body we are now is not yet the Body that we will be. Second, the parts of the Body have different gifts, all of which are necessary.[5] Some members of the Body have the gift of bearing the weight; they feel the burden of things more intensely. Others have the gift of bearing hope; they keep the group focused on possibility, on light, on energy. Third, the Body knows both the ability to stretch and the finality of limits. Institutions, like people, are mortal. Colleges and schools close, parishes consolidate, hospitals merge, resources diminish, and enthusiasm wanes. To be incarnate is to dance to an unending rhythm of ups and downs.

"Where is God in it all?" asks the person of faith. Jesus' answer is clear: "Where two or three are gathered in My name, there am I in the midst of them" (Mt 18:20). These words describe a God's-eye view of an organization—"two or three . . . gathered"—focused on a mission, congruent with its identity as a community of faith—"gathered in My name." In other words, we cannot say "we" or "us" without our God being in our midst. Though at times individuals and communities may obscure God's presence, though that presence may not be as tangible as we would wish, yet God is there, real, compelling, and life-giving nonetheless.

Jesus' words call those who are leaders to remember that the spirit/Spirit in a community or institution is always already there. It may need to be uncovered, pointed to, coaxed forth, led out, articulated explicitly. *But it was there before us.* We may need to name and claim it, stretch it, push it, strengthen it, make room for it to deepen and grow. *But the spirit/Spirit was and is always already there.*

Imagine that God is already there, waiting:

- when the staff gathers for a reflection day or to engage in a self-study;
- when the entire community commits itself to a service project;
- when the diocesan director visits;
- when the board of trustees faces a thorny issue, or has to search for a new leader;
- when the institution as a community listens deeply, struggles to express cherished beliefs and opinions, and works together to find the wisdom that is bigger than any one person.

INSTITUTIONS: SPIRIT-FILLED BODIES, EMBODIED SPIRITS

We have been trying to develop a language to express the inner reality of institutions as living entities open to grace and sinfulness, as bodies capable of being filled with the Spirit. We are not alone in this groping for a new grammar. Margaret Wheatley also speaks the language of spirituality in her consulting work with organizations. She writes, for example, about the power of love in institutional life: "What gives power its charge, positive or negative, is the quality of relationships. Those who relate through coercion, or from disregard for the other person, create negative energy. Those who relate to others and who see others in their fullness create positive energy. Love in organizations, then, is the most potent source of power we have available."[6]

Robert Quinn, a professor at the University of Michigan, and several colleagues are pioneering a new field, "Positive Organizational Scholarship."

They seek to describe patterns of positive organizing, drawn from leaders who have had the courage to open themselves to transformation. In turn, this deep personal change has had an impact on their institutions, which have emerged as productive, nurturing, energetic environments of people committed to values in common pursuit of their mission.[7]

As leaders you have embraced the task of putting a human face on your institution's Catholic identity. You do this:

- as you seek accreditation and appropriate recognition;
- as you pursue funding to support programs, grow your endowment, win grants;
- as you foster relationships with the communities within which your institution exists;
- as you engage your colleagues in meetings, interviews, evaluations, classroom interactions, conflict resolutions, negotiations about budget and personnel;
- as you try to include rather than exclude, cooperate rather than compete, within and beyond your institution, and teach others to do the same.

What difference would it make to see moments like these as opportunities to make a home for the Word of God in your midst, opportunities to allow the Spirit to be embodied in your institution?

SOCIAL SIN AND SOCIAL GRACE

Just as a person's life is never static but in a state of eternal becoming, so the life of an organization is always changing.[8] A group's choices, behaviors, gestures, words, and actions constantly orient it toward or away from the greater good, toward or away from God. Another way to name this reality is to speak of "social grace" and "social sin."

Walter Wink is one who believes firmly in the spirituality of institutions, and has developed its theory and theology. He spells out the link between the biblical notion of "principalities and powers" and the spirit or power of domination found in contemporary institutions like the Pentagon, the Mafia and multinational corporations.[9] Wink sees many of our societies and institutions as, purely and simply, sick. He speaks of the "diseased spirituality" of "systems and structures that have betrayed their divine vocations" and fallen captive to the "idolatrous values" of "the Domination System."[10]

Structures created by flawed humans, prone to the proverbial seven deadly sins, reflect and enlarge these flaws. Addictions, compulsions, and dysfunctions of every kind become routinized and institutionalized. All the anger, fear, and anxieties of individuals are embedded in and projected on the social systems they create. These systems in turn, taking on lives of their own, can use their corporate power to target persons deemed unimportant and ideas deemed dangerous. Theologian Mary Catherine Hilkert points to the weighty choice that confronts human communities who "hold the power to deny, and in that sense, to 'blot out' the image of God in those we consider to be 'other.'"[11]

Social sin wears many faces, according to theologian Stephen Duffy. It is "found in dehumanizing behavior patterns of institutions" that treat employees as expendable and clients as mindless. It "permeates cultural, including religious, symbols that grip imagination, fire hearts, and reinforce unjust institutional arrangements"—symbols, for example, like racist songs, nationalistic slogans, or advertising that feeds greed. As in Nazi Germany or South Africa under apartheid, social sin appears in the collective decisions and consent generated by "distorted consciousness," the intentional product of "institutions and ideologies that allows people to participate in a network of oppression with self-righteousness."[12]

Yet, the reality of sin that has nested in our hearts and our organizations cannot blind us to the abundance of grace that is present at the same time. How does grace appear in institutional life?

God's Spirit shows Herself, embodies Himself, in the way that groups act to make their best intentions real. The Spirit finds voice in a community that practices, worships, prays, serves, celebrates, forgives, and asks forgiveness. The Spirit looks through eyes that see the needs of those who remain invisible to society at large—the poor, elderly, homeless, illiterate, unemployed, outsiders. The Spirit reaches out in the caring touch of administrators and staff, in the hands of volunteers painting buildings, coaching sports, planning fund-raisers, decorating for special events, filling in during emergencies. The Spirit is present in the community's honest efforts to live its commitments faithfully, even if the results are not successful according to the world's standards.

Internal competition and external pressure can create an institutional climate heavy with blame, negativity, and self-pity. Resisting this downward pull, the leader must be a healer, accomplished in forgiving self and others, able to focus the group on its ultimate purpose without minimizing present difficulties. Hilkert comments on the challenge of embodying grace in institutions: "Human communities, and specifically ecclesial communities, reflect God's image when foot washing, forgiveness, and a common table open possibilities for relationships and reconciliations beyond our power or imagining."[13] Grace is always present when people are moved to do the good that previously seemed beyond their power.

But not even changed hearts are enough to dethrone the power of social evil; nothing less than conversion of structures is demanded. How might Catholic institutions do this? By a keen eye to existing injustice within our own structures first, of course. But the possibilities are enormous. Those who are leaders, whether in education, health care, or social services, can promote awareness of national and local legislation affecting our clients and students, try to partner with civic and other organizations committed to the common good, call attention to ethical implications of societal decisions, and work to hold public officials and corporations to standards of accountability, to name a few examples. Educational leaders have particularly rich opportunities to integrate service learning components into curricula at all levels and to promote student volunteer efforts, thus helping to shape future leaders who will continue to challenge social evil wherever it exists.

LEADERS: TENDERS OF SPIRIT IN ORGANIZATIONS

Leaders facilitate the movement of the Spirit in a group. They tend the spirit/Spirit at the heart of an institution. Parker Palmer's description of a leader is illuminating: "A leader is a person who has an unusual degree of power to project on other people his or her shadow, or his or her light. . . . A leader is a person who must take special responsibility for what's going on inside him or herself, inside his or her consciousness."[14] This suggests that the efforts of leaders to shape and transform the public, institutional world "out there" are deeply interwoven with, and often mirror, the journey of their own inner transformations. One cannot heal the world outside without paying attention to one's own vulnerabilities, limitations, weaknesses—even one's own sinfulness. In other words, a leader cannot heal external structures without faithful and disciplined attention to her/his own inner work. "Physician, heal thyself" (Lk 4:23). Spirit inhabits both inner and outer landscapes, and leaders do well to attend to both.

In the remaining sections of this essay, we explore some dimensions of the complex role of leaders who take seriously their embodied spirituality as institutions and as persons.

Seeing Things Whole

The leader's role is to see the organization as a whole, as a living body. In the crisp image quoted by Brian McDermott, the leader must regularly move "from the dance floor to the balcony."[15]

Eyes of faith see the organization as part of a web of relationships. Predating the institution by many generations is a social and ecological landscape. It exists in a neighborhood with its own story of creation and change, in a location shaped by rolling hills or city sidewalks, in a state or province whose early inhabitants, later settlers, cultural richness, and legal systems have marked it indelibly. Catholic institutions in twenty-first century North America belong to the most privileged society in the world. The circle of this self-awareness is incomplete unless it turns these institutions outward to embrace the reality of the rest of the world, where an estimated 18,000 children under the age of five die each day of hunger, and an estimated 800 million adults, two-thirds of whom are women, cannot read.

When faith-filled leaders seek to keep the whole picture of their institutions in view, they have more than five-year plans in mind. They open themselves to uncover patterns of life–death–resurrection. They learn to "distinguish between what's happening and what's really going on."[16] E. Glenn Hinson writes that our times demand "*horizonal* persons," those who can "look beyond the horizon of their age and culture and see what God is trying to bring into being."[17]

Helping the Group Discern Its Spirits

Forces, energies, dynamics, and powers operate in groups as truly as in individuals. Because these forces can lead in the direction either of good or of ill, they need wise and informed discernment. The leader's role is to help the group surface, name, and discern the forces or "spirits" that move within its life.

In this sense, spiritual leadership is fundamentally spiritual direction of a group. Feelings, energies, impulses—what we have been calling "spirits"—move in and through day-to-day administrative work; decisions about personnel, programs, and maintenance; discussions about money and property; issues of survival, diminishment, and growth; negotiations with board members, supervisors, and staff. Spirits move as leaders deal with institutional crises and personal family or health matters. Spirits move as leaders cope with the shifting, many-faceted demands of their role, and as they respond to systems and structures beyond their control.

Leaders need to sift and sort these spirits, discerning where they come from and where they lead. Do they arise from self-serving motives of competition or ambition, from residues of hurt, fear, anger, or revenge, from ego needs or compulsions? Or do they come from a place of peace and balance, where all parties seek to be open to God's inspiration? Does this spirit lead the group toward deeper freedom, greater generosity, stronger charity, and fuller energy in service of the mission? Does this spirit lead the institution toward or away from God?

Pushing the Envelope, Befriending Resistance

A leader needs to prod the group to do the difficult work that it needs to do even if it provokes resistance. Such "adaptive work," according to Brian Mc-Dermott, "involves some degree of loss, some measure of serious unlearning for the sake of new learning." Adaptive work "requires a change of behaviors and attitudes, and thus will provoke disequilibrium, anxiety, and other painful feelings because people feel they are being pushed beyond their present competence."[18]

Institutions, like persons, know the feeling of resistance. Of their nature, institutions resist change. What leader hasn't met the chorus of "We've always done it this way," or "Who do you think you are, to suggest a different process (or structure, or curriculum, or direction . . .)?"

Viewed in the light of spirituality, resistance signals a place where a person or institution may be wounded and vulnerable. That is always a privileged, holy place where the Spirit is at work, a growing edge where God waits to meet us. Endings signal change as much as beginnings do. Something has to end, die, move on, let go, to make space for the new, and humans resist it mightily.

But resistance has a positive face as well. One spiritual director counsels: "Resistance is the dragon that guards the precious treasure."[19] It is not always negative to resist. A leader faced with resistance might ask what precious treasure is being protected.

The leader continually reminds the group that they are about the work of conversion and transformation, about making space, over and over, for new life, for the Spirit's stretching. Thomas Merton wrote: "We are not 'converted' only once in our life but many times, and this endless series of large and small 'conversions,' inner revolutions, leads to our final transformation in Christ."[20]

For persons and institutions, the lifelong journey of faith rarely follows a smooth trajectory, and the experience of inner upheaval is itself part of the process of spiritual growth. Jesus testifies to this, climbing the hill of Calvary. So do mystics like John of the Cross and Teresa of Avila. The Carmelite writer Constance FitzGerald suggests that this very turning upside down and inside out is the work of God's Spirit, Wisdom-Sophia: "Sophia turns life upside-down, challenges my most deeply held beliefs and values, undermines what I have learned, claims whom and what I possess, and highlights the limitations and oppressive character of what I depend on most for satisfaction and assurance."[21] Whether we call it dryness, mid-life malaise, a crisis of faith, or the dark night of the soul, who among us hasn't known the taste and feel of this painful experience?

Now, imagine that your group, community, organization goes through the same dark night of wandering lost in a dark wood, feeling its cherished sense of self crumble, being propelled by forces within or outside to make radical changes—not just in logos and letterheads, but in its core identity. From one perspective, this feels like disintegration, dying, and loss of everything; from the other side of the tomb, or the cocoon, it feels like conversion, transformation, new life.

Margaret Wheatley uses the language of organizational transformation instead of conversion, but she is speaking about the same movement when she invites us to be willing to let go of "our most cherished beliefs, our greatest clarity" to clear space to create something new. "Look for the differences, those ideas and perspectives we find disturbing," she challenges us. She suggests that we allow ourselves to be "brought together by our differences rather than separated by them,"[22] and once in a while come together for the express purpose of changing our minds.

Wheatley's approach urges leaders to wrestle with God and let go of control by making an ally of disturbance and complexity. FitzGerald counsels us to befriend loss and upheaval. Loss or letting go of something precious breaks us open, makes space, stretches us, and expands us to be able to receive more. It can be hard to trust that, in the midst of being broken open, when the taste of loss is real. But when God invites us to let go, to surrender, to lose, it's always with the promise that we'll find something more. When a leader can shift energy from fear of divergent opinions and voices, or concern about maintaining control of the institution's life, to a felt sense that its present and future are held in the loving leading of God, it is truly a moment of grace.

CONCLUSION

The premise of this chapter is that the Spirit of the risen Christ inhabits our lives as a Body, our corporate, communal, institutional lives, as truly as the Spirit dwells deep within our individual hearts. A spirituality of institutions rooted in the Catholic way of interpreting life calls us to be grounded in the paschal pattern of Christ's living, dying, and rising. What would it mean for the organizations we lead if we lived as though we believed this?

Like the disciples who met the risen Christ on their disheartened walk to Emmaus (Lk 24:13–15), organizations walk the Emmaus walk, too. They move from initial excitement and enthusiasm, through crushed hopes and disillusionment, to purified and reawakened energy and commitment. A community rooted in faith can experience its hope returning, purified and sober, perhaps, but kindled anew, with a deeper awareness of the One in whom it puts its trust.

This book arose from a desire to raise to a level of conscious self-awareness the Spirit that is already present by grace in ourselves and the institutions we inhabit.[23] At a time such as ours, when every institution confronts the crisis of change and transformation to an unprecedented degree, learning to trust in that ever-present Spirit emerges as a powerful, saving grace. In this time of crisis and opportunity, the Spirit urgently seeks to partner with leaders who speak the language of spirituality and whose attentiveness to the spiritual dimensions of their ministries frees their colleagues to shape institutions even more responsive to God's working in their midst.

REFLECTION QUESTIONS

1. How would you describe the spiritual journey of your institution? Do you see parallels with your own spiritual story? With the story of Jesus' life, death, and resurrection?

2. How would you describe your institution as an incarnate body, growing into the Body of Christ? Is it in shape, trim, flexible—or creaky, uncoordinated, out of breath, out of touch? What does it look like to you and to others?

3. In what tangible ways does your institution embody grace and sin? How do its choices and behaviors affect the other bodies to which it relates, for example, the neighboring educational, religious, social service, and civic institutions?

4. Identify a time either when you felt that God's Spirit was at work within your institution or when you felt that there were other "spirits" or forces working against God's intention for your institution, as you understood it. On what do you base your discernment? How might you involve your colleagues in this discernment?

5. How do you and your institution embrace (or resist) calls to change and conversion? How does your institution deal with resistance? Does this essay offer any insights or approaches that might be helpful?

NOTES

1. Robert N. Bellah, Richard Madsen, William M. Sullivan, Ann Swidler, and Steven M. Tipton, *Habits of the Heart: Individualism and Commitment in American Life* (Berkeley: University of California Press, 1985); Bellah et al., *The Good Society* (New York: Alfred A. Knopf, 1991). The latter describes institutions as "patterned ways [we] have developed for living together, . . . normative patterns embedded in and enforced by laws and mores" (4, 11). In this essay I use "institutions," "organizations," and "groups" as interchangeable terms to refer to structures through which we express our communal life and mission.

2. Peter Steinfels, *A People Adrift: The Crisis of the Roman Catholic Church in America* (New York: Simon & Schuster, 2003), 13–14.

3. Cf. chapter 4 in this book.

4. Source unknown.

5. Cf. 1 Cor. 12.

6. Margaret Wheatley, quoted in Bennett Sims, *Servanthood: Leadership for the Third Millennium* (Cambridge, MA: Cowley, 1997).

7. Cf. Robert Quinn, *Building the Bridge as You Walk on It: A Guide for Leading Change* (San Francisco: Jossey-Bass, 2004); *Deep Change: Discovering the Leader Within* (San Francisco: Jossey-Bass, 1996).

8. In the words of Mary Daniel Turner, chapter 12 in this book, leaders must "respond with exquisite attention to the bewildering process of institutions' never-ending births" (p. 159).

9. Eph. 3:12. Cf. Walter Wink's four volumes, "The Powers": *Naming the Powers* (Philadelphia: Fortress Press, 1984); *Unmasking the Powers* (Philadelphia: Fortress Press, 1986); *Engaging the Powers* (Minneapolis: Fortress Press, 1992); and *The Powers That Be: Theology for a New Millennium* (New York: Doubleday, 1999).

10. Wink, *Engaging the Powers*, 8–9

11. Mary Catherine Hilkert, O.P., "*Imago Dei*: Does the Symbol Have a Future," lecture, Santa Clara University, April 14, 2002. www.scu.edu/bannancenter/eventsand conferences/lectures/archives/

12. Stephen Duffy, "Sin," in *The New Dictionary of Catholic Spirituality*, ed. Michael Downey (Collegeville, MN: Michael Glazier/Liturgical Press, 1993), 900–901.

13. Hilkert, "*Imago Dei*."

14. Palmer, "Leading from Within," *Noetic Sciences Review* (Winter 1996): 32–37, 45–47.

15. Cf. chapter 7, pp. 87–88 in this book.

16. In other words, in, through, and underneath the events of each day ("what's happening"), God is active in the world, shaping the total Body of Christ ("what's really going on"). The terminology is from the manual for the Ignatian Spiritual Exercises for the Corporate Person (ISECP); cf. www.isecp.org.

17. E. Glenn Hinson, "Horizonal Persons," in *Communion, Community, Commonweal: Readings for Spiritual Leadership*, ed. John Mogabgab (Nashville: Upper Room Books, 1995), 181.

18. Cf. chapter 7, p. 87.

19. Miriam Cleary, O.S.U., personal conversation with author.

20. Thomas Merton, *Life and Holiness* (New York: Doubleday, 1969), reissue edition.

21. Constance FitzGerald, "Desolation as Dark Night: the Transformative Influence of Wisdom in John of the Cross," *The Way*, Supplement 82 (Spring 1995): 100.

22. Margaret Wheatley, "Disturb Me, Please!" www.margaretwheatley.com/articles/please disturb.html.

23. See this book's preface (p. xiii), citing the concept of Karl Rahner.

9

Embodying the Spirit
of Those Who Came Before

Sean Peters, C.S.J.

Catholic institutions exist as living legacies, witnesses to the faith and de-termination of those who brought them to birth. Even if the mission has changed over time, it still bears the stamp of their seminal vision. In this es-say Sean Peters, C.S.J., offers both a conceptual rationale and practical sug-gestions for claiming the heritage of the past and drawing on its energy as a resource for today. She includes summaries of the Catholic intellectual tradition and Catholic social teaching, precious elements of the legacy com-mon to all Catholic institutions.

Ministries exist to accomplish a mission. The mission of any organization de-scribes not only its purpose but also how that organization will accomplish that purpose. If there were no difference in the "how," all organizations with the same task would act essentially the same. For example, both Neiman Marcus and Wal-Mart have department stores. "What" they do (sell a variety of items) does not distinguish them, but "how" they do it certainly does. One sells quite expensive items with considerable personal attention from staff; the other offers less expensive merchandise with a high expectation that cus-tomers will serve themselves. The values that underlie the completion of the task create a distinct mission for each organization, resulting in diverse or-ganizational cultures. Only by understanding the culture of an organization can we help to accomplish its mission.

Placing the organization in both a horizontal and a vertical context helps us to elucidate its culture. For example, a Catholic school holds many things in common with other Catholic schools in the diocese or the church (the hor-izontal dimension). At the same time, the school exists in a vertical context; it has founders who had a seminal vision and a history that has expanded, enriched, and embodied that founding vision. But the mission of an organization does not belong only to the past or to those who are currently implementing it. Those who will serve this ministry in the future also own the mission. The present leaders act as stewards, holding the mission in trust and enhancing it for posterity.

This essay will consider the context for mission—especially the vertical dimension—delving into how we can use the work of those who preceded us to carry out the mission today. It will define some terms, explore the value of mining the wealth of the vertical context, and describe some of the heritage all Catholic ministries hold in common. Finally, the chapter will discuss some practical ways to use this rich heritage in a faith-based institution.

SOME DEFINITIONS

In order to discuss the vertical dimension of the context for mission, we must define some terms. Mission, history, heritage, charism, and sponsorship all have a part to play in our understanding.

Mission

The mission of an institution has several dimensions. Chief among these are the goal of the organization and how those who implement the mission plan to accomplish that goal. As one Catholic elementary school principal said,

> If all I aim to do is provide a safe, disciplined environment for the children where they can learn enough to get good state test scores, how am I different from the public school down the street? Yes, we need safety, discipline and good test scores, but we must accomplish all this in the context of the Gospel mission. Faith formation must be the primary work of the Catholic elementary school. The tentacles of faith formation must reach into everything we do—how we teach a subject, the atmosphere in the school and how people treat one another. Otherwise, we have no reason to continue the institution.[1]

What we do is important. How we do it is equally important. If a leader focuses on only one part of the mission in a faith-based organization, she misses the point.

Not only the leader but also all those in the institution—faculty, staff, administration, board members—must understand and commit to the mission. For example, Monika Hellwig admonishes, "If the faculty does not share the ideals of the founders, those ideals will not remain the philosophy and spirit of the institution."[2]

History and Heritage

The history and heritage of the organization help those currently serving in the ministry to appropriate the mission. Knowing the history—who did what when—helps give a context. But more important than simple facts and dates is the heritage of the group—the core culture and values of the organization passed down from those who have gone before. The stories, traditions, and rituals of the organization embody the heritage.

Charism

A charism is a specific gift given to a group by God for the good of the whole. For example, each religious congregation embodies its specific gift in a particular way. Related to the founding story or myth of the congregation, the charism attracts those who share this charism to come together in community. The charism also creates a force that binds the group together, points toward deep values of the community, and gives focus to its work. Those institutions founded by a group that has a clear, strong charism will find support for their mission in exploring how that charism can give life and strength to the current ministry.

Sponsorship

A relatively recent concept, sponsorship, in the broadest terms, means that some group—usually a religious congregation, but sometimes other groups within the church—provides a base out of which a given ministry grows. While sponsorship has no one generally accepted definition, most understandings of this concept hold some characteristics in common.

All agree that sponsorship describes a relationship between the congregation and the sponsored institution; demands mutuality with neither the sponsor nor the institution totally responsible for maintaining the relationship; allows the congregation to expand its mission; and helps give foundation and direction to the mission of the sponsored institution. Those developing a definition of sponsorship must make clear the distinctions between sponsorship and other mission-related aspects of the sponsorship relationship such as founders, heritage and mission integration. While all of these support or impact sponsorship, none of them defines the totality of the sponsorship relationship.[3]

Even where written documents exist, sponsorship is a dynamic relationship. Leaders of any sponsored ministry would do well to meet periodically with the sponsor to clarify the sponsorship relationship and foster the mutuality that makes sponsorship a valuable resource for mission.

Dioceses oversee many ministries in the church either directly or through their parishes. The culture and history of a given diocese can also provide context for the mission of an institution. Most dioceses also have considerable and often underused resources—including skilled persons who are available to assist all of the diocesan and parochial ministries.

THE VALUE OF DRAWING ON THE
HERITAGE OF FAITH-BASED MINISTRIES

Energy flows through an organization when workers recognize themselves as part of a larger whole. Knowing and appreciating the heritage of a ministry helps me to realize not only that other people are engaged in this ministry and similar ministries right now, but also that they have been carrying out this work for years—sometimes hundreds of years.

Just as a sense of identity gives focus and purpose to an individual person, a clear sense of organizational identity gives focus to the ministry and helps us to carry out its mission. Stories of those who preceded us in this ministry tell us the values of the institution in a way that makes learning the values easy and gives personality and depth to the knowledge of what "counts" in this particular embodiment of the Gospel.

Knowing the history can also give us courage and hope, because it reminds us that we are not the first to take up this mission. Often the stories of the founders tell of overcoming almost impossible odds to initiate some ministry. Recounting particular crises that may have significantly changed the direction or even the mission of the institution in the past reminds us of the ebb and flow of all living things, including institutions. When we look at how a school or social service ministry modified itself to meet new needs or significantly changed in response to dwindling resources, we can find insights into how we can meet our current challenges. What may have looked like the end of the ministry, going into a crisis, reveals the birth of a stronger or more needed ministry looking back. How like the Paschal Mystery: what looked like death and defeat turns out to be salvation and resurrection. Storytelling gives us courage and hope. "If they could do it, so can we."

Traditions link us to our institutional ancestors who have walked these same halls ahead of us. Useful traditions must highlight some core value of the mission and remind us of all those who have witnessed to this value by engaging in this same activity in the past. Though we might not initiate a given tradition in this day and age, participating in it helps us to understand the mission through a different lens, the perspective of an earlier time. Traditions can lead to a greater understanding of the institution and each person's part in it, helping the faculty and staff deepen their connection to the school and its mission. It is almost as though, through participation in this annual tradition, invisible threads bind the participants ever more tightly to this ministry.

Rich rituals also help us to embody institutional values, enflame the heart, and foster zeal for the mission in all the participants. In a familiar, safe environment, symbols, action, and word embody the deepest beliefs of the Gospel and help us to recognize ourselves as part of something so much greater than we are. As one leader said, "It really grabs the listeners when they begin to realize that they are part of a much larger endeavor, something that has been going on for fifty, a hundred or even hundreds of years. They see themselves as adding a chapter to something that has served others for ages. They tell me that suddenly they see this work more like a vocation than a job, as having a significant spiritual dimension."[4]

Storytelling, tradition, and ritual all remind us of our role as stewards. If our predecessors passed on this ministry to us, we must do all that we can to strengthen and enhance this organization so that we pass on a vibrant ministry to those who will come after us.

OUR RICH HERITAGE

When we join a Catholic ministry, we are called into a rich heritage and a critically important mission, described by Louis Dupré.

> The awareness of a transcendent presence at the heart of human activity has gradually disappeared from culture and morality. Our very existence as spiritual beings has thereby come into crisis. Religion has withdrawn into isolation, protecting itself against the secular onslaught in a sterilized environment of its own. Culture and morality, on the other side, having mostly lost their awareness of a transcendent Eros, have become impoverished. Without the religious dimension, culture and morality become hollowed out, formalistic, shallow; without culture, religion loses what it most seriously needs, namely, an embodiment in moral practice and cultural symbols. The vocation of the Catholic [institution] in our time is, against all odds, to keep the disparate elements of our culture together within an integrating transcendent perspective.[5]

But only an awareness of the fruitful tradition that supports this mission will inspire staff and faculty in their work. Let us explore some of the rich heritage from which we can draw strength.

Catholicism at its best is based on three fundamental premises. First, Catholicism embraces all reality and is inclusive. This distinguishes Catholicism from sects that only allow certain types of members. This characteristic of enfolding all reality underlies the Catholic demand for inclusivity rather than exclusivity. The Catholic Church is universal and inclusive—open to all races, all people, and all parts of the world.

Second, Catholicism accepts the goodness of creation and the goodness of the human. Whatever has been made by God is good and is included within the Catholic understanding and embrace. Catholics also recognize that humans sin, both individually and as societies, and that people sometimes fail to live up to the full potential of creation. Redemption, however, overcomes all our human failings and restores humanity to the fullness of life. While beliefs about creation ground the Catholic acceptance of and openness to all existence, Catholics believe that redemption, too, touches all reality, including humanity. Redemption creates a new heaven and a new earth.

Third, in Catholicism, God and the divine are mediated to us through creation and the human. For Catholics, everything holds the possibility of revealing the glory of God. The sacramental system emphasizes this importance of creation. God comes to us through the stuff of earth. Some have even described Catholicism as an "earthy" religion—as opposed to the more disembodied belief systems in some other religions.

These three aspects of Catholicism—universality, the inherent goodness of creation and, thus, of humans, and the mediation of God through creation and the human—underlie the characteristics of the Catholic intellectual tradition.

The Catholic Intellectual Tradition

After the Gospel itself, the thousand-year-old Catholic intellectual tradition provides perhaps the richest resource for Catholic educational institutions. Many formulations of the tradition exist, but all agree that the Catholic intellectual tradition recognizes that reason and faith are not antagonistic or unconnected, that questions of transcendence, meaning, significance, and value must form part of the curriculum, and that there is no such thing as a value-free education. Schools in the Catholic tradition take philosophy and philosophical thinking seriously. They do not see questioning as antithetical to faith, but encourage individuals to understand as fully as possible the rational basis for what they believe. Catholic institutions demonstrate by their programs, which are open to all disciplines and arts, that the whole purpose of education is to draw the person out of her narrowness and continually expand the intellectual horizons of all. A Catholic education upholds the dignity of each person, recognizes that individuals exist in community, and fosters a collaborative style of interaction. Catholic schools resist reductionism, neither accepting the tenets of faith without reflection nor agreeing that empirical data is the last word. The Catholic tradition takes symbolism and mysticism seriously, admitting that there are ways of knowing and understanding beyond the reach of reason alone. Catholic education is not elitist, but cares for the poor. This concern for the poor not only inspires service to the community but also encourages those in the institution to use their power to influence political philosophy and social theory.

In some form these basic characteristics of the Catholic intellectual tradition should inform a Catholic educational institution at any level. Those leaders in Catholic schools who find ways to help their faculties make the elements of the Catholic intellectual tradition their own will see staffs more eager to demonstrate how the mission of their institution implements this broader tradition.

Catholic Social Teaching

Catholic social teaching, drawn from the heart of the Gospel message, provides another strong foundation for any Catholic institution. Some of its elements overlap with the Catholic intellectual tradition, but reflection and study of this resource reveal subtle nuances that will enhance the mission integration of the individual institution. The critical characteristics of Catholic social teaching include belief in the inherent dignity of the human person, who is both sacred and social. Belief in individual dignity and in community form the foundation of all Catholic social teaching. Other basic tenets of Catholic social teaching affirm that human dignity can be protected and a healthy community can be achieved only if institutions protect human rights and all persons meet their responsibilities, that the moral test of a society is how it treats its most vulnerable members, that all people have a right to participate in the economic, political, and cultural life of society, and that the economy must serve people, not the other way around. All workers have a right to productive work, to decent and fair wages, and to safe working conditions. The state, as an instrument to promote human dignity, protect human rights, and build the common good, has a positive moral function. The principle of subsidiarity holds that the functions of government should be performed at the lowest level possible, as long as they can be performed adequately. Catholic social teaching recognizes that the goods of the earth are gifts from God and that they are intended by God for the benefit of everyone. Because we are one human family, our responsibilities to each other cross national, racial, economic, and ideological differences. The promotion of peace, which is far more than the absence of war, involves mutual respect and confidence between peoples and nations, collaboration, and binding agreements. Anyone who looks seriously at a Catholic institution should see these characteristics manifested, not only in its documents, but also and more importantly in its daily life.

HOW TO DRAW FROM THE
HERITAGE TO SUPPORT THE MISSION

While understanding the value of the institution's heritage is important, good leaders realize that understanding alone is not sufficient. Heritage will have no power unless leaders, recognizing mission integration as their primary role in the institution, find ways to translate this understanding into actions that will infuse the mission into all aspects of the school. Let us explore some ways to achieve this mission integration.

Tell Stories

Storytelling is perhaps the most powerful tool available to the institutional leader. Jesus frequently used stories in his ministry, to name values, to illustrate points, and to provide an easy form of learning for his followers. Providing a brief history of the school which tells the story of the founders can give inspiration to all those involved in the school. Since few institutions are the work of one or two people, remember to include all those who collaborated with the original founder. One institution that has good archival material highlights a former teacher, student, parent/family, or alum each month, telling some story about that individual which illustrates a key value that the school holds dear. Interviews, visits to the school, bulletin boards, pictures, and stories all help show why the school community is proud that the selected person worked or studied at their school. Last year the school's first choice was the maintenance man who had worked at the school for many years. Everyone knew him as a person who went above and beyond his job description to serve others. His witness was particularly powerful because the theme that school year was "Using my best gifts for others."

Those in institutions associated with a religious congregation can visit the archives or heritage room of the congregation to help the school board, faculty, and staff see how, along with the other works of the congregation, they participate in something much larger than themselves. They can draw strength from this shared work. Members from the founding community who worked in the particular ministry in earlier times can also tell wonderful stories that highlight the values of the school.

Ask members of the congregation to host a retreat for the board or the staff of the sponsored institution that elucidates the charism of the congregation and helps people to see how the mission of their particular institution echoes the mission and charism of the founding community. The more the board, faculty, and staff of an institution deepen their appreciation of the charism, the more that charism will inform and strengthen the mission of a sponsored work.

Diocesan-sponsored ministries can use the archives of the diocese to give context to the work of their institutions, demonstrating how the founding parish or other diocesan entity embodied their values in this particular institution. Archives often contain stories of overcoming hardship and the joy of successes that can give depth to present-day celebrations. Diocesan personnel might be invited to describe how this particular ministry fits into the overall mission of the diocese. Leaders in the institution can show how the mission statement and goals of the institution reflect the overall mission statement and goals of the diocese. Former employees of the local institution can be invited to participate in story-telling events and anniversary celebrations. (The diocesan personnel office can offer assistance in locating former employees.) All these activities help current employees realize that they minister in a long line of dedicated and enthusiastic people who set goals and achieved them.

Provide Orientation

Orientation experiences provide excellent opportunities to share the mission and culture of an institution. As individuals enter into a new culture they tend to be open, even eager, to learn about this culture. Some leaders design an orientation program that extends over three or four months, giving them a chance for more intensive teaching about the Catholic intellectual tradition and Catholic social teaching that helps the new employees understand the basis of the school culture. Many institutions end their orientation experience with a missioning ceremony during which the newer board members and employees are not only welcomed into the community, but also pledge to use their gifts to foster the mission of the institution.

Foster Prayer and Ritual

Good ritual and prayer can transform an institution. One principal assembles the entire school community in the church each morning for a brief prayer and motivational talk. Each Friday, as part of the school's Gospel catechesis, the principal presents a reflection on the Gospel reading for the upcoming Sunday with a suggested application. The Sunday readings also form the basis for the religion lesson in each classroom on Fridays. This modification in the curriculum, along with the Friday morning prayer and ritual, changed the students' understanding of the Gospels. But the transformation did not stop there. The principal reports that faculty members have told her that, although they are lifelong Catholics, they have never really broken open the readings before. She also hears faculty saying to one another, "This is what I think this Gospel means. What do you think?" Parents have indicated to her that at times they had no intention of attending a weekend liturgy, but the children came home so excited to hear the word proclaimed that they changed their minds and accompanied them to Mass. The morning assembly and the new curriculum help to integrate the mission into all parts of the school community.

Begin staff meetings with more than a cursory prayer. Rather, develop an environment that gives people the tools that enable them to see the deeper meaning of their work and their connection to a larger purpose. After insti-tuting this prayer style in the workplace, one leader commented, "At first I feared that people would see these prayer experiences as a waste of their time, but instead they have told me that they love this opportunity for si-lence and reflection in this harried world. It has helped them see their work, not as a job, but as a ministry."[6] Recognize that your staff, board, and stu-dent body might include persons from a variety of religious backgrounds. Make certain that the prayer experiences provide opportunities for them to express their understanding of God and how God works in them and through this ministry.

Reverence Traditions

Traditions embody some value of the community, connect us to those who have gone before, and help us to see that this particular mission has been implemented in this place over time. For example, one school had a tradition of allowing students who contributed through work or funds to some charitable purpose to dress down instead of wearing their uniforms on Fridays. This fostered several values of the school: that a particular style of dress is appropriate in given situations, that privileges like dressing down are earned, and that we use our resources to assist others. Traditions may be tied to a particular historical era and become outdated, but rather than throw them out completely, creative leaders take the essence of a tradition and update it to fit a new time. One school hosted a pageant each year to highlight the history and values of the school. Eventually the school popu-lation began to decline and the resources for the pageant were more lim-ited. The school substituted a founders'-week celebration which included student activities as well as events for the parents and the parish commu-nity. Thus, the tradition changed, but the energy derived from recognizing the heritage continued.

Celebrate Almost Everything

Celebrations and parties provide a good opportunity to highlight what a given community holds dear. Mark the institutional or religious congrega-tion's patron saint, founders' days, student achievements, alumni successes and any other likely event. Relate the virtues of those who are honored to the mission of the institution, to inspire greater commitment.

Celebrations also promote community—an essential characteristic of Catholic institutions—and allow for the appropriate crossing of boundaries in the school community. Much of the time, groups divide by role. The fac-ulty at one level meets separately from that at another level. Staff meetings occur independently from faculty meetings. Parents most often meet individually with a child's teacher. Parties allow all these groups to encounter each other as people, not as roles. This can make a big difference in how people work together, enjoy one another's gifts, and allow for each other's mistakes. One diocesan superintendent of schools claims that he tells all new administrators that building community is a three-step process. The group must first play together—taking time to get to know one another as more than the task-related single dimension of teacher, administrator, and maintenance worker. In step two the group prays together, breaking open the Word. Only then, says the superintendent, can the community really work together to foster the values of the school.

Parties need not be elaborate. One principal invited faculty, staff, parents, board members, and even older students to stop by her office for tea between 2:30 and 3:30 on Thursday afternoons. While some regulars came weekly, most people stopped in two or three times a year. For the price of tea bags and a few inexpensive cookies, she manifested her strong commitment to approachability and community spirit. Besides that, she easily kept her ear out for rising concerns and could often nip rumors in the bud.

Make Connections

Leaders in organizations must continually encourage the board members, staff, and students to make the connections between the heritage of the institution and what occurs today. Questions such as, "Do the judicial policies used by the Student Disciplinary Council reflect Catholic social teaching?" and "Do these new curricular changes embody the principles of the Catholic intellectual tradition?" should become ordinary parts of reflection and decision making in the institution. Many organizations use a decision-making matrix for all major decisions. Such a matrix, listing a series of questions, reminds those embroiled in the decision-making process what the institution values as they hash out a resolution.

Name Values

We may believe that the institutional values springing from our mission are so long-standing and obvious that anyone can name them, and perhaps they could. But there is no harm in naming them clearly as well. One institution worked with the board, faculty, and parents to formulate the five major values flowing from the mission. These values were then printed on book covers, emblazoned on school bulletin boards, and passed out on bookmarks from the library. Soon everyone, even the youngest students, could name at least some of the values of the school. The faculty began using the values to form the basis for their classroom discipline. The parent-teacher organization used one of the values as a theme for each of its meetings, structuring its prayer and speakers around that theme. The principal used these values in her fund-raising efforts.

Naming values helps build a school identity. It sensitizes people to expect to see certain things. They notice examples of the named values and begin to see themselves as implementers of those values. As more and more people see the named values and take on the responsibility to implement them, the identity of the institution deepens with each cycle.

Tag lines, short phrases of no more than seven words that name the mission and values of the institution succinctly, provide another way to name values. For example, one all-girl high school used the tag line, "Empowering Catholic women for leadership and service." These values became so much a part of the school's culture that by October of a student's first year, she could cite numerous ways in which she had already experienced these values.

Letters, memos, introductions at public events, and homilies also allow leaders to name the values of the mission. For example, in a thank you note to a faculty member, one principal wrote, "Thank you for taking your students on the field trip to the homeless shelter. It manifested again your continuing commitment to our value of Christian service." At a fund-raising event, the person introducing the speaker remarked, "Because this school community values working together in peaceful ways, we are pleased to have Mr. Pocatelli, who has manifested such a collaborative spirit in his work with other business leaders." These reminders of the mission take no special funding and no extra time. They are included in already required tasks. But they serve as a constant reminder that this work supports a larger purpose. This is not just another job; this is a ministry, a service to the Gospel message.

Visuals

In addition to written communications, visual communications can convey the continuing mission of the institution. At one school, a banner listing the major values of the institution led the procession at ceremonial events, such as the opening assembly and graduation services, and in the meantime hung prominently in the foyer of the school. Bulletin boards, letterhead, posted pictures of faculty and students engaged in valued activities, and announcement signs in front of the school provide other opportunities to display the core values of the mission.

Resources

Some institutions or groups of institutions with the same heritage collect and share mission integration ideas. Having the history and values, prayer services and commitment ceremonies, orientation materials and homily ideas gathered in one place provides an invaluable resource for any leader who takes seriously his or her responsibility for the mission.

CONCLUSION

This essay emphasizes the need for each new leader to appropriate and implement the mission of those who have gone before and to steward that mission for those who take it up in the future. The heritage that all Catholic institutions share, combined with the dynamic history of a specific ministry, gives the leader a rich resource for mission integration. When leaders employ this resource well, they will agree with one principal who rejoiced,

> Our students and our staff see clearly that being Catholic isn't *part* of who we are, it *is* who we are. All the decisions, all the challenges, all the joys we face must come from the spirit of that Catholicity. The reason for the existence of our school is that spirit—that Catholic tradition of education, not for any academic program or our sports program, but because we are Catholic schools. We are grounded in the Gospel.[7]

REFLECTION EXERCISE

1. In a small group (six to eight people), tell the story of the founders of the institution. If no archival material or history book describes this story, tell a story of the more recent past which someone in the institutional community can relate.
2. Consider: (a) what values this story elucidates, and (b) what the core values of the institution are today. Reflect on the relationship.
3. Share the results of this reflection in the group. For those values described in the original story that match the current values, describe specific ways these values are fostered in the community. For those values present today that do not match the story, consider whether this occurs because the mission of the institution has changed by design or because the institution has drifted away from the founding vision.
4. With this as a background, consider how the institutional community might better use the spirit of those who have gone before to inform such things as the curriculum, the social service experiences, the ritual and traditions of the institution.
5. Choose at least one but no more than three specific activities that would embody the spirit of those who have gone before in ways that strengthen the values practiced in the institution today. Set a time to evaluate the impact of these activities after they are completed.

NOTES

1. Katherine Arseneau, C.S.J., interview by author, Albany, NY, February 11, 2004.

2. Monika Hellwig, "The Intellectual Tradition in the Catholic University," in *Examining the Catholic Intellectual Tradition*, eds. Anthony J. Cernera and Oliver J. Morgan, vol. 1 (Fairfield, CT: Sacred Heart University Press, 2000), 17. See also *Issues and Perspectives*, vol. 2 (Fairfield, CT: Sacred Heart University Press, 2002).

3. Sean Peters et al., "Beyond the Present: The Shape of Sponsorship in the 21st Century," *Current Issues in Catholic Higher Education* 23, no. 2 (Summer 2003): 69.

4. Nancy Roche, S.S.J., interview by author, Albany, NY, February 17, 2004.

5. Louis Dupré, "The Task and Vocation of the Catholic College" in *Examining the Catholic Intellectual Tradition*, ed. Anthony J. Cernera and Oliver J. Morgan (Fairfield, CT: Sacred Heart University Press, 2000), 31–32.

6. Danielle Bonetti, C.S.J., interview by author, Albany, NY, February 18, 2004.

7. Focus group interview by Zeni Fox and Regina Bechtle, S.C. Newark, NJ, March 13, 2002.

IV

THE ROLE OF THE SPIRITUAL LEADER

In this concluding section we return to the person at the core of the community, who carries the Catholic institution and its mission in sacred trust. He/she knows that leading this kind of community demands more than managerial expertise and professional savvy. It requires a level of spiritual maturity that is both gift and goal. The following essays invite leaders to pay attention to the mystery of God's activity in their unique stories and, through their daily administrative work, to confront contradictions between ideals and behavior without losing hope or humor, to engage questions and tensions in fidelity to the pursuit of truth, and to mentor others with generosity and humility. Above all, those in authority must be clear about power—what it is and is not, where it comes from and what it is for, always with profound openness to the Spirit's transforming, empowering presence.

10

"Grace Given to Each": Spirituality and Administration

Dolores R. Leckey

Because we are body-spirits, our lives have both an interior and an exterior dimension; in this chapter, Dolores Leckey charts the way both are part of spirituality and, more precisely, part of a spirituality of administrators as they lead groups in mission. She tells the stories of three persons, one a saint of the fifteenth century and two contemporaries. Through these accounts she notes key moments in all spiritual journeys and central virtues of administrators.

St. Paul assures the people of ancient Ephesus and—by extension across time and cultures—all of us that grace is given to each according to the measure of Christ's gift (Eph 4:7). And for Paul, Christ's gift to the Church includes apostles, prophets, evangelists, pastors, and teachers. So what about administrators—those who are overseeing the day-to-day functioning of a parish or a diocesan agency, a school, or some other institution? I submit that administrators, too, have been and are grace for the Christian community.[1] This is an important factor to probe and understand in this particular historical moment when lay leaders are increasingly assuming certain roles formerly enacted by pastors, religious superiors, and even bishops. How the Church's business is conducted surely matters to its members, and it surely matters to the new administrators who are following a vocation and who daily face issues of responsible decision making. To understand this evolving role, it helps to encounter the inner life of the men and women whose work is to manage and lead the Church in the most authentic way possible. Therefore we will explore the inner and outer lives of three church administrators, whose lives and ministries span time, cultures, and styles.

ST. CATHERINE OF GENOA (1447–1510)

Serge Hughes, a translator of the teachings of St. Catherine of Genoa, says this about her:

> Just imagine:
> In Genoa, a saint among administrators!
> Maybe there's a chance
> For us, too?[2]

Caterinetta Adorna, known to history as Catherine of Genoa, did not set out to be an administrator; she did set her heart, however, on being a saint, what today we might characterize as her response to the universal call to holiness.[3] In many ways, she serves as a prototype for the layperson whose ministry is wholly or partially that of administration. A member of Genovese nobility, she married at age sixteen, a marriage that was politically and financially beneficial for her family. In fact, it was an arranged marriage. During the first ten years of her marriage Catherine experienced intense loneliness. Her husband, Giuliano, squandered their financial resources and, worse, was unfaithful to his marriage vows, fathering an illegitimate daughter. These betrayals deepened her sense of isolation and depression. At the same time, this period of withdrawal and inner suffering called forth her natural contemplative tendencies. Evelyn Underhill, the outstanding twentieth-century student of "practical mysticism," describes a point of conversion during Catherine's valley of darkness. Underhill writes, "The center of interest was shifted and the field of consciousness was remade."[4] Catherine's profound prayer did not lead her deeper into depression; quite the opposite. It propelled her into the busy life of the city. She began to walk daily through the slums of Genoa, where she came into direct contact with the poor. At the same time, she was determined to deal with her husband's bankruptcy (a total disgrace in Genovese society), and in so doing was honing administrative abilities. For whatever reason—Catherine's generosity, her prayer, sheer grace—Giuliano experienced a conversion and became a Franciscan Tertiary. He and Catherine moved into a humble house near the Pammatone Hospital, which had vast wards of the sick poor. There they lived for the remainder of their lives, dedicated to works of mercy.

Catherine's love spilled out into total acceptance of Giuliano's child and the child's mother and complete forgiveness of her husband, a decidedly countercultural stand for her time and place. Clearly Catherine's spiritual experiences informed the totality of her life. For most of their years at the Pammatone Hospital, Giuliano and Catherine performed a variety of volunteer services, becoming skilled in nursing care and many practical tasks.

In 1490, Catherine became director of the hospital, and when the plague struck Genoa three years later, her administrative leadership was evident.

She transformed the open space behind the hospital into a huge tent hospital, thereby extending the institution's capacity to care for patients. For many months she supervised doctors, nurses, volunteers, priests—a whole complex staff in the service of the sick poor. And by all accounts she enacted her tasks, including her financial duties, with consistency and integrity. Giuliano died during this period and in tribute to his wife, left her what remained of his diminished fortune. This legacy enabled her to continue the work they had done together for the poor of their city and "to provide the means for her continuing to lead her quiet, peaceful and spiritual mode of life."[5]

During Catherine's lifetime other seekers after God were drawn to her rich inner life. They saw, simply through the way she lived, that it was possible to be a contemplative while engaged in active life. One follower, Ettore Vernazza, a young wealthy businessman, became the founder of several institutions dedicated to prayer and the care of the poor. Vernazza is also the source of much information about Catherine's life, ministry, and teaching.

One of her teachings pertains to purgatory. Catherine's insight about life after death, born of her mystical experience, is unique for her time and perhaps for all time. Catherine teaches that purgatory is strangely consoling. She says the souls are at peace in God's will, yet the opposition remaining in the soul to God's will is the occasion of pain. Still, there is an ever-increasing happiness in purgatory, insists Catherine. And the soul, once purified of self (ego), comes to abide in God. "Its being *is* God," she says.[6] Catherine's mystical knowledge regarding purgatory as a place of moving ever more deeply into God signals her conviction of the power of God's love. That sense of *God as love* was enormously influential not only in the Catholic world but among Protestants as well. (She died at the beginning of the Protestant Reformation.) Her spirituality formed a natural bridge into many worlds, and she is, I believe, a mentor for today's ecclesial administrators. Why?

Her personal biography is a major factor. She was a laywoman, married, and for a significant period of time, in an unhappy marriage, marked by financial problems and infidelity on the part of her husband. She experienced depression, largely related to her marital situation, but also perhaps because of a predisposition. In the midst of these troubles, Catherine came into what might be called "a second conversion," a sense of her call that grew out of her attentiveness to the inner world to which she was drawn, initially through sorrow and travail. The cultivation of her contemplative life drew her more fully into the rhythms of daily life in the city of Genoa, relating her to her extended family (whom she had previously avoided) and to the larger human family, particularly those poor and in most need. As an unsuspecting herald of the Second Vatican Council, Catherine taught that *perfection* (holiness) was as available to the laity as to the ordained and religious. For so long a major assumption in Church life had been that the pathway of holiness belonged to those who lived *outside* of secular reality.

Holiness occurred in monasteries and convents, in seminaries and papal courts: so went conventional thinking. Her life and works demonstrated that holiness is realized in the web of human relationships, an understanding affirmed by the Second Vatican Council.

What Catherine offers to a spirituality of administration is, above all, the necessity of a balance between intentional attentiveness to the inner life and courageous and committed action. She is, in a way, an icon of balance: probing the deepest recesses of the inner life, attending to relationships, bringing competence and integrity to daily work, and maintaining what Michael Downey calls a vision of the "larger worlds of which the enterprise is a part."[7]

Historically, one sees a certain pattern in the formation of authentic leaders, namely, a period of withdrawal or solitude followed by activity and accomplishment. The pattern is everywhere, in secular as well as religious endeavors, and notably in the lives of artists of all kinds. It is certainly so in the lives of religious leaders. Jesus and Paul immediately come to mind. So does Teresa of Avila, who spent many years in her Carmelite monastery trying to pray and meditate, without much to show for it, according to her own account. Then around age forty, the prayer deepens, her mystical consciousness awakens, and her entire being is energized. What does she do with this newfound energy? Spend more time in the chapel? No. A contemporary statue of her in Avila vividly depicts her life *after* solitude. She is setting forth, staff in hand, a woman on the move. And indeed, until her death in her mid-sixties, she was intensely active, reforming the Carmelite order, establishing new foundations, living out the inner Word that reverberated within her.

Central to this pattern of oscillation, of moving between solitude and activity, is detachment, the opposite of willfulness. Detachment allows for a radical openness to doing things differently, that is to say, creatively. The Hebrew Scriptures emphasize the necessity of time apart, Sabbath time, for *everyone*, in order to be fully human. In our own time, with the high value placed on efficiency, it can be difficult to incorporate solitude and contemplation into the rhythm of home life and work schedules. Yet, if we deny this dimension of life, we invite imbalance and problematic leadership. The challenge for contemporary leaders, and especially administrators, is to honor both solitude and engagement, to demonstrate a more fully human, balanced life.

Catherine's life and teaching are a model, for they are infused with several qualities of true spiritual leadership. *Conversion* is the foundation of her life. *Collaboration* is everywhere evident: in her work with the poor and in her personal relationships. And the *balance* of "resting in God" and active mission is central. If saints show us what is possible, St. Catherine of Genoa, a married laywoman and administrator, is worth some pondering.

GEORGE NOONAN, DIOCESAN CHANCELLOR

As more and more laity assume positions of administrative leadership in the Church, questions about the proper spiritual formation for these new leaders are in the forefront of responsible discussion. Can the new lay leaders receive a preparation comparable to that of clerics and vowed religious? How might that happen?

Clearly there is a need for formal theological and spiritual formation, but at the same time, there has been a growing consensus that the primary place for spiritual formation is in the family. Although parents (and certainly children) do not speak in the language of mystical consciousness or technical theology, the fact is that values and beliefs—and practices—are absorbed in the dynamics of family life. And this formation can and does plant the seeds of Church service in a totally committed way. That service may of course draw one into ordained ministry; it is just as likely to lead one to lay ministry. George Noonan, currently chancellor of the diocese of Kansas City–St. Joseph in Missouri, is such an example.

One of the truest things one can say about George Noonan is that he knows his roots. The fourth of eight children, he grew up in Springfield, Massachusetts, in the same house where his father grew up. And his parish (his great-grandparents were among the founders) was like an extension of his home. George's grandfather lived next door, and aunts and cousins seemed to be everywhere. This was a familiar and secure environment, with a recognizable center.

But in the late 1950s and early 1960s, the neighborhood where "everyone knew everyone else" began to change. African Americans were moving in, and white flight began. George's parents refused to flee. Both of them were veterans of the Second World War, and perhaps it was their experiences in Europe and in the South Pacific, experiences of real danger, that helped them instill in their children a sense of fairness toward others and courage regarding new developments in their neighborhood.

The parish, too, was gripped by change. Where there used to be many Masses on Sunday morning, now there were fewer. Catholics were among the fleeing. But the pastoral leadership—the priests and the Sisters of St. Joseph—challenged the fears and the rumors that were constantly springing up. George says of these childhood leaders, "They understood ordinary life."

It is not surprising that in eighth grade George was mulling over whether he should go to the minor seminary for high school. The elder Noonans sought guidance from two priest friends (members of a religious congregation), who suggested that it might be best if their enthusiastic son waited awhile. Their advice was accepted, but the pull toward commitment did not disappear, even when he went to St. Michael's College in Vermont, and even when he met Maureen (later his wife), who was a student at the University of Vermont. As their relationship grew, his desire to be of service took the form of a question: priesthood or marriage?

St. Ignatius of Loyola tells us to examine our desires to help locate God's will for us. George decided to major in philosophy and religious studies—that's where his heart was. But he also loved Maureen, and he wanted a family. Were these desires mutually exclusive? He solved the dilemma, for the moment, by focusing on an academic path of Church service, and at the same time planning on marriage immediately after graduation. The academic plan was to be realized in Toronto, where George would pursue a Ph.D. in theology.

George and Maureen found the Toronto environment intellectually stimulating. The employment prospects, however, were poor, and both he and Maureen needed to work to make "the plan" work. Realizing that total poverty would likely put an enormous strain on their new marriage, they headed for home in Massachusetts, where George had a job waiting: teaching religion in high school. The school rector, a priest, saw leadership in George and suggested that he consider an M.A. in theology at Yale Divinity School. Furthermore, there was money available for scholarships at Yale.

I first met George in 1979 when he was a Yale student. He and Henri Nouwen (the Dutch priest-psychologist and author, who at the time was on the Divinity School faculty) came to my office at the United States Conference of Catholic Bishops. The purpose of our meeting was to arrange a pastoral visit of bishops on the Laity Committee to Yale Divinity School. They hoped the bishops would be open to dialogue with the lay students who believed they had a vocation to Church service, and who were being trained for that service in an ecumenical setting. George had been active in organizing the Catholic students to come together for conversation about their Catholic faith and how it was both challenged and strengthened in the Yale environment. He was invested in making Catholic connections.

Several bishops did, indeed, visit Yale, and the Catholic students made a favorable impression on them. They were particularly touched by the testimonies of young men and women who spoke of their "call," and how they were willing to sacrifice to honor that call. I remember that day as grace-filled.

Henri Nouwen, like others before him, recognized George's leadership qualities and urged him to remain at Yale for a third year to complete a Master of Divinity degree. George and Maureen were both open to the idea, but then, as before, money was a problem. George did not know where he could find the tuition. Nouwen said he would take care of it, so much did he believe in George's vocation.

George not only continued his theological studies, but he continued to exercise certain administrative gifts on behalf of his fellow students, as well. He realized that for Catholics there was a missing piece in the curriculum. Other students had access to the polity systems of their churches; Catholics did not. So George approached John Whealon, the archbishop of Hartford, and asked him to remedy the situation. George wanted a course in canon law. Whealon saw the request as an opportunity to connect the archdiocese with the educational institution and, at the same time, to contribute to the formation of future lay ministers. The archbishop wanted these new ecclesial ministers to have an excellent education. It was he who first used the term "ecclesial" in reference to lay ministry, terminology that was later incorporated into the U.S. bishops' statement, *Called and Gifted*.[8]

George's first full-time ministry after receiving his divinity degree was as Catholic chaplain to the prep schools in the northwest corner of Connecticut. There was concern that Catholics in those schools were disconnected from the local churches. Archbishop Whealon provided funds for the position.

Being on the move from school to school was clearly hard, but it was also a chance for George to refine further his natural organizational skills. He had to work with people who had different theological perspectives from him and from one another, or who were indifferent to the place of theology in everyday life. In those early years of administrative ministry, George learned that he liked the "big picture." He learned that if you applied yourself, took the needs of others into account, listened carefully and attentively, you could be successful and have a sense of satisfaction. Still, George felt a certain restlessness. He wanted to do more.

When a pastoral planning position in another diocese opened, he applied for it. He felt a natural alliance with planning and saw the work as a way to bring people together. He did not get the position, however, and for the first time since he began his ministerial journey from Springfield, Massachusetts, he experienced a deep disappointment.

Knowing how central family had always been in his spiritual life, George turned to his new family, especially to Maureen, to help him find his center. Maureen, an artist who is acutely aware of the grace coursing through ordinary life, helped him navigate this restless period. George refers to her as his reality check.

In truth, something new was on the horizon. Within a year, he was appointed director of the Center for Pastoral Life and Ministry for the diocese of Kansas City–St. Joseph, a position he held for eleven years. Nine years ago, he became the chancellor of the diocese.

George likes being chancellor, but it *is* a lot of work. Again, he references family in trying to understand the meaning of this work he has chosen—or which has chosen him. "My father worked all the time," he says. "That's my life script too. I'm doing what I love." He adds that he and Maureen have learned to carve out time for their relationship and for their parenting—there are three sons—a new factor which contemporary ministers must take into account.

After twenty years in diocesan leadership, George is still convinced he is following a call. This is not to say that there are no tensions. With some regularity, the question surfaces: "Is there really a vocation here?" He would like a sabbatical to think through such big questions. He would appreciate intellectual and spiritual stretching. The pressing issues that weigh on thoughtful people—the role of women in the Church, inclusion of laity in decision making, courageous leadership—weigh also on George. He is especially concerned that he, and others, be authentic leaders and not simply managers. He wants to ponder such things. As a new member of the Yale Divinity Alumni Board, he may have some unexpected opportunities to do so.

One could easily describe George Noonan as a "born administrator," but that would be a partial description. He exercises his faith over and over again. He is unafraid of questions and the *conversions* they lead to. He is *committed* to family and the larger community that flows from families. His roots are strong within the Church but his horizon is expansive. He is theologically curious and searching. George Noonan is a sign of hope for the Church of the twenty-first century.

CULTURE AND MINISTRY

Both Catherine of Genoa and George Noonan were influenced by their particular cultures. In fifteenth-century Genovese society, Catherine became acutely aware of the contrast between her own elite social standing and the impoverished people of the slums, and that experience turned her toward finding a centerpoint within her own consciousness. When the plague devastated Genoa, Catherine's developed sense of responsibility led to the recognition and exercise of her administrative abilities.

George came of age in the 1960s, exciting years of change both in society and in the church. In some ways, these two realities were woven together. Racism affected both the civic community and the church community, and George was growing up in both these worlds. He was able to navigate the tumultuous time because of mentors—his parents and his pastors—who made it clear that racism was not an option. What George learned about courageous response to crises came straight out of the culture of his time.

As their responsibilities grew, George and Catherine responded to their cultures in two main ways: through reflection and through participation in the rhythms of daily life. For both of them, *family* was a critical factor. For Catherine, it was initially a cauldron; for George, it was (and is) a consolation. As they moved into administrative ministries, their histories led them to locate the Spirit's leadings in the *quotidian* (that which is familiar) as much as in the quietude of prayer.

I think we can say the same thing about lay ministry, and particularly lay *ecclesial* ministry in the post-conciliar period. The new ministers have not come by the old pathways. Like George (and Catherine long ago), they are being formed in domestic settings, often seeking professional theological training in conjunction with their work. New ministries seem to rise up in response to expressed needs and to cultural urgencies. Consequently, practice often precedes theology. Michael Downey suggests this moment is characterized by bricolage, i.e., the gathering of insights "from whatever is at hand." And even though it is necessarily partial, it does release a creative dynamism that utilizes the ordinary. An artful example of bricolage is quilting.[9]

Quilting is not only about pieces and patches. In American history it also reveals a philosophy, a way of life. One quilter, an elderly woman interviewed for a history of quilting, recalled her mother's journey in a covered wagon, from Missouri to west Texas.

> During the long journey, the new bride worked out of her "piece bag" making a Star of Bethlehem quilt that still remains in the family. Her first home was a dugout house, underground. There in the dugout, her mother made the best quilts "because that was when she needed something pretty." Through dust storms, through loneliness when her husband was away, through worry about her endangered gardens, through her desire to raise her children in a house above ground, the woman in the dugout quilted. It was as if this pioneer woman built a base with her quilts and used them as a plan for her next project, an *above-ground* house. "At each step she sank her roots deeper into the earth. At each level she changed, built her surroundings. . . . Then the community came next. Roots reaching out from one ranch to the next . . . a whole network, a grid of support."[10]

I suggest that this quilter's tale can be viewed as an analogue for the development of lay ministers, including lay administrators. Three decades ago a small band of lay ministers were metaphorically in dugouts. Using what was available, guided by the Spirit, the lay ecclesial ministers at the beginning of the twenty-first century are not only above ground, but they are creating communities and networks and supporting a vision of mission, as well.

The third administrator whose narrative offers insight into the spirituality of administration is *not*, in usual parlance, a layperson. She is a vowed religious who is canonically a layperson, the status accorded all women in the Code of Canon Law.

A more cogent reason for including the following story is that the history of lay ministry has strong ties to the post-conciliar ministry of women religious.

> As Sisters moved from classroom teaching to leadership in non-school religious education, they became the daily pastoral presence in parishes. And frequently

laywomen were drawn into ministry by the DRE [Director of Religious Education] who knew what women could accomplish. . . . Furthermore, bonds between sisters and laywomen have been strengthened through the ministry of spiritual direction. . . . For more than a generation, laywomen and women religious have invested the word "sisterhood" with new meaning.[11]

SISTER SHARON EUART, R.S.M.—ADMINISTRATOR AND QUILTER

When Mercy Sister Sharon Euart began quilting, she was an associate general secretary of the United States Conference of Catholic Bishops, the first woman to hold that position. She was a key national administrator of the church in the United States. A canon lawyer (she is now president of the Canon Law Society of America), she was at the heart of the programs and projects generated by the national church. The immediate motivation for her quilting was to engage in some kind of creative work that was nonverbal and that was not on behalf of someone else. Her work at the Bishops' Conference was done in the name of the bishops. Her mother's seventy-fifth birthday was the occasion to create something that originated with her, that was her design.

Sharon's life goal was not to be an associate general secretary of the Conference of Bishops. In fact, she did not envision her life as an administrator. Her vision was to be a Sister of Mercy, where she knew her gifts, whatever they were, would be valued and put in the service of the Church. This vision came clearly to her when she was a student at Mt. St. Agnes College in Baltimore, under the tutelage of the Sisters of Mercy. She entered the community immediately upon her graduation from the college. The year was 1966, when change engendered by the Second Vatican Council was touching every aspect of church life, including religious communities.

Sharon had met the Sisters of Mercy earlier in her life, in junior high school in Atlanta, Georgia, one of the many places she lived with her military family. And it was to Mercy High School that she returned for her first assignment after religious profession. There she taught Latin, Spanish, and religion. She truly loved teaching. But before long, some senior sisters asked if she might be interested in administration. She was, but reluctant to give up teaching, she managed to combine both responsibilities for a while. During this time, she lived in a convent of eighteen sisters, twelve of whom taught in the school. A van transported them back and forth to school.

Gradually, teaching decreased and administration increased, as Sharon became vice principal. During those nine years, she grew in confidence about her own possibilities for leadership. So, when the position of principal opened up, she felt ready to apply. She was one of two finalists, but was not chosen, and she was both surprised and disappointed. As she prayed, she began to realize that it was time to do something else. The Sisters of Mercy agreed.

About the same time, a new program opened in the Archdiocese of Baltimore, a place familiar to Sharon. It was an internship for women in church management. Archbishop William Borders, who had written a groundbreaking pastoral letter on the role of women in the Church, saw this program as a natural implementation of his pastoral letter. Sharon was selected as one of seven interns, and a wider door for understanding the inner workings of the larger church was opened to her. As an intern, she worked in a variety of areas, but the one that really appealed to her was *planning*. When her internship was completed, she was hired by the archdiocese, first as associate planning director. In 1985, she became the director. From that vantage point, Sharon saw that a crucial issue in the church was governance. She felt an inner desire to study canon law. Her own leanings were confirmed by the Sisters of Mercy and the archbishop, who jointly sponsored her studies at the Catholic University of America. She had not yet completed her doctorate in canon law when she was approached to assume the position of planning director for the United States Conference of Catholic Bishops.

As she reflects on her ministerial journey, Sharon is aware that she never explicitly sought ministries; rather they developed as a result of what she had been doing. There is, however, a clear thread of coherence and consistency. With her first experience of administration, it was evident that she felt her gifts blossom. And with planning, both in the Archdiocese of Baltimore and in the Bishops' Conference, she realized how essential it is for someone to have an overview of the entire mission and how the different parts, the different roles, serve that mission—or should.

When Msgr. Robert Lynch (now the bishop of Tampa) became the general secretary, he asked Sharon to leave planning aside and become an associate general secretary. One church glass ceiling was shattered. If planning afforded an overview of the organization, the position of associate general secretary enabled her to see the conference of bishops, and indeed, the entire Church in America in relationship to the universal Church. Because she was interested in finding a way to "make things work," she brought a positive attitude to sometimes intricate and difficult problems. This is not to say that attitude alone solved the problems. What it did do was to provide a spiritual basis for living a faithful life of mission. She has come to believe that *voice* is important, that there should be a place "at the table" for different people to truly experience the richness of the Catholic Church. This is particularly important for women, she believes, who have for so long been left out of decision making. Voice is an instrument of influence and a gift of the Holy Spirit, and so exclusion is, in essence, a denial of the gift.

When Sister Sharon came to the United States Conference of Catholic Bishops, her living arrangements dramatically shifted. She began professed religious life in a community of eighteen, then twelve. When she was in canon law studies at Catholic University, she lived in a building with other sisters in graduate studies. Then she shared an apartment with one other sister. From her time as associate general secretary until now, she has lived alone.

The solitude has been an essential part of her spiritual life. When she was immersed in the bustle and activity of the Bishops' Conference, the contrast of home was welcome. She came to appreciate that in solitude and silence her life was becoming more reflective, more centered, more prayerful. When disappointment colored her life (and it did when she was not reappointed associate general secretary), again the solitude enabled her to enter fully into that experience, and to finally emerge ever more trusting in God's will. An equally important aspect of her life, however, is community. She spends weekends in Baltimore with her religious community. There she shares Mass and meals and faith with the women who have mentored her and cared for her as she followed the golden thread of her vocation. Now she uses her talents and considerable executive experience as a consultant to dioceses, to the Bishops' Conference, and to church organizations. She began her term in 2004 as president of the Canon Law Society of America. Much of her current work is informing the people of God about how church governance should work and what laity can do to help it work better. The lessons of administration are finding an ever wider audience.

WHAT LIFE STORIES TEACH

The three administrators featured in this chapter are in some ways different from one another and in some ways quite similar. Certain spiritual qualities appear in all of them. None of them set forth with a predictable life map. Rather, each followed the first beckoning of the Spirit in their lives, and they responded to the call to seek God with trust. For each of them, disappointment and even suffering played a crucial role. Perhaps they learned to trust God even more in the dry and desolate times. All three experienced at some point the essential truth that growth in the spiritual life requires balance, a balance between the soul's solitude with God and human connectedness to others: in family and/or in community and ultimately in mission. Even the great mystic Catherine of Genoa knew that the authenticity of her experience was tested in relationships. Catherine had no formal theological training, and it is thought she was illiterate. She did, however, keep track of her experience, and others wrote down what she saw, what she learned, and what she deeply believed. Her teachings, preserved by others, influenced the lives and work of many generations, to this day. George and Sharon, living in a different time and culture, pursued excellent theological education. They sought to be well prepared for the work that was unfolding in their lives.

It is true that the ministries of Catherine, George, and Sharon were gradually enacted on ever larger stages. Yet, their inner qualities of leadership—conversion, collaboration, commitment, creativity, compassion, and courage—are relevant to all ministries, to administrators in a variety of settings, from school principals to treasurers, from parish managers to health care administrators and Catholic Charities' managers. Authentic leadership, characterized by these qualities, is needed everywhere. And it is possible to cultivate these qualities, as we see in the life stories recounted in this chapter. The main requirements are trust, willingness, and mentors.

REFLECTION QUESTIONS

1. Chart your own life journey in terms of the qualities illustrated in Catherine's life, of conversion, collaboration, and balance of solitude and activity. Where has each of these been exercised? How can you attend more to each?
2. In George Noonan's story we note a centrality of relationships, with his family of origin, his wife, his teachers and mentors, and church leaders. What relationships are central in your story? How do you carve out time for these relationships?
3. Sr. Sharon experienced a gradual flowering and expansion of her gifts. How has this been true for you? How have you dealt with the times when disappointment colored your life?

NOTES

1. Administrators are specifically mentioned in the First Letter to the Corinthians, 1 Cor. 12, NAB translation.
2. Serge Hughes, trans., *Catherine of Genoa: Purgation and Purgatory, the Spiritual Dialogue*, The Classics of Western Spirituality Series (Mahwah, NJ: Paulist Press, 1979), 67.
3. See *Lumen Gentium*, #40.
4. Evelyn Underhill, *Mysticism* (New York: E. P. Dutton, 1961), cited in Hughes, *Catherine of Genoa*, 4.
5. Hughes, *Catherine of Genoa*, 16.
6. Hughes, *Catherine of Genoa*, 36.
7. See Michael Downey, "Without a Vision the People Perish," chapter 2, p. 26 in this book.
8. The terminology of lay ministry has been evolving, from "ecclesial lay ministry" to the preferred language of the twenty-first century, "lay ecclesial ministry."

9. See Vincent Miller, *Consuming Religion* (New York: Continuum, 2004), 154–57, for a discussion of bricolage and modern culture. Also, Michael Downey, chapter 2 of this book.

10. Patricia Cooper and Norma Allen, *The Quilters*, cited by Dolores Leckey in *Women and Creativity* (Mahwah, NJ: Paulist Press, 1991), 32–33.

11. Leckey, *Women and Creativity*, 45.

11

In the Between: Reflections on Educational Institutions and Communities of Faith

John S. Nelson

In this chapter, John Nelson explores a number of complex questions with significant bearing on the work of Catholic educational institutions—and without easy answers. Each question revolves around a relationship, for example, the relationship between a school and a parish or between a Catholic school and the members of its multiple communities (students, parents, faculty) who are not Catholic. These are questions of our age, the age of a global village in which many faiths and cultures have an impact on our Catholic communities, from without and from within.

I am honored to share some ideas on the spirituality of lay leadership, especially as this spirituality interrelates educational institutions and communities of faith.

My wife Cathy has spent most of her professional life in church-related schools. She has worked hard and has done well; over the years she has reserved as a kind of therapy her right to complain in the teacher's room about the pay scale for laypersons in ministry.

Just recently Meg, our twenty-three-year-old daughter (herself a teacher in a Catholic school), was involved in an auto accident on her way to work. Despite Cathy's concern for Meg, when she learned that Meg was not hurt physically she started her teaching for the day.

During first period Cathy's principal came to her classroom, inquired about Meg's condition (and that of her auto), then told her that he had enlisted the help of a replacement so that Cathy was free to pack up her books and go to Meg. Later Cathy commented: "I felt very good being on the staff of a Catholic school." At times membership in an educational institution and membership in a community of faith seep into one another.

Two phenomena in particular call for interrelating educational institutions (schools, colleges, universities) and communities of faith (people coming together for worship, service, mutual support). One is the historical fact that religious movements, not only worldwide ones such as Islam, Judaism, and Christianity, but also local-centered people and charismatic groups, have tended to assume responsibility not only for the religious instruction of the group but also for the whole education of children and students from nursery through graduate programs. The second phenomenon is more particular to Catholic Christianity. Over the course of centuries, through such leadership personnel as Basil and Macrina in the East and Augustine and Benedict in the West, communities of vowed religious and ordained priests became the educators not only of their own members but also of the whole Catholic body. As these communities have decreased in number, especially in the last half century, the ministry of educating has been taken up by the laity.

My reflections on the interrelationship between faith and education cluster under five foci:

1. Church: how necessary is community as an expression of faith?
2. God: how do we assess the passage from a universal divine presence of God to the emergence of a tribal deity claimed as its own by a chosen community of believers?
3. Catholic schools: how does a school founded on Catholic Christian faith continue its mandate to the local and universal faith communities?
4. Ministry: by what norms do Catholic school administrators rate passing or failing grades?
5. Moving forward: is it a time to zig or a time to zag?

First, Church: how necessary is community in expressing one's faith? How church and faith interrelate follows a continuum. At one end we have an exclusive view of church, that is, one particular church and one alone is necessary for union with God. In the words of Cyprian of Carthage in the mid-third century, "the one who does not have the church as mother cannot have God as father." At the other end the understanding of church is inclusive, that is, people view church as a gift that is available through the mediation of all religious traditions. In the classic Christian text of the first century, "God wishes all to be saved and to come to the knowledge of the truth" (I Tm 2:14). At various stations along the continuum line, just about all religious traditions consider faith community to be a source of union with God. They are increasingly reluctant to engage in debate about "the one true church."

In Catholic Christianity on this topic we are witnessing a paradigmatic shift of enormous proportions. We are moving from an exclusive perspective that sees salvation as a privileged gift through the Catholic Church to an understanding of salvation as an invitation extended to all humankind of goodwill. On the relationship of church and faith we are moving beyond the ecumenical vocabulary of half a century ago to an all-inclusive view. We experience this paradigmatic shift, it seems to me, especially in the living faith of groups of Catholic Christians, particularly in such areas as personal morality, marital values, and social justice.

Second, God: how do we assess the passage from a universal divine presence of God to the emergence of a tribal deity claimed as its own by a chosen community of believers? Sports announcer and former big league catcher Joe Garagiola tells this story about himself. A batter for a team against whom he was playing would bless himself before stepping into the batter's box. Garagiola kidded him with the remark: "Why don't you let God sit back and enjoy the game?" There is some truth in his statement, but it should be more nuanced. Prayer is more than asking that the sun will get in the centerfielder's eyes. St. Ignatius Loyola is said to have advised that we should pray as if everything depended on God and act as if everything depended on our human selves.

Belief is traditionally tripartite: a) what a community of faith holds to be true; b) how members express this belief in sign and symbol; and c) the shared code of behavior by which members live. This chapter tries to go beyond this tripartite understanding of belief to a more basic stance vis-à-vis God present in each of our lives.

By "belief" is not meant, at least primarily, acceptance of a body of religious truths such as those affirmed in a creed or catechism or sacred writings, or patterns of prayer and worship as expressed in a faith community's sacramental system, or a code of conduct such as that articulated in the Ten Commandments. A better word for what I intend by "belief" is "faith," except for the fact that "faith" does not have a verb form in ordinary English. I include here treatment of these levels of belief because in Catholic schools a fair number of teachers, parents, and young persons themselves confuse them, and thus make more difficult stating and achieving the school's or college's religious goals and objectives.

I admit that I am torn when I read the sacred scriptures, compose a catechesis from them, or hear them proclaimed during the church's liturgy. They are rich in insight, persuasive for the mind and heart, claimed by Israel as their own. As a sign that this is a dialogue of faith with the Lord, the people of Israel attributed them to their greatest leaders: Abraham for faith, Moses for history, David for poetry, Solomon for wisdom, prophets such as Isaiah or Hosea for reminders how we should be living out our covenant with Yahweh. To some extent, we can parallel this list with women of Israel's covenant, such as Ruth and Naomi. Further, we see a similar pattern in the men and women of the Christian community and in their scriptures. What they have in common is an avowal of belief that God is our god, that other gods are false gods. In anthropological terms, God becomes a tribal god who, yes, owns us, but whom we also own as our own. Is that true faith or accurate theology? Clearly God is other than a tribal deity, but how can God be addressed more fittingly?

Further, I am torn not so much when I hear the scriptures appeal to God as though God were a tribal deity answering prayers as when I read in the daily newspaper or watch on the evening news how religious belief is politicized and militarized. For many traditions in both East and West, the God in whom they believe has increasingly evolved into a tribal deity. A tribal deity fights on the side of its believers, rewards those who suffer in combat, and punishes those who sacrifice for the other side.

The health and happiness of the inhabitants of this planet should not be put at risk for the sake of crusades or holy wars. It is for historians to judge whether Urban II was right or wrong in the late eleventh century when he called for the first crusade with a "God wills it." Today, it seems to me, it is neither moral nor responsible to claim that God, whether God be Allah or Yahweh or the Father of Our Lord Jesus Christ, wills our modern wars.

My third focus is Catholic schools: how does a school founded on Catholic Christian faith continue its mandate to the local and universal faith communities?

Through family and school, through parish and diocese, through seminaries and religious life, my generation of Catholic Christians in the United States has been the product of socialization. This process continues today, but with a different vocabulary. In the mid-twentieth century, at a postwar period of numerical strength, vowed religious and ordained priests staffed Catholic educational institutions. Their worldview was one of ministry. Its influence has continued into the present, as can be seen in the mission statements which grace the lobby walls at the main entrance of so many Catholic schools.

In the second half of the twentieth century the decline in the number of vowed and ordained Catholic personnel had at least three effects. First, Catholic parishes, dioceses, and religious communities struggled to maintain the schools into which they had invested so much of their limited resources. Second, the vowed and ordained explored new arenas for their apostolic energies, such as houses of prayer, media communication, and computer-aided instruction. Third, and most important for our topic, a transition has been taking place in the staffing of the schools. For the most part, laypersons are now the teachers and administrators.

This difference is important because, although lay and religious personnel may be likeminded, often they do not think alike. As mentioned above, in expressing how they understand what they are doing in schools, the vowed and the ordained still incline toward the vocabulary of "vocation" and "mission." In ranking their top ten values laypersons are more likely to head their list with "professional competence."

There is evidence for this diversity of paradigms in the options that teachers take when they are offered freedom of choice. They gravitate toward secular disciplines in what courses they take, in what books they read, in what projects they assign and mentor.

We are tempted to set the humanistic and the religious over against one another, as do at times classical religious authors such as Thomas à Kempis and some contemporary writers. Yet, there is another way. We can see them as enriching one another, as two dimensions in the academic growth of the one person.

We can phrase this section in terms of problem or gift. Is an integrated religious/humanistic education a gift or a burden? Christian education comes down firmly on the side of gift. As a consequence of our faith in the Incarnate Word, we search for, welcome, and celebrate all that is human.

In the light of a half century of learning and of helping others to learn, I would like to image the teaching/learning process in the metaphors of adoptive agent and of midwife. These two metaphors wander a bit from this chapter's topic, but they have helped me find direction in the path I have followed.

I function as adoptive agent in that I invite young people freely to make their own the insights and ideas which other thinkers have already brought to birth. My input aims to present the wisdom of my discipline in the clearest and most appealing light. Books serve to put students in contact with key writers in the field. Guided assignments are intended to make sure that students have read and understood and made their own the mental offspring of the best minds on a topic.

As a midwife, I try to assist young people as they give birth to the thoughts of their own minds and the values of their own hearts. Sometimes the labor is painful, yet the issue is joyful. This midwifery takes place by my helping students to internalize and to personalize what they are studying. Their receptivity to books and lectures hopefully is active and creative through critical reflection, discussion, and composition. The end term of our combined efforts should enable the young person to claim: "This I know, this I value, this is my own."

My fourth focus is ministry: by what norms do Catholic school administrators rate passing or failing grades?

Today the world of education is one of testing, observing, improving. If our area to be evaluated is the spirituality of Catholic schools, by what yardstick do we measure how well or how poorly they are doing?

First of all they are schools. A school is a school is a school. It is a structured collection of persons, usually in a designated place, where people teach and learn according to the disciplines that have come to be recognized as worth pursuing. There are similar agencies that overlap schools in their purpose, but they should not be confused with school. Examples of these similar agencies can be church or temple, scouting, organized athletics, bands and orchestras, etc. In evaluating the spirituality of their schools, the first question that administrators have to ask themselves is, "Are we running a good school, given the resources available to us?"

Second, these schools are Catholic (with both upper and lower case). We have to include in our evaluation what is distinctively Catholic about them. Sociologists have provided us a methodology to isolate what is different about one group as distinctive from another: intensity factor. A subject responds to an item, such as prayer or scripture reading, not by a simple "yes" or "no," but according to its strength as "very much," "very little," or some degree of intensity in between. Thus, again by way of example, both Protestants and Catholics may be said to be at home with their bodies, but Catholics more so. What the text asserts here is that the Catholic tradition harbors, even celebrates, what is diverse, even ambiguous. In the poem "Pied Beauty" of priest-poet Gerard Manley Hopkins, we hear praise for this insight in his cry of praise, "Glory be to God for dappled things."

At the heart of the Catholic tradition is living with, even celebrating, the tension of both/and rather than resolving it in favor of either/or. Both/and rather than either/or is a commonplace in Catholic doctrine and theology: God *both* transcendent *and* immanent, the Word *both* divine *and* incarnate, both sovereign grace and human freedom, the Eucharist both as sacrament and as sacrifice. It extends beyond doctrine and theology: both a vertical cultivating of inner union with God in prayer and a horizontal serving of men and women spiritually and corporally; both canonization for our sainted elite and compassion for ourselves as sinners; public devotions at the risk of superstition, sacramental symbols at the risk of magic; both celebrating human sexuality in a sacrament and giving special honor to celibacy and virginity for the kingdom's sake; trying to be both priestly and prophetic, developmental and liberational, incarnational and eschatological; both reverence for life here and hope for life hereafter; a strong but qualified yes to human philosophy, human culture, human folkways.

Finally, the schools are meant to be Christian. It is in this arena we still experience both most tension and most collaboration between the "educational institutions" and "communities of faith," around which this chapter revolves. Consider how they influence one another with regard to social standing and financial resources, leadership and authority, and gender and marital status. We could examine and reflect upon each of these dynamics insofar as they form chapters in our personal and corporate stories.

I would prefer, however, to reach back into early Christian history and hear what it has to tell us about ministry and education in the faith community. To provide a focus for our reflection, I would look to some vignettes we have of Christian women.

How familiar are most Catholics with these four Christian women of the first century: Priscilla, whose husband was a tent maker in Rome, Corinth, and

Ephesus; Phoebe, who served as a deaconess not far from Corinth; Mary, the mother of Mark and aunt of Barnabas, in whose house in Jerusalem the first Christians used to meet; and the better known Mary, mother of Jesus, among his earliest and most constant disciples?

What did these and other women do in the first-century communities? What was their role? For the most part, women gathered together the Christian community through a ministry of hospitality; they instructed people in private through a ministry of teaching; they stayed with Jesus and his disciples through a ministry of familial fidelity.

Take, for example, what we know of Priscilla. She and her husband, Aquila, were forced to leave Rome because they were Jewish. This turned out to be fortunate, because they went to Corinth and just happened to be there when Paul arrived to start a Christian community. Paul came to live with them and teamed up with Aquila in making tents. A year and a half later, when Paul moved on to Ephesus, Priscilla and Aquila went with him and set up a household that became a center for the young Christian community.

One day a very intelligent Jewish Christian named Apollos arrived in Ephesus from Egypt. He had been instructed in the way of the Lord, but he still had much more to learn. When Priscilla and Aquila heard him speaking fearlessly about Jesus in the local synagogue, they invited him to their home and instructed him in greater detail about their faith. Apollos went on to become an important teacher in the Christian communities. In this way, Priscilla and Aquila blended the two ministries of hospitality and of teaching.

We may be tempted to look for parallels in faith communities today. That is a worthwhile enterprise. These ministries still abound in church and world. We can make them our own and share them with others. Yet, the search may be somewhat empty, because there were, technically, no lay leaders in the first century. That category did not yet exist; it developed in later centuries. As the early church structured itself in ways to accomplish its mission, gifts were widespread, but as Paul reminded the enthusiastic Christian community in Corinth, "To each individual the manifestation of the Spirit is given for some benefit" (1 Cor 12:7).

Moving forward is my final focus: is it a time to zig or a time to zag?

It is difficult to project the future. It is especially difficult when that future is happening all around us. The difficulty intensifies when we recognize that for some scenes we are more than the audience of a drama someone else has written. Some of the dialogue, some of the action, is our very own.

The task is one of discernment. Through prayer, reflection, and consultation we try to make out the way God is leading us and the means we are offered to get there. As a church, our journey in faith has been limited. We have lectured into the air, and often the wind has carried away our words. We have written on the sands of the beach, and the incoming tides have washed away what we have written.

Against the backdrop of our corporate history, may we employ a few images more to illustrate and clarify the interrelationship between educational institutes and communities of faith:

Zigs and Zags

Being a lay leader, as a catechist or religious educator, has been like crossing a body of water in a sailboat rather than in a rowboat. With a rowboat, we can set our sights on a destination on the far shore and head directly toward it by pulling evenly on both oars or by adjusting our rowing according to wind, tide, and current. Ideally, we make our way in as straight a line as possible. With a sailboat, it often makes better sense to take advantage of these same winds and run with them for a while, even though they may threaten to lead us too far off course. Then, either because wind or tide or current shifts, or because we recognize we are getting farther off course than is wise, we use sail and rudder to tack in a different, a balancing direction.

Evangelization and Humanization

The topic most hotly debated in the first decade after the Second Vatican Council concerned the mission of the church in the modern world. It dominated the agenda for the episcopal synods over which Pope Paul VI presided. The contrasting images are clear. The first-world churches favored evangelization, that is, the freedom to preach the gospel in word and sacrament. The third-world churches looked to humanization as the task of the church, that is, to improve the quality of life, especially of the poor and oppressed, so continuing the mission of Jesus. Pope Paul VI offered a resolution to the question by affirming that the essential mission of the church is evangelization, but that it is closely linked in many ways with humanization.

Leaven and Lever

A final set of images can close these clusters of reflections on educational institutions and communities of faith, that of leaven and lever. They correspond to the manner of response that a community of faith gives to a world of human values. Leaven is a *yes*. It penetrates from within. It looks upon the world the way that God saw it when it was first created: "God found it very good" (Gn 1:31). Lever is a more reserved, more hesitant, more prophetic response. It echoes the words put on the lips of Jesus, who would not even pray for this world (Jn 17:9).

In the rhythm of ordinary life, school and its books get closed for a while. Prayer and worship punctuate our times and seasons, but we usually do not make a career of them. There is something within ourselves that awakens us, keeping us alive to ourselves and to one another. Since in faith we recognize this inner drive as spirit, may we not link it with spirituality, a special kind of spirituality, that of lay leadership, that meets a special need of the church today?

I look to the scriptures to clarify my thinking, but what I find only increases my confusion. My eye is caught by the story of Mary and Martha, the two sisters of Lazarus, the close friend whom Jesus loved and later brought back to life. They are having a meal together. Mary sits at the feet of Jesus, listening to his teaching. Martha is doing all the preparing and serving. She complains about this to Jesus: "Lord, do you not care that my sister has left me by myself to do the serving?" In his response Jesus sides with Mary: "Mary has chosen the better part and it will not be taken from her" (Lk 10:38–42).

But wait a moment. Isn't Jesus more restating the problem than solving it? Aren't the lay leaders in the church still mainly to be found among its Marthas? Are we urging them, especially the young, toward monastic piety? These statements have their truth on all counts. Yet, if we turn them around they still have their truth. To be vital and flexible is of the very essence of the church. How is leadership to navigate the bark of Peter? Where does it zig and where does it zag? How do we discern for our decision making a proper reliance upon *both/and* over against *either/or*? And to introduce a final image to describe the dynamism of the church, how do we integrate time devoted to making plans face-to-face (thus building community) with energy spent outward shoulder-to-shoulder (thus sharing in a mission)?

These reflections on how educational institutions and faith communities interrelate leave several questions unanswered. By way of a forward-looking summary, I voice a few of these questions and suggest responses to them:

1. What are the bases for proposing as a kind of thesis that the educational and the religious overlap, share a common ground, complement one another? Their histories constantly merged them, their understandings of the human person opened them to dialogue, their belief in God as present and active enabled them to pray and worship as a community.

2. Why don't we imitate what has sometimes been proposed among some Catholic Christians in history, that is, reserve the cultivation of "spirituality" to vowed religious and ordained clerics? That is precisely what we are trying not to do. Our ideal is rather that all members of faith communities share together the spirituality to which all are called, according to the gifts and talents that are theirs.

3. It is sometimes said sadly that Catholic Christianity as we have known it is dying, if it is not already dead. How accurate are such prognoses?

Hopefully even now the Holy Spirit is bringing fresh life to us as we continuously reform and renew ourselves.

4. Yet, there are counterforces having their influence in our society. We can ask the question prophetically put to each new generation of men and women of faith and intelligence: Is there no way out? Yes, there is a way out. It is a spirituality for all persons, with a particular appeal to and for lay leaders.

5. What distinctive words can sum up the spirituality of lay leaders? This spirituality should be as deep as individual personal faith, as broad as communal bonding, as high as God transcendent, and as near as God immanent. We can learn from the first experience of church in the way that two disciples met the Risen Lord on the road to Emmaus. It is true that the first encounter with Jesus as Risen featured the leadership of the early community. Yet, interestingly enough, those whom today we would call ordinary lay Christians, such as the women at the tomb and the two disciples on the way to Emmaus, were chosen to exemplify this extraordinary spirituality.

REFLECTION QUESTIONS

1. What are the implications of the paradigmatic shifts occurring in the Catholic community today for the faculty and students of your school, relative to your understanding of the Church's role in salvation?

2. What are the implications for the prayer life of your school, relative to your understanding of how God relates to the Church and to persons of other faiths?

3. Using the categories developed by John Nelson, in what areas would you give yourself and yours a passing grade? A failing grade? (You might also ask some members of your school community to grade you in these areas.)

12

Power and Authority: Rooted in and Fashioned by the Spirit

Mary Daniel Turner, S.N.D. de N.

Power and authority—these terms delineate a minefield in today's world. When those who exercise power do so without a firm grounding in human rights and Gospel values, Mary Daniel Turner, S.N.D.deN., points out, abuse and injustice too often result. Turner's discussion of power and authority refreshingly widens our perspective and offers leaders a space to probe their personal beliefs and behaviors on the topic. Her contemplative approach reminds us that power is a spiritual energy and a sacred trust, a gift of God that demands constant tending. As those in a role of authority (vested power), leaders are invited into partnership with the Spirit in service of the mission.

> God's love has been poured into our hearts
> through the Holy Spirit who has been given to us.
>
> —Rom 5:5

INTRODUCTION

Power and authority: terms pregnant with a complex of meanings, values, and attitudes! Like all words, these two terms carry centuries of variegated experiences, stories of multiple relationships, narratives of personal biographies, and chronicles of organizational and societal life. The terms power and authority, and the meanings we ascribe to them, undoubtedly shape the texture and character of relationships, interpersonal and institutional. When mined, these terms disclose what we believe and what we value; explored, they also reveal worldviews that shape our perceptions; examined, they uncover the ethos generated by the dynamics of power and authority. Yes, these two terms are mines waiting to be explored. The exploration will tell us much about ourselves and the contexts we use in understanding, embodying, and evaluating our myriad uses of both power and authority.

ORIENTATION

An Invitation to Reflect

Before you begin to read this chapter I invite you, the reader, to reflect for a moment on the terms power and authority. Consider, "What do these terms mean to me? What do they *not* mean?" Reflect on a personal experience of authority or power. How would you describe this experience? Was it a source of life for you and others? Why? Or was it disempowering? Why? Identify the energies you felt within yourself during the experience: were they wholesome or toxic? In addition, what were the external conditions that played a part in the experience? Does this reflection illuminate your understanding of power and authority?

I suggest this inquiry because, as we well know, our respective journeys make a difference in how we name, understand, embody, and exchange power and authority. For example, at a meeting of the laity with Pope John Paul II a spokeswoman remarked, "Unity, not division, is our goal; service, *not* power, is our mission." Why dissociate service and power? Why separate power and mission? Similarly, during a meeting in Rome with the U.S. hierarchy, Cardinal Innocenti, Prefect Emeritus of the Congregation for the Clergy, asserted that women who want to be ordained are motivated by a desire for power, *not* service. Why do those who have institutional power (authority to govern) speak pejoratively of power? Why do they place power and service in opposition?

Initial Observations

Definitely we must not allow ourselves to flee from the power that is ours, personally and collectively. On the one hand, we must resist all temptations to deny that we have, and that we need, power. On the other, we must transcend the propensity to act as though we do not want power. The denials and pretense effectively dispense us from our responsibilities as moral agents: we call into question our capacity to make moral judgments and decisions. The denial of power, personal and corporate, permits us to be uncritical and unquestioning about uses of power. If we claim we do not have power, we cannot then hold either ourselves or others responsible for how power is exercised. Negating the power we have, we cast ourselves as victims and acquiesce in the victimization of others. Consciously or unconsciously, we reinforce systems of oppression, domination, and exploitation. In the words of Rollo May, we cultivate a kind of pseudoinnocence when we deny that we have power. We opt for powerlessness. Inevitably, violence is spawned.[1]

Tragically then, when we deny that we have power and abdicate the responsibility to use it, we betray ourselves and others. We become alienated from ourselves; we become estranged from others, even from God. Knowingly or unknowingly, we participate in dehumanizing environments and relationships. Rather than engage in the daunting tasks power and authority exact, we choose impotence.

Neither can we allow ourselves to internalize understandings and definitions of power that recognize only its demonic embodiments, for example, a designation that power corrupts. This orientation often serves to legitimate autocratic exercises of power. We determine that only a few *special people* can be trusted with the authority power bestows. We even allege that some, usually minorities and women, need to be protected from the evil implicit in power. Sometimes we even assume that those denied access to institutional power are grateful. We further assume that they do not want to deal with the temptations, the tensions, and the conflicts that often accompany the exercise of power.

However, abuses and negative definitions of power do not justify the abdication of personal and corporate use of power. In fact, biased definitions and the abuses of power make an uncompromising claim on us to invest in creating alternative definitions and embodiments of power and authority. The prevailing and unenlightened approach to power compels us to articulate a *context* for understanding power and authority that births a wholesome ethic and ethos of power and authority.[2]

CONTEXT: THE GIFT OF THE SPIRIT TO THE CHRISTIAN COMMUNITY

Thus, critical to any analysis of power and authority is our individual and collective orientation to these two realities in our daily lives. What we think and feel and judge about authority and power will fashion how we use, or abuse, or fail to use power and authority. Similarly, it will determine whether we hold ourselves and others accountable for exercises of power. Indispensable then to a wholesome appropriation of power and authority is the context out of which we derive their meaning and purpose.

The Scriptures are replete with images of the Spirit of God as the source of power, of energy, of transformation. In Genesis, the Spirit moves over the face of the waters, creation happens; God blows the Spirit into Adam, a human is born. The Spirit anoints the prophets, God's message is proclaimed; the Spirit overshadows Mary, Jesus is conceived. The Spirit anoints Jesus, his ministry begins; the Spirit descends on the apostles and disciples in the Upper Room, the church is begotten. Throughout the ages, the Spirit has summoned peoples of different races and creeds and nations to oneness, to union with God and with one another—to community.[3] Ceaselessly, the Spirit dwelling within all creation, and not limited to any one church or group, summons and gifts us for newness of life. Persistently, the Spirit invites transformation, personal and corporate. Where the Spirit is welcomed, good things happen.

Undeniably our interior dispositions render us finely tuned or stone-deaf to the movements of the Spirit. Alert with an open mind, or sedated by a closed one; sensitive to voices that cry out to us, or tone-deaf to the messages of others; alert to the differing contexts of diverse situations, or domesticated by a single perspective, our responsiveness to the daily stirrings of the Spirit makes all the difference in the kind of Spirit-agents we incarnate. Similarly too, receptivity to the Spirit, or the lack thereof, influences (if not determines) the kind of systems and institutions we construct.

However, when imaginatively faithful to the ministry of leadership, we root and fashion our exercise of power and authority in the grace of the Spirit's indwelling within us and within our universe. Compelled by this indwelling, we pledge ourselves to lay bare the ethic and the ethos of power and authority that govern us and the institutions of which we are a small yet significant part. For it is incumbent on church leaders to craft mission statements, formulate policies, determine priorities, establish structures and procedures, adopt budgets, and design evaluative mechanisms as copartners of the Spirit.

POWER: A SACRED TRUST

Even if we accept the indwelling of the Spirit as the context for our understanding and exercising power and authority, we still must ask how we understand power. Simply stated, power is energy. Not a univocal term, power has many and diverse embodiments. Its numerous manifestations can be named; its myriad effects can be judged.

For example, daily we experience the energy of electrical power; we know its effects. Tragically, through Hiroshima and Chernobyl, we know the destructive energy of nuclear power. We feel the energy of economic power as it affects the commonweal or woe of the body politic. We experience, sometimes simultaneously, both the life-giving and death-dealing energies of political power. At home and abroad we witness the power at work in globalization as it affects the cultural distinctiveness of all peoples, no matter how primitive or sophisticated. We are never not affected by the diverse energies different embodiments of power beget.

As earth dwellers and members of a cosmic community, then, we must acknowledge the awesome responsibility inherent in the use of power and authority. A most fragile yet paradoxically treacherous energy, power demands tending. Its embodied possibilities require attention. Gifted with the energy power generates, we are accountable to God for the stewardship of this most wondrous trust.

MORAL POWER

In this chapter we consider specifically *moral* power. A spiritual energy, moral power has its source in the Spirit's rejuvenating and steadfast presence. It gifts us to attend responsibly to the character, purpose, meaning, and effects of power's various embodiments. Remarkably, moral power facilitates the discovery of what God is asking and gracing us to do and to be. At the same time, the quality of our response to moral power molds our values; the fidelity of our response shapes our character, individually and collectively. The quality and the character of responses to moral power likewise generate an ethic and an ethos of power that distinguish a people. Moral power has the incredible potential to engender finely tuned women and men who appreciate their elemental kinship with the human and cosmic community. Similarly, moral power, responded to, brings about men and women who apprehend that little in life is ever wholly private: one's most personal spaces and an institution's most private spheres have import for the public weal. In other words, moral power, understood as the grace proffered by the indwelling Spirit of God, exacts (1) a commitment to image the common good; (2) a pledge to take steps to bring it about; and (3) choices—personal and institutional—compatible with the *image* and the *pledge*. When responsive to the indwelling Spirit, we experience the persistent call to be moral agents who copartner with the Spirit in making visible and credible the reality that indeed God intends the fullness of life for all beings.

AUTHORITY: VESTED POWER

As copartners with the Spirit, and as relational beings, we organize to advance our dreams and hopes and aspirations. We articulate a vision to which we freely commit ourselves. We take measures to institutionalize hoped-for outcomes. In doing so we assign specific and limited power—*authority*—to designated persons. Through differentiated roles we entrust authority to one or few or many. The roles, as it were, become the media through which we embody, express, exchange, structure, systematize, and channel authority for the fulfillment of the organization's mission. Both those who entrust authority and those entrusted with authority pledge themselves to an ethic of power rooted in and fashioned by the Spirit.

Clearly then we must understand and appreciate the value of roles as unique instruments of authority: they help bring about the purpose and meaning as well as the spirit and mission of an institution. Carefully described, roles identify (1) the functions of a service (specific responsibilities accompanied by a concomitant authority); (2) the expectations linked with specific roles (the anticipated scope of the service); and (3) the obligations of those served by roles. Unquestionably, roles, and the authority they bestow, serve as formidable catalysts for the realization of an institution's most cherished ambitions.

Yet, roles can lure us into believing we *are* our roles. Beguiled, we are seduced. Foolishly we derive our identity from roles, even when not functioning from them. Mechanically we think and feel, perceive and act, observe and judge, not from the interiority that the Spirit's indwelling creates, but from ungrounded role expectations and/or from our unexamined ego needs. We act as though the authority entrusted to our care is our possession to be used according to personal whims or prejudices. Thus seduced, we betray the very purpose for which roles exist, namely, the exercise of authority for the well-being of an institution in relation to both those serving in and those served by the institution. Anesthetized to the indwelling of the Spirit, we become so politically correct and socially acceptable that inevitably our hearts wither; our minds become numb; our deeds routinized; our spirit dwarfed. Without knowing it, we squander or abuse or neglect the authority placed in our care. We forget that authority vested in roles is intended to be a reliable resource for promoting the moral agency of a group. We forget that authority is intended to be a graced resource for the Spirit to speak to the community about its deepest longings and burning passion.

When we appreciate roles, however, and the authority vested in them as sources for the Spirit to summon us to fidelity, we stay attuned to the possibilities roles offer for transformation, both personal and institutional. We respect roles. Valuing the raw material roles provide for the daily birthing of institutional life, we depend on our partnership with the Spirit to carry out the roles. Thus, we have confidence that however fallibly we fulfill our respective roles, the Spirit will transform our creaturely uses of power into wholesome embodiments of authority.

Partnering with the Spirit, we intuit that roles participate in the painstaking and delicate work of a midwife. Like midwifery, the exercise of authority (through differentiated roles) calls for judicious attention—that is, sensitivity to movements, changes, and rhythms. Like midwifery, authority roles also demand that we learn stillness, that we take time, that we accept the fact that we are not in control. Partnering with the Spirit in the midwifery service that authority begets, we appreciate that we are graced to respond with exquisite attention to the bewildering process of institutions' never-ending births. We cherish authority as a wellspring of the Spirit.

TASKS FOR THOSE WHO PARTNER WITH THE SPIRIT

Institutionalizing Power

Collaboratively, those entrusted with authority must take leadership in the institutionalizing of an organization's moral power. Not the work of a lone individual, or a chosen few, the institutionalizing of power requires the goodwill of both those entrusted with authority *and* the other members of the group. The former never cease being members; and the latter never cease being potential informal leaders. In fact, the relationships and interactions between and among named leaders (those in authority) and informal leaders (those recognized, for example, for their knowledge and experience, or for their competency and skills) definitely contribute to the ethical persona of a group. The quality of these relationships and interactions reveals the depth of their responses to the indwelling of the Spirit within and among them. When steadfastly attentive to the grace of the Spirit, lay leaders: (1) cooperate with one another to create *conditions* that ensure both individual and institutional well-being; (2) collaborate to promote *environments* that nurture both personal and corporate growth; (3) work together to design *structures* that facilitate interpersonal and systemic interactions; and (4) labor as a team to formulate *policies* that promote personal integrity and organizational cohesion. An organization marked by life-giving conditions, a wholesome environment, easily accessible and workable structures, and fair policies gives witness to women and men purposefully responsive to the power and grace of the Spirit's indwelling. Such an organization makes visible and credible that indeed the reign of God is its consuming passion.

Decision Making

Undoubtedly, the skills of those entrusted with authority play a significant part in whether decision making is in fact a spiritual activity. Those with designated authority have the distinct privilege of stewarding decision making in ways that reverence the work of the Spirit in the life of an organization. Indispensable to the fashioning of spirit-filled decisions is the ability of those in authority to engage others in the process of decision making in ways that foster the integrity of the members and of the institution.

In designing decision-making activities, it is imperative then that those exercising authority cultivate *conditions* that invite critical listening and honest inquiry. It is equally imperative that they foster *environments* that allow for the emergence of tensions, and even of conflict. Of similar significance is the ability of those in authority to develop *processes* that welcome into decision-making procedures each and every voice, no matter how differently oriented or conflicted. Critical listening and inquiry, differing perspectives and tensions, and inclusive processes provide the groundwork for decision making that respects a group's mission, honors the inviolate worth of each person, elicits the collective wisdom of the members, and takes into account the claims of those served.

When these components come together, an organization learns to be *at home* with complexities and ambiguities. It begins to trust that chaos can be the raw material for creativity. So inclined, an organization intuits that the Spirit "is not against chaos, nor, as many claim, does chaos make God's creative action impossible."[4] When the art of decision making is rooted in and fashioned by the Spirit, we learn, not simply from history but from our lived experiences, that the Spirit of God is an ever-immanent birthing presence. We are not alone in the work of institutionalizing power as graced energy; we delight in our cocreativity with the Spirit!

A CALL TO CONVERSION

No matter how appealing an ethic of power rooted in and fashioned by the Spirit, it is not easily achieved. It doesn't simply happen. It requires hard work; it demands steadfastness; it exacts courage. It calls for conversion.

The Transformation of a Western Worldview[5]

Socialized in a western worldview, we must liberate ourselves from the dominant western way of using power to control. We have become too skilled in *rank-ordering* relationships, such as men and women; white and black; thinking and feeling; clerics and laity. Adept in establishing *hierarchies,* we identify one of the pair as superior; the other as inferior. For example (although not always consciously), we rank men superior to women; whites better than blacks; thinking more trustworthy than feeling; and the clergy more spirit-filled than the laity. Prone to dichotomize rather than to note distinctions, we fail to make connections. For all intents and purposes, we ignore the radical oneness that inheres in creation.

Ingenious in rationalizing this order, we easily put down or out those who are different from us. We decide they are deficient. We then discount their perceptions, trivialize their analyses or insights, belittle their customs or practices, and dismiss their ways of interacting and making decisions. In fine, we disrespect their culture. We write them off. More often than not, power embedded in a western worldview is used to control, to exclude, and to divide. Its uses maintain the status quo. Thus, it is most difficult for the Spirit to break through barriers that patriarchal and matriarchal systems of a western worldview establish.[6]

When power is used to control, it breeds a toxic ethos. It engenders an ethic of authority that legitimates domination, rewards passivity, encourages compliance, and demands unquestioning obedience. As leaders, it is imperative that in our exercise of power we free ourselves from the matriarchal and patriarchal prisons that a western worldview constructs.

However, we don't simply take off one worldview and put on another. Painstakingly we engage in the task of acknowledging we are a part of a *man-made* history that is partial and biased (even as this chapter is). We admit that knowledge can and does change. We concede that new and different experiences can alter and even supplant what we once accepted as sacred and certain and permanent. We welcome the personal and corporate transformation that new knowledge may evoke. We know a welcoming spirit is indispensable for leaders who desire to stay attentive to the movements of the Spirit.

Freeing ourselves from a western hierarchal bias, we begin to recognize that differences are evidences of pluralism. However faintly, we glimpse that pluralism is not an enemy of order or unity. It is not antithetical to community. It is, rather, a fundamental principle of creation. We cannot simply decide to take it or leave it. It is not something that occasionally we tolerate. In fact, the worldview emerging from contemporary ecological insights and the new physics compels us to make friends with pluralism and the differences it generates.

From the perspective of the new cosmology, pluralism (the holding up of differences) and unity (the holding together of differences) are partners, not competitors. Awakened by the perspective of the new physics, we begin to intuit, however diffidently, that pluralism reflects the lavish largesse of God's creative Spirit. It is imperative that those who have authority promote pluralism, not simply tolerate it, much less attempt to suppress it.

Thus, pluralism challenges us to develop the capacity to see all persons and things as interactively connected, not as isolated and competing phenomena. It invites us to approach each day's epiphanies of reality as multi-centered, multifaceted, and multidimensional, each having its own integrity and yet intimately related. Pluralism likewise calls us to look at experiences and events and situations holistically (not as unrelated happenings); it pushes us to become skilled in articulating distinctions (not constructing dichotomies). Pluralism urges us to dare originality and risk taking (not to stay wedded to the security of conventional wisdom and the status quo). Befriending pluralism, we give up closed and inflexible systems. We embrace open and adaptive systems, an indispensable quality for church leaders responsive to the movements of the Spirit.

Espousing both pluralism and unity is an undeniable challenge for those who have been entrusted with authority and who have the power to make a difference. It is a clarion and urgent call to conversion.

Living in a Global Village[7]

Repeatedly we are told we live in a global village, a most difficult place for subscribers of a western worldview to feel at home. Yet, in many instances, that village exists right where we live and work and socialize. Many parishes and other diverse catholic institutions reflect the makeup of a global community: people of different races from diverse nations; from different ethnic backgrounds; from varied church affiliations, or no affiliation; and sometimes (but all too rarely) from mixed economic classes. However, where we are is the best place to learn how to clothe ourselves with a new worldview. Where we are is where we must learn the disciplines and skills and virtues to copartner with the Spirit in the embrace of a global community.

When, as leaders, we choose *to participate* in the well-being of the global village, and not simply be distant observers of it, we behave differently. We translate our western worldview into a global seeing that transforms myopic viewpoints, narrow perspectives, and biased perceptions. Awakened to a global seeing (an alternative to matriarchal or patriarchal perspectives), we grasp that whatever our skin color, our national identity, our ethnic heritage, our religious convictions, our economic status, none of these renders us superior. Pledged to be global citizens where we are and with those with whom we rub elbows, we (who have been formed by a Western worldview) give up any claim to a superior niche in the village. Sensitized by a global vision, we respond to the summons to share power and authority as agents of the Spirit. We witness to the truth that those who are different from us are as fully graced by the Spirit to exercise power and authority as we are. The Spirit does not discriminate, and neither should we. Together we share power to work for the commonweal of this global village, a tiny spot in the household of God's universe.

Humility: An Indispensable Virtue for Embracing a
Worldview Distinguished by a Global Vision

Surrendering an old worldview and putting on a new one marked by a global vision is the work of folks at home with the Spirit's persistent calls to conversion. Attentive to the stirrings of the Spirit's movements, we are not astonished that we must forego the messianic compulsions that a western worldview has instilled in us. We are not surprised that moral maturing is a lifelong process. We make friends with our limitations, shortcomings, and deficiencies: we clothe ourselves with humility. Yet, we appreciate that we are not simply or only our insufficiencies and inadequacies. We are the dwelling place of the Spirit. Humbly we put our trust in the Spirit's promise: "A new heart I will give you and a new spirit I will put within you; and I will take out of your flesh the heart of stone and give you a heart of flesh. I will put my Spirit within you" (Ez 36:26–27). Even as creatures, we nevertheless have confidence in ourselves and in others.

Clothed with humility, we pledge ourselves to deal creatively with our propensity to control and to dominate when we have authority. For example, we will welcome the piece of truth each person is; we will welcome the collective wisdom of the community. When exercising authority, we will draw on both our radical oneness and the riches of pluralism. We will value, not resist, the fact that we *are* related; that we *are* interdependent; that we *need* one another.

Similarly, humility summons us, as bearers of authority, to recognize the deceptive power of self-serving ideologies and the part they play in hardening "hearts of stone." Building stones of the western worldview, ideologies trick us into believing that we possess the truth, that our way is the best, that our traditions are divinely sanctioned. Humility, however, alerts us to the fact that all human artifacts, whether the creation of the mind (like ideologies) or of the heart (like symbols) are simply that: creaturely. We need to hold them lightly. We need to give them up when invited to go beyond habits of mind and heart that enslave. Wondrously, humility graces us to acknowledge that we must be women and men for whom conversion is a way of life, not a rare expedition.

Institutions in the hands of leaders who have learned humility are especially graced. These institutions will be distinguished by an ethic and ethos of power rooted in and fashioned by the Spirit.

POSTSCRIPT

In one of her poems, "The Avowal,"[8] Denise Levertov reminds us of a most sobering yet reassuring faith conviction: the indwelling of the Spirit is pure gift. We don't earn it. We don't have a right to it. Our good actions do not make the Spirit available to us. Rather, the indwelling Spirit graces our efforts. Transformed, they become deeds consonant with God's reign. As Levertov says, "no effort earns that all-surrounding grace." How wondrous the transforming power of the Spirit, working in our lives and our institutions!

REFLECTION QUESTIONS

I end as I began, by inviting you to a reflection, this time both alone and with your colleagues and coworkers. As you think about this chapter, consider:

1. What challenged you in this chapter, and why? What called you beyond your current beliefs and convictions about power and authority, in particular, and why?
2. What did you find yourself resisting, and why? (Remember, the feeling of resistance is neither good nor bad. Usually the feeling illuminates something we value and that we feel may be threatened. This is a call to look at the value and to discover what the Spirit is asking of us: to hold onto the value, to let it go, or to refashion it. Like challenges, resistances, more often than not, are the movement of the Spirit at work in our hearts.)
3. What questions were answered as you read this chapter? What questions remain unanswered? What new questions emerged?
4. What steps might you take in your institution to work for an ethic and ethos of power rooted in and fashioned by the Spirit?

NOTES

1. Rollo May, *Power and Innocence* (New York: Dell, 1972), 51–57.

2. In the context of this chapter, I use *ethic* to signify a community's efforts to identify, define, and determine the values and principles that are to inform its lived faith; in other words, that are to shape the praxis of a community. I use *ethos* to signify the spirit or character or culture of an organization that a given ethic begets.

3. For a fuller treatment of the indwelling of the Spirit, see Elizabeth A. Johnson, *Truly Our Sister, A Theology of Mary in the Communion of Saints* (New York: Continuum, 2003), 78–79, 235–36, 251–54.

4. Robert Russell, "Contemplation and Science: Converging Streams and the Human Futures," paper presented at a Carmelite Seminar, Baltimore, 1990.

5. "For most of history, the task of imposing order on an unruly world was left to a few dominant powers, from Sargon of Mesopotamia in the twenty-fourth century B.C., through the empires of Asia and Europe, to the Cold War powers forty-three centuries later. For all that time, the idea of order was traditionally hierarchical and usually absolute. In the Middle Ages, 'world order' was a natural ladder in which men and women knew (or were supposed to know) their places before God and king. In the Modern Age, the idea of order became secular, rational and scientific—but remained hierarchical and largely absolute. The world's course was directed by European colonial powers and then the superpowers: in politics and alliances, in economics and development, in social trends and culture, and in war." Robin Wright and Doyle McManus, *Flashpoints: Promise and Peril in a New World* (New York: Fawcett Columbine, 1991), 218–19.

6. When I use the term *patriarchy*, I intend to signify that, in the abstract, men simply because of their gender are identified as normative, superior, and the determiners of values, structures, systems, etc., that govern a people. While individual men may not see themselves as such, patriarchy defines men as the source of what is of value; power and authority reside in men simply by the fact of their gender. Similarly, "matriarchy" identifies women as normative, superior, and the determiners of value. Simply by the fact of their gender, women are considered to be invested with power. In my use of the term, I intend to signify women's use of power in ways that bring about systemic injustice. Gerda Lerner (*The Creation of Patriarchy*, Oxford University Press, 1987) believes that no matriarchal society has ever existed, although some feminists disagree with this.

7. See the following for a reflection on the global village: Julian Filochowski, "A Theology of Protest in a Globalized World," paper presented at the Twenty-fifth Annual Conference of the National Justice and Peace Network, July 11, 2003. This article can be obtained from the United States Catholic Mission Association, 3029 Fourth Street, NE, Washington, DC, 20017 (e-mail: usmca@uscatholicmission.org or website: www.uscatholicmission.org).

8. Denise Levertov, *The Stream and the Sapphire: Selected Poems on Religious Themes* (New York: New Directions, 1997), 6.

13

Spiritual Leadership: The Leader as Formator and Mentor

Margaret Benefiel

Margaret Benefiel introduces us to three leaders who are seeking to live in sync with the Spirit. Mentors have nudged, challenged, and inspired them, so they in turn look for ways to pass on what they have received, forming and mentoring others for leadership. "The gift you have received, give freely" (Matt.10:8, adapted). From the stories of elementary and secondary school principals Benefiel crafts a portrait of the spiritual leader—encourager, torchbearer, carrier of the community as a whole—that will surely resonate with those who mentor and are being mentored in mission-focused institutions of all types.

INTRODUCTION

How do lay leaders of Catholic institutions keep the mission alive? How do they internalize the charism after the vowed religious have left? How do they ensure that the Catholicity of their institutions will be passed on to future generations? This chapter will consider the leader as formator and mentor, using as examples the stories of lay principals of Catholic elementary and secondary schools. It will examine their spiritual leadership as they keep the mission of their institutions alive.

Spiritual leadership, first and foremost, involves attending to the spiritual life of the group. Spiritual leaders find ways to celebrate the group's spiritual life, for example, on feast days and significant times on the institution's calendar. They introduce spiritual discernment into decision-making processes. They nurture opportunities for growth as a faith community.

Spiritual leaders mentor and form others—department heads, staff, board members, faculty, and those they serve. Leaders seek opportunities to pass on to others what they have learned about the mission of the institution. And they invite others to work shoulder-to-shoulder with them in leadership, seeking mutuality in leadership.

Spiritual leaders experience the asceticism of leadership. They run interference for those they lead and those they serve. They live without seeing immediate results from their work. They experience the strain of being a public person, always on view. They live with the loss resulting from the shift in relationships with their once peers.

Spiritual leaders understand formation and mentoring deeply. They themselves have often experienced extraordinary formation and mentoring, and they feel compelled to offer the same to others. They understand deeply how the Holy Spirit is a partner in the mentoring process, and they seek to be sensitive to the Holy Spirit's presence and movement.

The following stories of three New Jersey principals illustrate these themes.

PHILIP MEEHAN: ENCOURAGER

Philip Meehan, principal of St. Cassian's Elementary School (the school affiliated with St. Cassian's Parish) in Upper Montclair, New Jersey takes seriously his responsibility to be spiritual leader of the school. He feels deeply his responsibility to "make these kids good, Christian human beings," and he understands the importance not only of teaching the principles of Christ, but also, above all, of living by them, if he is to make an impact.

Philip's staff share his sense of mission. The process of formation and mentoring begins early in a teacher's relationship with the school, with the interview process. Philip carefully reads through fifty to seventy-five applications for each position. He schedules two interviews with each finalist, including in the second interview a teacher and/or the pastor of St. Cassian's Parish. The interviews consist of questions about how well the candidate understands the school's vision of faith formation for its students and about how the candidate would carry out that vision, in addition to the standard questions about educational qualifications. The result is teachers who live the values.

Although there are no longer any vowed religious on the staff at St. Cassian's, Philip believes that the "intensity and fervor of teaching Catholicism hasn't suffered." Once faculty are on board, Philip continues to act as ongoing formator and mentor to his staff in a number of ways. First, he raises up the mission statement so that it becomes second nature to his staff. "We stamp it on their foreheads," he says figuratively. It's not unusual for staff to refer to the mission statement in faculty meetings or when giving a public presentation at the school. Second, he seeks to support his staff in living out the mission. For example, the Director of Religious Education of St. Cassian's Parish offers workshops for teachers on the principles of Catholic education on in-service days. In addition, teachers who want further mission training are funded by the school to pursue such training. Philip also sees to it that teachers get whatever materials they need to forward the mission.

Elated with the results, Philip muses, "How could I be so lucky, to have such a wonderful group of teachers? They give a hundred percent. They are totally committed and dedicated to the youngsters they teach." The challenge for St. Cassian's, and for Catholic education in general, Philip believes, will be to continue to recruit and retain such dedicated and faith-filled teachers amid the rising costs of education.

In addition to the formation of teachers, Philip nurtures the spirituality and mission of the school as a whole in schoolwide worship and celebrations. The school holds a weekly liturgy, which staff and students attend. Special celebrations mark holidays. For example, Advent and Christmas and Lent and Easter are lifted up and celebrated as important faith-filled seasons in the life of the school.

With all of the faith formation of teachers and the community as a whole, what is the result for students? What is it like where the rubber hits the road, in the classroom? For the most part, students respond very favorably to the teachers, both in learning the academic material and in absorbing the faith. Because the teachers demonstrate credibility, integrity, and relevance with regard to the mission in their own lives, they inspire respect and pass on their values to the students. The mission also gets conveyed spontaneously on the playground and in the hallways, where students learn to live by the values in the nitty gritty of everyday life.

Philip is especially pleased with the new advisory groups established for middle schoolers to help them with all aspects of their lives. Because St. Cassian's is a small school and doesn't have a guidance counselor on its staff, the advisory groups serve as a place for students to talk to someone who isn't an administrator or a teacher who is grading them. Each advisory group has a teacher assigned to it, and while there are designated formal meeting times for these groups, many of the teachers have also gone the extra mile to provide special extras for the students in their group. Sometimes they will invite students to come hang out before school with doughnuts and hot chocolate, or after school with pizza. Advisory groups help students in many ways: with academic needs, with spiritual needs, and with emotional needs. For example, one student whose parents were fighting and apparently about to separate sought out the teacher who led his advisory group and received the help and support he needed. Philip remarks, "So we've built in our own Guidance Department where kids who need counseling—it can be something very simple or it can be something very complicated—have a place to go. They don't have to leave this building feeling empty." Philip's mentoring and formation of his staff thus get trans-ferred to mentoring and formation of students.

JENNIFER MORAN: GROUNDED IN PRAYER

Jennifer Moran, principal of the Academy of the Holy Angels, a School Sis-ters of Notre Dame girls' secondary school in Demarest, New Jersey, experi-enced her own mentoring and formation into the SSND charism in three ways. First, when she became assistant principal in 1987, the principal (a School Sister of Notre Dame) deluged her with books, documents, and other information about the history and mission of the SSNDs, believing that it was essential that Jennifer understand deeply the SSND charism. Although at the time Jennifer felt it was "just a lot of extra things I was being asked to do," she now looks back on it as the first "blessing" she received in her role as ad-ministrator, because she came to understand that her job was not just about administration but was first and foremost about living the mission.

The second blessing built on the foundation of the first. When the School Sisters decided to form an international network of their secondary schools, the Academy of the Holy Angels joined, and Jennifer and the principal at-tended the meeting of representatives of the member schools. To her sur-prise, Jennifer found herself in the position of articulating the network's vi-sion, as her colleagues asked her to assume the role of architect of the founding document. This mammoth task caused Jennifer to reflect deeply on the history and mission of the School Sisters, digging beneath the surface of the historical accounts to retrieve the treasure at the core, and then re-articu-lating that core vision in the context of late twentieth-century secondary schools. Because of the international character of the network, Jennifer's task included shaping a vision that schools in Africa and Asia could claim as eas-ily as could American schools. The process took a year and a half, and then the group worked on the document each year at its annual meetings until it was approved and published. Jennifer found that, even more than she shaped the document, the process of working on the document shaped her.

The third blessing occurred in 2000, after Jennifer had been serving as principal for five years. The president of the school, a School Sister, sug-gested that she and Jennifer travel to Germany to visit the birthplace of the congregation. Their pilgrimage took them from the first tiny school that was opened, to the first secondary school, to the mother house in Munich, to many other significant sites along the way. Seeing the sites firsthand, staying in the convent of the first secondary school, breathing the air that the foundress had breathed, all served to imbue Jennifer with a powerful sense of carrying a hard-won vision forward.

Jennifer's own formation and mentoring prepared her to form and mentor others in the SSND way. As principal, she carries the community as a whole.

She holds them in her heart, seeking opportunities to nurture their growth as a faith community. In many creative ways, she attends to the spiritual life of the group.

First, the school's celebrations all lift up the SSND charism. The school celebrates all the significant SSND dates, as well as focusing its other celebrations around SSND themes. For example, on October 24, SSND Foundation Day, Holy Angels holds a prayer service, connecting it to the United Nations, which shares the same foundation day. Because the congregation is international and emphasizes preparing young women to enter the wider world, linking the two foundation days serves to underline the SSND charism. On the Foundation Day of the school itself, the community celebrates by remembering the story of the school's foundress and by awarding the scholarships named after her, the Mary Nonna Dunphy Scholarships. When the school celebrates International Women's Month in March, the community not only celebrates women of a different culture each year with food, art, and music, but also links the celebration to its peace and justice emphasis by, for instance, raising funds to improve the lives of women workers in that culture.

Second, corporate prayer figures regularly into the life of the school. Not only do feast days and other schoolwide celebrations include prayer, but the school also gathers each morning as a community in prayer. In addition, faculty meetings and committee meetings begin with prayer, reminding participants that God's presence grounds their business. Jennifer relates,

> We had a beautiful prayer yesterday at the faculty meeting. It was so tailored to us and our situation that someone looked up after the prayer and said to the faculty member who had offered the prayer, "Carol, did you write this?" She said, "Yes, I did." I think that kind of nourishment is very helpful to faculty.

Third, spiritual formation occurs in the way things are done in the daily life of the school. Jennifer believes that spirituality doesn't have to be a prayer service or a ritual. It also emerges "in the manner in which you do things, in the tone that you set." Authenticity is the hallmark of Holy Angels: "If we say it, we do it." Jennifer cultivates practices of dialogue, consensus, and honest and patient questioning and working together.

Fourth, faculty retreats serve as opportunities for formation. Each year's retreat carries a different theme. For the year of preparation for the 125th anniversary celebration of the school, two School Sisters presented the history of the congregation and its educational mission, the changes that have occurred over the years, and how, despite the changes, the core mission has continued. Another retreat focused on the social teaching of the Church, and on how the peace and justice ideals that are part of the SSND vision can be incorporated across the curriculum. Retreats also allow ample time for individual prayer and reflection, giving teachers much-needed quiet time to replenish their souls.

In addition to faculty retreats, new faculty receive their own orientation. At the beginning of the school year, their orientation includes watching a video on the seven ministry ideals of the School Sisters. Then they discuss which one of the seven ideals most stands out to each of them, and how they can see themselves living out that ideal in their ministry at Holy Angels. Later in the year they watch a video about the foundress of the American branch of the School Sisters and discuss further how they are living into SSND ideals.

Jennifer finds that nurturing her own spiritual life is foundational for her spiritual leadership. In addition to regular liturgy and participation in the prayer life of the school, Jennifer believes that spiritual leadership requires personal prayer: "I think you have to have a deeper prayer life and you have to do that every day and find the time for it, so I do. That might mean less sleep than I would have gotten if I hadn't, but I have to."

JACK RASLOWSKY: TORCHBEARER

Jack Raslowsky takes up where Jennifer Moran leaves off. While Jennifer has served as formator and mentor to the school as a whole, and has begun the task of imbuing faculty with the SSND charism, she admits that her next step (and the SSNDs' next step) is the fuller formation of the faculty. Jack Raslowsky and the Jesuit network in which he serves have done extensive work in this area, reflecting on and practicing deep formation of lay faculty in the Jesuit way.

While serving for eleven years as principal of St. Peter's Prep, a Jesuit secondary school for boys in Jersey City, New Jersey, Jack was the torchbearer of the Jesuit mission and vision. He gave careful thought to faculty formation and dedicated time, energy, and resources to the process.

First, the hiring process at St. Peter's includes attention to the Jesuit mission. In their interviews, candidates discuss any experience they may have had of Jesuit education and of the Society of Jesus. They spend at least one entire day on campus meeting with the principal, with the department chair, with other faculty members, and with students. They have lunch with a faculty member not involved in the search. They observe classes. Jack remarks: "I think they get a real sense of what the institution is about, of its being a community of learners and a community of believers. The ethos of the place, I think, shines through when you're there."

Second, new faculty orientation, in addition to introducing faculty to the nuts and bolts of life at St. Peter's, and to teaching, introduces the mission. Of the three days given to the new faculty retreat, a day and a half focuses on such themes of Jesuit education as the history of Jesuit education, pedagogy, and what it means to "form men for others." Then, for two to three years, new faculty continue to meet regularly in small groups to discuss mission and values and how these are lived out at St. Peter's.

Third, St. Peter's provides ongoing formation for faculty. Each year begins with a faculty retreat day, followed by two days set aside during the academic year for faculty to focus on Ignatian themes. For example, one retreat focused on the Ignatian theme, "finding God in all things." Two panels of faculty, most lay, shared their experience of trying to find God in all things. Jack relates, "It was wonderful, moving and honest and revealing stories of struggles and joys, some consolation and in some stories, more desolation. People were willing to share their stories with sixty or seventy colleagues and say, 'Here is who I am and where I am and how God is working in me.'" Faculty too found the stories moving, inspirational, and informative, and the sharing helped them know and respect one another more deeply, laying the groundwork for respect and mutuality in working together back in the daily life of St. Peter's.

Another year's opening faculty meeting focused on a booklet published by the Jesuit Secondary Education Association, "What Makes a Jesuit High School Jesuit?" As faculty discussed the ten principles elaborated in the booklet, they raised questions that would continue to engage them throughout the year: What is Jesuit pedagogy and how does it differ from good pedagogy in general? What is evangelization in the context of the interfaith community of our school—how do we simultaneously engage in interreligious dialogue and evangelization? How can we be sensitive to the poor and immigrant community, thus living out the Jesuit commitment to the poor? Faculty then continued to discuss these questions, not only in the two designated faculty days during the school year, but also in regular faculty meetings, in departmental meetings, and in individual conversations. Discussions of the Jesuit mission at St. Peter's are regular and intentional. As Jack observes, "If you're going to work to deepen the mission and people's understanding of it, you really have to commit time to it."

Fourth, St. Peter's Prep lives within a larger context of Jesuit schools. The Jesuit Secondary Education Association (JSEA) has a staff of six full-time people in its national office, and each province has at least one Secondary Education assistant. JSEA holds a national five-day colloquium for over 500 participants every three years, to which St. Peter's sends about a dozen people. A major focus of the colloquium is mission and identity, and those who attend return and share their experience with faculty who didn't attend. The JSEA also sponsors regional gatherings of interest groups, for example, gatherings of campus ministers or Christian service coordinators. In addition, the provinces organize gatherings of faculty and administrators in their provinces, sometimes by department. Recently, History Department faculty from the New York province met to discuss what it means to be history faculty in Jesuit schools, considering such questions as: Do we have a particular focus on and attention to questions of justice? If not, how do we begin to deal with that topic in our history classrooms?

Thus, Jack has done an excellent job of mentoring and forming teachers in the Jesuit way. His careful, thoughtful attention to the matter, and his dedication of time and resources to it, have yielded abundant fruit.

In reflecting on the work of the principal, Jack also speaks to the asceticism of spiritual leadership. During his time at St. Peter's, he saw himself as being there to serve his faculty, to care for them so they could thrive. At the same time, he wonders who is caring for the principals and presidents. The role of principal can be a lonely and thankless job: "I think the good principals are caring for their faculty, providing them opportunities for professional and personal growth, for time away, for advancement, for challenge. I don't know that we have people in spots that are doing that for the principals and presidents." Jack worries about stress and burnout among principals and presidents, and seeks to encourage them to be open to support when it is offered them.

CONCLUSION: THE HEART OF IT ALL

What do all these principals have in common? In their hearts, they carry the vision, they carry the charism, they carry the wisdom of Catholic education. As lay spiritual leaders, they have all experienced formation and mentoring in their schools' charism, and they each in turn pass on that formation and mentoring to others. They share a deep commitment to Catholic education, and they have devoted time, energy, and creativity to envisioning what it should look like in the twenty-first century and beyond. They carry in their hearts their teachers and students.

Coupled with the vision at the heart of each school are the principals' ingenuity and practical skill. They know how to translate vision into action. They have made manifest the charism. The stories of these three leaders illustrate and illuminate the role of all lay leaders in Catholic institutional ministries. As these leaders and others like them follow in the footsteps of their institutions' founders, they will not only keep alive the charism for today, but they will also continue to inspire future generations of lay leaders who will keep the charism alive for tomorrow.

REFLECTION QUESTIONS

1. In what ways have you exercised spiritual leadership similar to that of Philip Meehan, Jennifer Moran, or Jack Raslowsky?
2. What can you learn about spiritual leadership from these three spiritual leaders?

3. What events in your life of leadership have been or could be blessings, even though you, like Jennifer Moran, may not recognize them as such at first?

FOR FURTHER READING

Benefiel, Margaret. "Leadership." In *New Dictionary of Christian Spirituality,* ed. Philip Sheldrake. London: SCM Press, 2004.

Cobble, James, and Charles Elliott, eds. *The Hidden Spirit: Discovering the Spirituality of Institutions.* Mathews, NC: Christian Ministry Resources, 1999.

Heifetz, Ronald. *Leadership without Easy Answers.* Cambridge, MA: Harvard/Belknap, 1994.

Moxley, Russ. *Leadership and Spirit.* San Francisco: Jossey-Bass, 1999.

Palmer, Parker J. "Leading from Within: Out of the Shadow, Into the Light." In *Spirit at Work,* ed. Jay Conger. San Francisco: Jossey-Bass, 1994.

Terms for Reference

Body of Christ: Refers to the Risen Body of Christ, to the Real Presence of Christ in the Eucharist, and to the community of Christians united with Christ and one another. While there is a unity in these references, at times one or the other is intended, in a more narrow sense of the term.

charism: A key theme word in the New Testament, denoting the free gift of God, especially the saving will of God communicated to humanity through Jesus Christ. Often focused as a divine spiritual gift to individuals or groups for the good of humanity. All Christians receive charisms; sometimes gifts given to one person become embodied in a group, such as a founder's charism within a religious congregation

Church: The Christian community, all the baptized, also called the Body of Christ and the People of God, embracing both the living and the dead. A visible *and* spiritual communion of persons. At times designates the Roman Catholic Church, those of the Roman rite united with the Pope of Rome. In common usage, at times imprecisely refers only to the hierarchy (pope, bishops, priests) or to the institutional aspects of the Church (e.g., visible structures).

culture: The web of expressions of the human spirit consisting of behavior patterns, beliefs, institutions, art, rituals, symbols, and narratives, a web which shapes both those who have expressed the culture and those who inherit it.

ecclesial: Referring to the church (Lat. *ecclesia*); ecclesiology is the branch of theology that reflects on the nature and mission of the church.

Incarnation: The doctrine that teaches that the Second Person of the Blessed Trinity took on human nature, conceived by Mary, becoming one of us to save all of humanity, as the one divine person, the Son of God.

lay ecclesial ministers: The name given by the bishops to those laypersons providing leadership in ministry, usually in parishes.

mandatum: A document granted to a theologian by the local bishop that attests the theologian teaches in communion with the Church. Initiated by Pope John Paul II, the requirement to seek a mandatum, or mandate to teach, was instituted by the bishops in the United States in 2001. It applies to Roman Catholics who teach Catholic theology, Church history, morality, scripture, or canon law at Catholic colleges. A private matter between bishop and theologian, there is not clarity about the consequences of not seeking the mandatum.

mission: (1) Belongs first to the Trinity: the Son proceeding from the Father, and the Spirit from the Father and the Son, *sent* in a saving mission to the world. (2) The Church continues the mission of Christ, *sent* in the power of the Spirit, preaching by word, action, and example the gospel, the good news, that the reign of God is among us. Each Catholic institution, and each individual Christian, continues the mission of Christ, preparing the way for the fullness of the reign of God.

ministry: The ministry of Jesus encompassed all of his works of preaching, teaching, healing, celebrating, reconciling, saving. Christians today continue the ministry of Jesus, each based on the charisms received, in the works of service they perform, individually and together.

praxis: Actions that are (at least potentially) transformative. It can simply signify "action" in contrast to non-action, indifference, neutrality, or anomie. It has been described as "reflected-upon-action and reflection-acted-upon."

reign of God: A way of speaking about the world as it will be when God has God's way in the world, a world in which holiness, truth, justice, love, and peace prevail. It is the reign of God that Jesus preached and for which he died.

social grace: Because all that is created holds a dimension of the goodness of God, and because all has been redeemed in Christ Jesus, not only individuals but also communities and even structures (institutions, cultural norms, common practices, laws, etc.) partake of the Creator's goodness and the Redeemer's salvation. Individuals and communities are called to discern the ways in which the Spirit draws all toward the fullness of God's reign, to cooperate with the grace given (individual and social), and to resist the counterforces (social and individual).

social sin: In the Old Testament, the word most used for sin could be translated "to miss the mark." Another word used means "a straying," leaving the path so that the destination is lost. Social sin describes the missing of the mark, the straying, which is embedded in the structures of society (our institutions, cultural norms, common practices, laws, etc.) in so far as they do not embody the values of the reign of God. Social sin includes injustice, oppression, discrimination, etc. On the one hand, no one individual is responsible for the social sin of his/her setting; on the other, each person is called to work toward the values of God's reign so that social sin may be overcome.

spirituality: Refers not simply to one dimension of the Christian life, such as prayer, recollection, discernment, or ascetical practice, but to the whole of one's life in response to the gift of God in Christ Jesus through the presence and power of the Holy Spirit. It is nothing more or less than being conformed to the person of Christ, brought into communion with God and others through the gift of the Spirit.

sponsorship: Describes a relationship between a religious congregation and a sponsored institution. Characteristics of this relationship: it demands mutuality, with neither the sponsor nor the institution totally responsible for maintaining the relationship; it allows the congregation to expand its mission; and it helps give foundation and direction to the mission of the sponsored institution.

theology: Faith seeking understanding; the process of consciously and reflectively trying to give expression to the mystery of God's self-communication as experienced by persons and communities.

tradition: In Catholic understanding, the good news proclaimed by Jesus is a living message, handed down by the community of believers, safeguarded from error by the Magisterium (the teaching authority of the Church). The Scriptures, as well as the entire life of the Church, comprise the tradition, not a dead letter but an ever-renewed, living incarnation of the Gospel in each age and place.

Trinity: The doctrine central to Christian belief: God is Father/Creator, Son/Redeemer, and Spirit/Sanctifier. We are saved by God, through Jesus Christ, in the power of the Holy Spirit.

universal call to holiness: Teaching of the Second Vatican Council that the call to holiness is for everyone: "all the faithful of Christ of whatever rank or status are called to the fullness of the Christian life and the perfection of charity" (*Dogmatic Constitution on the Church*, 40). Love of God and love of neighbor are the essentials of holiness.

Vatican Council II: The twenty-first general council in the history of the Church, 1962-1965. The Council, pope, and bishops of the world together promulgated sixteen documents, which became part of the teaching of the Church.

SOURCES CONSULTED

Catechism of the Catholic Church. Libreria Editrice Vaticana. Washington, DC: United States Catholic Conference, 1997.

Richard P. McBrien, General Ed. *The Harper Collins Encyclopedia of Catholicism*. San Francisco: Harper, 1995.

Karl Rahner and Herbert Vorgrimler. *Theological Dictionary*. New York: Herder and Herder, 1965.

(See also the essays in the present volume.)

Index

The Active Life (Palmer), 12
adaptive work, 87; vs. technical work, 87, 92
Adorna, Caterinetta (Catherine of Genoa, Saint), 130
agere contra, 37
Alison, James: *The Joy of Being Wrong*, 88, 97n2
Allen, Norma: *The Quilters*, 137
Altogether Gift (Downey), 17, 29n2
Americanism, 58, 60
analgesic society, 93–94
Apollos, 149
Apostolicam Actuositatem (Decree on the Apostolate of Lay People), 51n4
Aquinas, Saint Thomas: *capax Dei* (capable of God), 33, 34
Areopagai, 21, 24, 26
Areopagus, 21, 40
Aristotle, 40
Arrupe, Pedro, S.J., 38–39
Arseneau, Katherine, C.S.J., 114
Asian Catholics, 89
assimilation into American culture: and election of John F. Kennedy, 60; vs. prophetic distance, 55
Augustine, Saint, 33, 37, 144

authority, 153–54; analogy to midwifery, 158–59; ethic and ethos of, 155, 157, 164n2; roles, danger and value of, 157–59; as vested power, 157–59
"The Avowal" (Levertov), 163

Balance Sheet for Catholic Elementary Schools (Kealey), 71
Baltimore, Council of. *See* councils, Church
baptism, 18, 21, 25; universal call to mission in, 45; variety of callings in, 46
Basil, Saint, 144
Bayley, James Roosevelt (first bishop of Newark), 77
Beaudoin, Tom: *Virtual Faith*, 91
belief: definitions of, 145; politicization of, 146
Bellah, Robert N.: *The Good Society*, 110n1; *Habits of the Heart*, 100
Benedict, Saint, 39, 144
"Beyond the Present" (Peters), 115, 126n3
Bible, the: Acts of the Apostles, 46, 50n1; Gospel, the, 117, 121; of John, 6–7, 34; John 1:11, 35; John 6:38, 6; John 17:9, 150; of Luke, 45, 50n1;

About the Contributors

Regina Bechtle, S.C., Ph.D., is Director of Charism Resources for the Sisters of Charity of New York. She researches, writes about, and offers retreats and programs on Vincentian spirituality, religious life, and leadership. She has served on her congregation's leadership team, coauthored a resource manual for women religious new to leadership, and directed a center for leadership and spirituality at the College of Mount Saint Vincent in New York. Coeditor of a three-volume collection of St. Elizabeth Seton's writings, she has also published essays and poetry in religious and theological journals.

Margaret Benefiel teaches at Andover Newton Theological School in Boston, in the area of spirituality, leadership, and organizations. During the 2003–2004 academic year, she held the O'Donnell Chair of Spirituality at the Milltown Institute in Dublin, Ireland. She coedited *Hidden in Plain Sight: Quaker Women's Writings 1650–1700,* and is working on another book, *The Second Half of the Journey: Leading Organizations through Spiritual Transformation*. Her articles have appeared in journals of spirituality and organizational management. She holds a Ph.D. from the Catholic University of America and lives in Boston and Dublin with her husband and dog.

Michael Downey is Professor of Systematic Theology and Spirituality at St. John's Seminary, Camarillo, and the Cardinal's Theologian, Archdiocese of Los Angeles. The first layperson to receive the Ph.D. in theology from the Catholic University of America, Dr. Downey is author or editor of seventeen books, most recently *The Heart of Hope* (Pauline Books and Media, 2005). His essays and book chapters number in the dozens.

Elinor Ford, Ph.D., has a long and distinguished career in Catholic education. She served as Superintendent of Schools for the Archdiocese of New York, then as the first Director of Nonpublic Education in the Graduate School of Education at Fordham University. While at Fordham, she and Fr. Vincent Novak, S.J., then Director of the Department of Religion and Religious Education, cosponsored a doctoral program for church leaders. She has also served as CEO and President of the William H. Sadlier Company, a major publisher of religion and academic materials for parishes and schools. Currently she teaches graduate courses at various Catholic universities and is a consultant to dioceses and educational, catechetical, and parish ministries.

Zeni Fox, Ph.D., is Professor of Pastoral Theology at Immaculate Conception Seminary, Seton Hall University, South Orange, N.J. Author of *New Ecclesial Ministry: Lay Professionals Serving the Church* (Sheed & Ward, 2002), the FADICA (Foundations and Donors Interested in Catholic Activities) white paper, *Laity in Leadership Roles in the United States Today*, and various articles, she has lectured and taught in dioceses, schools, and universities across the country. Since 1994, she has served as an advisor to the United States Catholic Conference of Bishops Subcommittee on Lay Ministry.

Doris Gottemoeller, R.S.M., is the Senior Vice President for Mission and Values Integration at Catholic Healthcare Partners, a multistate health care system headquartered in Cincinnati, Ohio. She has served in leadership within the Sisters of Mercy and on numerous health care, higher education, and social service boards. Other ministry experience includes writing and lecturing throughout the United States and abroad on topics of ministry, ecclesiology, and religious life. She holds an M.S. in chemistry from the University of Notre Dame and an M.A. and Ph.D. in theology from Fordham University.

Monika K. Hellwig, LL.B., Ph.D., Executive Director of the Association of Catholic Colleges and Universities, was formerly the Landegger Professor of Theology at Georgetown University, where she taught for three decades. She has written and lectured nationally and internationally, in both scholarly and popular contexts, on Catholic systematic theology and interfaith studies, and is a past president of the Catholic Theological Society of America. Her published books include: *Understanding Catholicism, Jesus the Compassion of God, The Eucharist and the Hunger of the World, Sign of Reconciliation and Conversion,* and *Guests of God: Stewards of Divine Creation.* She is the mother of three now grown adopted children: Erica Hellwig Parker, Michael Hellwig, and Carlos Hellwig.

Dolores R. Leckey is a Senior Fellow at the Woodstock Theological Center, Georgetown University, and former director of the Family, Laity, Women, and Youth Secretariat for the United States Conference of Catholic Bishops. She has lectured and led retreats in the United States, Europe, and Australia, and authored or coauthored a number of books, including *Facing Fear with Faith*, a book of spiritual reflections on September 11, 2001, and *Spiritual Exercises for Church Leaders* (Paulist Press, 2003).

Richard Liddy is the University Professor of Catholic Thought and Culture at Seton Hall University. Msgr. Liddy is also a member of the Religious Studies Department and Director of the Center for Catholic Studies, and a priest of the Archdiocese of Newark. His areas of scholarly interest are interdisciplinary dialogue and the works of Bernard Lonergan and John Henry Newman. Among his publications are *Transforming Intellectual Conversion in the Early Lonergan* (Liturgical Press, 1993), and "The Catholic Intellectual Tradition" in *As Leaven in the World* (edited by Thomas M. Landy, Sheed & Ward, 2001). Another article, "A Shower of Insights: Autobiography and Intellectual Conversion," will appear shortly in *Method: Journal of Lonergan Studies*. He is currently working on a book on intellectual conversion.

H. Richard McCord is Executive Director of the Secretariat for Family, Laity, Women, and Youth at the U.S. Conference of Catholic Bishops. Before joining the Bishops' Conference staff in 1988, he served in a variety of pastoral leadership positions for the Archdiocese of Baltimore. He holds master's degrees in theology and religious education, and a doctorate in adult education from the University of Maryland, and writes frequently for Catholic News Service and occasionally for church-related journals and other publications. He and his wife, Denise, have been married since 1976 and have an adult son, Andrew.

Brian McDermott, S.J., rector of the Jesuit Community and professorial lecturer in theology at Georgetown University, was previously a faculty member at the Weston Jesuit School of Theology. He holds a Ph.D. from the University of Nijmegen in the Netherlands. His publications include *What Are They Saying about the Grace of Christ?* (Paulist Press, 1984), and *Word Become Flesh: Dimensions of Christology* (Liturgical Press, 1993). His teaching and writing interests include Christology, theological anthropology, Ignatian spirituality, and authority and leadership, an area in which he has also collaborated with faculty at Harvard University's Kennedy School of Government.

John S. Nelson, Ph.D., is Professor Emeritus of Theology and Religious Education in Fordham University's Graduate School of Religion and Religious Education. With his wife, Catherine Zates Nelson, he has contributed as author and editor to Sadlier's *Coming to Faith* program for junior high school students and to the *Journey in Faith* series on the senior high level. He has published numerous articles on religious education and the theology of the Catholic Church.

Sean Peters, C.S.J., Ed.D., a Sister of St. Joseph of Carondelet, currently serves as Executive Director of the Association of Colleges of Sisters of Saint Joseph—a group of eight colleges that span the country from Boston to Los Angeles. She has held faculty and administrative positions at various colleges and led her religious community for eight years as Province Director. She has developed a resource kit of heritage materials for institutions sponsored by Sisters of St. Joseph and has written articles and presented workshops on sponsorship, the Catholic intellectual tradition, and Catholic social teaching.

Mary Daniel Turner, S.N.D.de N., coauthored *The Transformation of American Catholic Sisters* (Temple U. Press, 1992). An experienced facilitator, with graduate studies in philosophy and theology, she was one of the early members of the Sister Formation Conference and its National Chair during the 1960s. She later served as president of her congregation, the Sisters of Notre Dame de Namur, and as Executive Director of the Leadership Conference of Women Religious. For over twenty years, she has lived in a biracial and intergenerational community, and counts it as one of the most profound and challenging graces of her life.